Press acclaim for *Why Blame*

'This book is an essential guide t[...]
Israeli debate. In the current roll[...]
progress it can be used with confid[...]
the roots and evolution of the con[...]

Martin Gilbert

'A important book ... essential reading for anybody who wants to have a fair, up-to-date account and understanding of Israel's history.'

Jewish Telegraph

'Incisive, informed, well-written. Amidst a mass of books published on the Middle East, this stands out as an unusually fair and accurate account from someone who is neither Jew nor Arab.'

Tom Gross, commentator on Middle East affairs for CNN, the *Sunday Telegraph* and the *Wall Street Journal*

'A rare combination of a book one wants to read for its narrative, in addition to keeping it on one's bookshelf for reference.'

George Jonas, *National Post*

'A timely, erudite study that deserves to be read.'

Good Book Guide

'Israel, lest we forget, is the only country in the Middle East that any feminist, atheist, homosexual or trade unionist could bear to live in. Yet there exists a quite striking bias against the state of Israel. Neill Lochery's excellent, accessible book is a must-read for anyone wanting a tonic to this persistent and illogical prejudice.'

Julie Burchill

'The received wisdom is that the terrorism to which Israel is regularly subject is a product of its own behaviour towards the Palestinians. Neill Lochery's superb book is a useful antidote to this grotesque distortion.'

Stephen Pollard, *Mail on Sunday*

'A necessary book. So much discussion of the Arab–Israeli conflict fails to rise even to the level of being wrong. This scrupulous, well-written and eminently sane book will go far to set things right.'

Bret Stephens, Editor-in-Chief, *Jerusalem Post*

WHY BLAME ISRAEL?

NEILL LOCHERY

ICON BOOKS

Originally published in the UK in 2004 by Icon Books Ltd

Reprinted 2004, 2005

This edition published in the UK in 2005
by Icon Books Ltd, The Old Dairy,
Brook Road, Thriplow, Cambridge SG8 7RG
email: info@iconbooks.co.uk
www.iconbooks.co.uk

Sold in the UK, Europe, South Africa and Asia
by Faber and Faber Ltd, 3 Queen Square,
London WC1N 3AU
or their agents

Distributed in the UK, Europe, South Africa and Asia
by TBS Ltd, Frating Distribution Centre, Colchester Road
Frating Green, Colchester CO7 7DW

This edition published in Australia in 2005
by Allen & Unwin Pty Ltd,
PO Box 8500, 83 Alexander Street,
Crows Nest, NSW 2065

Distributed in Canada by
Penguin Books Canada,
10 Alcorn Avenue, Suite 300,
Toronto, Ontario M4V 3B2

Published in the USA in 2005 by Totem Books
Inquiries to: Icon Books Ltd, The Old Dairy,
Brook Road, Thriplow, Cambridge SG8 7RG, UK

Distributed to the trade in the USA by National Book Network Inc,
4720 Boston Way, Lanham, MD 20706

ISBN 1 84046 624 3

Typesetting by Hands Fotoset

Printed and bound in the UK by Clays, Bungay

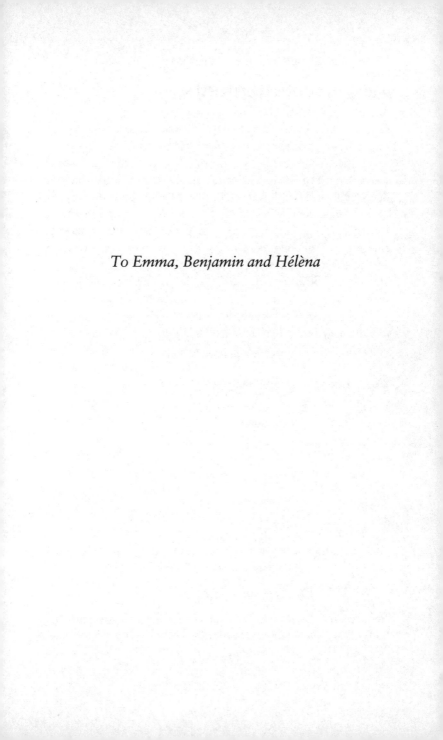

To Emma, Benjamin and Hélèna

Acknowledgements

I owe a debt of gratitude to Sir Derek Roberts, the former Provost of University College London, for giving me the idea that there was a need for a good book – aimed at the 'general reader' – that went beyond the headlines of the Arab–Israeli conflict and the development of Israel. As ever, I am deeply indebted to my agent, Louise Greenberg, whose drive, input and nagging are always welcome. To Jeremy Cox at Icon Books who was extremely supportive even when he didn't agree with some of the content, and to my editor Duncan Heath whose attention to linguistic and factual detail transformed the manuscript into its present form. This book would not have been possible without the help and support over a number of years of Natasha Hassan, John O'Sullivan, Martin Sieff, Bret Stephens, and the Syd Barrett of the newspaper world, Dean Godson. Finally, I wish to thank my family who had to put up with endless cancelled trips and late night working sessions over the long hot summer of 2003.

Neill Lochery,
University College London,
December 2003

NEILL LOCHERY is 39 years old, married with two children, and is currently Lecturer in Modern Israeli Politics and Director of the Centre for Israeli Studies, University College London.

Neill has written numerous scholarly articles and two scholarly books, *The Israeli Labour Party* and *The Difficult Road to Peace*, as well as filing weekly background pieces for UPI, *The Scotsman*, the *National Post*, the *Chicago Sun-Times* and the *Jerusalem Post*, among others.

Contents

List of Maps

Introduction to the Paperback Edition

In between the publication of the hardback edition of the book and this paperback version, Yasser Arafat died in Paris on 11 November 2004. Though I subscribe to the view that one man does not make a conflict – nor does he make peace for that matter – the death of Arafat marks the single most significant event in the Middle East for decades. I first became aware of the serious-ness of the decline in Arafat's health in March 2004 when BBC World Service Radio asked me to update his obituary. I recall thinking to myself at the time that we have been here before. My memory was cast back to the premature reports of his death in Jordan during the Jordanian–PLO war in September 1970, his evacuation from a compound surrounded by the Israeli army in Beirut in 1982 and the air crash in the desert from which he miraculously walked away as the sole survivor. This time, however, there was no escape from death as Arafat slowly passed away in a Paris hospital chosen years previously because of the extremely strict French privacy laws that grant control and access only to the next of kin – in this case, Arafat's estranged wife, Suha.

It is much too early to fully understand the impact of Arafat's death on the Palestinians and the conflict with Israel. Needless to say, there will be much talk and speculation about the oppor-tunities that lie ahead. This is the Middle East, however, and I would caution against over-optimism. History has shown us time and time again that just when one problem or obstacle dis-appears, a new, previously unseen one raises its head, leading to a renewed round of violence. In truth, much will depend on how willing and able Israeli and Palestinian leaders are to make political concessions, given the lack of popular will on both sides for such moves to take place. Arafat's death, in short, moves the region into uncharted waters and these are bound to get a little choppy before progress towards some resolution of the conflict is made.

Prior to Arafat's death, George W. Bush was re-elected President in the United States with a much clearer mandate to govern than during his first term. The success or failure of any future political dialogue between Israelis and Palestinians will depend much on the efforts of the second Bush administration. The second Clinton administration was derailed by sexual scandal and the resulting impeachment, with disastrous effects for the Middle East which are outlined in Chapter One of this book. President Bush must not make the same mistake that President Clinton made in his Arab–Israeli policies of over-engagement in trying to resolve the conflict.

As the Postscript of the book argues, the overall parameters of a deal between the Israelis and Palestinians are already in place via the Geneva Accords, which themselves have their origins in the Abu Mazen–Beilin Plan of the mid-1990s. What is now imperative is finding ways for the respective political leaders to be able to sign a peace agreement without having to commit domestic political suicide. This remains the biggest challenge for Israelis and Palestinians in the post-Arafat era. The decisive election victory of Abu Mazen in the Palestinian Presidential elections held on 9 January 2005 and the formation of a new broad-based government of national unity in Israel (including both the Likud and the Labour Party) the following day would appear to provide a new opportunity for progress. Accepting that the actors are in place and that all parties have a good under-standing of what a final deal will look like, the key issue would appear to be how to get to the endgame. The coming months and years are likely to present very difficult challenges for Israeli and Palestinian leaders, as well as for the American, British and European mediators involved in attempting to bring an end to Israeli–Palestinian conflict.

Introduction

Josiah Bartlet, the fictional President in the US television drama, *The West Wing*, recounts a story to his Chief of Staff of a dialogue between a distinguished professor and his student about the intractability of the Middle East conflict. The professor argues that there is endless conflict in the region due to centuries-old disputes over religion and land. No, says the student, it's because it's hot, and there isn't enough water.[1] For those keen to go beyond the narrow parameters of the professor's explanation and to discover just how complex – and often hijacked by other issues and events – the Arab–Israeli conflict and Israeli history have become, then read on. Yes, to some degree, the dispute is about two conflicting ancient claims on a single piece of land. To non-Jews or non-Muslims, however, such claims of legitimacy to ownership of the land dating back to ancient times do not constitute sufficient grounds for favouring one claim over the other. In reality, the conflict is dominated by questions of power (both political and economic), military might, the international order of the day, and yes – even water.

It is often said that when an effective Israeli leader speaks he does so using all three tenses at once: past, present and future. In doing this he is relating Jewish events in the past to the present – often seeking legitimacy for his government's actions and policies – while keeping an eye on the future problems and challenges that lie ahead for the state.[2] Any history of Israel must do likewise in terms of using the past to understand the present and exploring the ways in which the past and present are likely to shape the future. Accordingly, the last chapter is devoted to highlighting past mistakes and summarising the lessons that need to be learnt if Israel and the Arabs are to move towards some state of peaceful co-existence in the foreseeable future.

The Arab–Israeli conflict is also often referred to as the battle of the maps; from maps purporting to show when the first Jewish community in a particular area was established (and did it pre-date any Arab village there?) to the more sophisticated attempts of the international powers to divide the lands in various ways and using various criteria. The latter was particularly significant during the period of British rule over what was then termed Palestine, when first Britain and France effectively carved up the Middle East between them with the Sykes–Picot Agreement, and during the subsequent British attempts to divide or sub-divide Palestine between its Zionist and Arab populations (see maps 1–4). Israel, it should be remembered, has never enjoyed secure borders, and consequently the map of Israel has evolved as the direct result of wars. Today, with Israel's borders unchanged since the return of the Sinai Desert to Egypt over twenty years ago, two highly related maps dominate the political agenda: the map of Israeli settlement in the Disputed Territories (or the 'map with the red dots') and the Oslo Redeployment map (known as the 'scrambled egg map' – see map 11).[3]

Alongside the map, the visual image – either television or photograph – has come to play a central role in legitimising Israel's existence, its borders and its conflict with the Arabs. In recent years, two images have come to characterise Israel and the Disputed Territories. The first is of a badly mangled bus with only its basic structure intact – the latest target of the now terrifyingly routine strategy of suicide bombing. Such attacks have turned Israeli cities into war zones, reducing everyday life in Tel Aviv and Jerusalem to a perverse game of Russian roulette (or the 'odds game' as some Israelis prefer to term it).[4] The second image is of an Israeli soldier firing on a Palestinian, and the wounded Palestinian being carried to a waiting ambulance. Both images are brutal, and help stoke the embers of hatred in the region. No matter how tragic, however, they merely reflect news editors' obsession with the humanistic story over the developing of a deeper understanding of the complex arguments. Somewhere along the line, the deep-lying arguments over Israel and its fight for its existence have been lost in the rush to play the blame game or the 'who's right, who's wrong' set of arguments.

Sadly, nowadays it would appear that most images are used in conjunction with largely ill-informed reporting. The reports are shown by television companies dominated by a left-of-centre political culture, to reinforce stereotypical perceptions such as the notion of the Palestinians as victims and the Israelis as oppressors. Coverage of the alleged massacre of Palestinians by the Israeli army in the refugee camp at Jenin in 2002 illustrates this in-built political correctness. Many television companies were quick to act as judge and jury and convict Israel of perpetrating a terrible crime against the Palestinians, relying on accounts by local Palestinians and second-hand accounts by aid workers in the area. As we now know, no such massacre took place and when the area was opened up to the international press, revised versions of events had to be put out by the news networks, who had in effect broken codes of practice in reporting such events. Once more, the humanistic story with pieces to camera by clearly anti-Israeli reporters had replaced hard facts. A specific difficulty with the BBC's coverage has been their refusal to label Palestinian suicide bombers as terrorists. To be fair, this policy has left many senior BBC journalists feeling uncomfortable, but the directive came from senior management in London, and reflects deep contradictions in the BBC's use of the term.[5]

Looking further afield, any quick glance at the Arab media reveals a more radical lexis of vocabulary than its Western counterparts. 'Occupation', 'Zionist entity', 'forces of repression', 'military might', 'curfew' and, yes, even 'Nazi' are commonplace. There is a strong tendency in editorials to talk of the injustice of the current situation, and an over-concentration on the past at the expense of analysing attempts to solve the conflict. Until the Oslo Accords of 1993, the majority of the Arabic media made no distinction between the two major political parties in Israel – the Labour Party and the Likud – or between a hard-liner and a moderate. There was little awareness of the internal dynamics that govern Israeli politics, and little in the way of cultural awareness. Clearly, the media need to focus on looking behind the headlines and at the key arguments and developments within Israel, which today remains a democratic odyssey in a region where civil society and political culture remain very much locked in the past.

There is an old joke that many a Middle Eastern expert has used to break the ice with audiences. So familiar are the various sides in the Arab–Israel dispute with the central arguments – the joke goes – that in negotiations they should merely shout out numbers at each other, followed by another number for the counter-argument. Such a methodology would save much time and wasted breath. In truth, when we look at Israel we cannot ignore such questions as the right to the land and the counter-arguments that the Arabs put forward. By simply agreeing, however, that both sides have merits to their arguments, we can help avoid the tortuous debate of the blame game that has characterised the conflict since its conception. It should be noted, though, that many Arabs argue that by taking this stand of starting from a level playing field we are, in effect, providing legitimacy for the current position of Israeli political, economic and military dominance in the region.

A survey conducted in the United States in the year 2000, and published widely in the American media, found that Israel topped the poll in two categories among the sample group of Americans questioned: the most popular country and the most disliked country. This seeming contradiction says much about the continuing polarisation of opinion about Israel as it enters the 21st century, and its 56th year of existence. Throughout its brief history there has been such a disproportionate interest in Israel from the media, academics, diplomats and politicians that it is important to remind oneself that Israel's population is only 6.5 million – a size comparable to the population of Scotland. In terms of impact, however, there can be few other recently created states that can match Israel. It is almost impossible to turn on the television news without hearing about the latest development in the peace process or the latest twists and turns in Israel's often turbulent but rarely dull domestic politics. Indeed, with the exception of the United States, Israel takes up more news hours than any other country in the world. Israeli leaders are recognised the world over, and in recent years have appeared to spend as much time abroad as at home during their period in office.

Since its creation in 1948, Israel has been in a state of conflict with the Arab world and has fought five major wars against Arab states (1948, 1956, 1967, 1973 and 1982). Throughout this time, Israel has remained engaged in a complex conflict with the Palestinians. Even during times of so-called tranquillity in the Arab–Israeli conflict there have been incidents, attacks and retaliations that have created the impression of a permanent state of war. As a region of great strategic importance, the Middle East as a whole has to a degree been shaped by its contacts with the external powers: the Turks, the British and French, and, following the Second World War, the USA and the Soviet Union. Israel's conflict with the Arabs has, at various times, and to varying degrees, been complicated by the intervention of one or more of these external powers. As Bernard Lewis points out, the intrusion of these powers has meant that there has been no clear resolution of the Arab–Israeli conflict, as no one side has been allowed to secure a total victory over the other.[6] The conflict has therefore taken the form of a series of relatively short wars that have been ended by the intervention of the key powers of the day before a tactical victory could be turned into a major strategic victory. As a result, the unintended consequence of international intervention has been to prolong rather than resolve the conflict.

Israel has had to endure economic boycott imposed by the Arab states both on Israeli goods and on companies that conducted business with it. At times, Israeli shipping has been excluded from using key waterways. As a result, Israel has remained to all intents and purposes isolated in the Middle East region, and has developed ties with European countries and the USA rather than its neighbours. In recent years, there have been signs of progress towards the ending of the Arab–Israeli conflict. Israel signed peace deals with Egypt in 1977 and Jordan in 1994, and deals have also been signed between Israel and the Palestinians, starting with the Oslo Accords in 1993. But at the start of the 21st century it is difficult to foresee an end to the conflict. Indeed, there has been a marked return to violence following the breakdown of the Oslo Accords and the start of the self-titled Palestinian Al-Aqsa Intifada in October 2000.

In writing *Why Blame Israel? The Facts Behind the Headlines*, the aim has been to present a clear and concise outline of the arguments that surround the birth and development of Israel rather than to present a comprehensive chronological account of the events and personalities. Given the heated debate that still surrounds Israel, this has been no easy task. Historians – Jewish/ Israeli and Arab – strongly disagree on key events in Israeli history. As researcher and author of this work I do not claim to be totally objective. I am, however, neither Jewish nor Arab, and nor do I have any particular axe to grind.

Though the Arab–Israeli conflict dominates the history of Israel, there are other areas that are no less emotive or divisive to Israelis. These include the absorption of immigrants, divisions between Ashkenazi and Oriental Jews, the secular–religious debate, and disputes over the distribution of the national economic cake. This book, as a result, also highlights the major arguments surrounding these areas that have been at the centre of the development of the state of Israel.

CHAPTER ONE

The Setting: Three Men Searching for a Political Lifeboat

In the summer of 2000, three men and their respective advisers sat in a log cabin at the US Presidential retreat of Camp David and attempted to resolve one of the most intractable conflicts of the 20th century. In truth, their meeting was born more out of personal desperation than any political rationality. An American President, Bill Clinton, led the cast list, in the twilight of his term of office and desperately seeking a place in the history books for his peace-making activities rather than his sexual deeds. To President Clinton's right during the pre-summit photo op was Ehud Barak, Israel's most decorated solider and now its Prime Minister, leader of a crumbling coalition government that had failed to address the most pressing issues of the day for the Jewish state: peace and the economy. To the President's left stood the Palestinian leader Yasser Arafat, who had been leader of the Palestine Liberation Organisation (PLO) when President Johnson was in office in the 1960s, and had seen six US Presidents come and go since that time. Arafat now headed the politically troubled and economically cash-strapped Palestinian Authority, a quasi-governing body which had been set up as a result of the Oslo Peace Accords he had signed with Yitzhak Rabin in September 1993.

After two weeks of tense and often acrimonious negotiations, the talks broke up without any agreement being reached. President Clinton could barely contain his frustration as he faced the world's media for the debriefing session. Unlike previous occasions, in which a failure to bridge the gap had been met with statements of cautious US optimism for the longer term chances of success, this time there was little attempt by the President to mask his disappointment. When Arafat telephoned Clinton following the failure at Camp David to praise his peace-making efforts, the President responded: 'I am a colossal failure because of you.'[1] Though Clinton may have said it partly in irony, the message was clear. Hillary Clinton was equally damning of Arafat: 'Unfortunately, while Barak came to Camp David to make peace, Arafat did not ... Arafat was never ready to make the hard choices necessary to reach an agreement.'[2]

Camp David was the swansong for the process that had become generally known as the Oslo peace process. The term itself is somewhat misleading, as it refers to a series of agreements signed by the Israeli government and the PLO. The first of these had been negotiated in secret in Oslo during late 1992 and early 1993. It was this agreement that produced the famous handshake between Yitzhak Rabin and Yasser Arafat on the White House lawn. This was followed by several other increasingly detailed agreements signed in Cairo and Washington, collectively known as the Oslo Agreements.

Putting aside all the detail and political history of the accords, the central philosophical feature of the process was an attempt to solve the core of the Arab–Israeli conflict, the Israeli–Palestinian dispute, by means of creating two states with a degree of open borders between them. This was considered to be important, as to a large extent the economic viability of the Palestinian state depended on large parts of its labour force being able to enter the Israeli jobs market and earn wages that they would subsequently spend back in the Palestinian state. This was no one-way dependency. For many years, Israel had been chronically short of cheap labour, and the Palestinians, many of whom worked without proper papers or employee national insurance contributions, filled an important gap, especially in the construction industry and domestic sectors.

The failure at Camp David put an end to all this. From here onwards there is a new set of terminology: separation, physical barriers and fences replace the vocabulary of co-operation, mutual dependency and integration. This marks a return to the peace-making strategies of the era of the late 1940s, when the United Nations General Assembly voted in 1947 to divide what was then Palestine into two states: one for the Jews and the other for the Arabs (see map 5). Under the UN proposals, the states were to be fully independent, with Jerusalem made an international city. The events of the next 50 years stem from two brutal facts: the Zionist leadership accepted the partition plan, while the Arab leadership of the local Palestinian population rejected the concept of partition in any form and moved to defeat the Zionists on the battlefield. Elie Kedourie makes the additional charge that not only did the leadership of the Palestinian Arabs oppose Zionism, they called in the Arab and Muslim worlds in order to help their cause. By doing this they took a local limited conflict and widened and raised its importance.[3] The wider Arab world took a similarly hostile view towards the Zionists, whom they regarded as little more than colonial settlers or 'outsiders' who would be only temporary residents of the region.

Before looking at who these Zionist immigrants were and where they came from, it is important to sketch the history of Palestine and the basic origins of Zionism. A word of caution here: both the history of Palestine and the development of Zionism lend themselves to separate comprehensive studies in their own right. Central to all this is the question: why Palestine?

Here, a brief look at key points in the history of Jerusalem and Palestine helps to illustrate the linkage between the Jews and the land.

Jerusalem's origins are said to date back some 4,000 years. In the beginning, around 1000 BC, King David captured the city and declared it the capital of the Israelites. Subsequently, David's son, King Solomon, built the First Temple there. Following Solomon's death in around 928 BC, his kingdom split into two: Jerusalem remained the capital of Judah (the southern part of the empire). Later, around 587 BC, the Babylonians conquered Judah and destroyed the First Temple, taking many Jews to Babylonia as prisoners. In 538 BC, however, after he conquered the Babylonians, Cyrus the Great, King of Persia, decided to allow the Jews to return to Jerusalem, and it was these returning Jews who built what became known as the Second Temple.

The period of Roman rule was marked by a major Jewish revolt that started in AD 66 and resulted in the seizing of the city by the Jews, until the Romans eventually retook it in AD 70. Subsequently, the Romans destroyed the Second Temple and much of the rest of the city's fortifications. Many Jews died during the Roman siege of the city and the ensuing battles, and those surviving Jews who weren't either executed or enslaved were sent into exile. Today, the Western Wall represents the only surviving part of the Second Temple.

Following the destruction of the Second Temple, Jews who have gone into exile have always desired to return to Zion (one of the biblical names for Jerusalem). Every year the traditional Passover meal, which commemorates the exodus from ancient Egypt, concludes with the phrase 'next year in Jerusalem'. For centuries, however, this desire was only a fantasy, and Jews living in the Diaspora adapted to their new countries. Zion, which had been under Muslim rule since the 7th century, remained possible for only a small number of Jews able to make the tortuous journey and to have a means of existence once there.[4]

At the start of the 19th century, the population of Palestine was less than 300,000, of which around only 5,000 were Jewish. Palestine itself was a small part of the Ottoman Empire that encompassed much of the Middle East and had been ruled by various Turkish dynasties since 1517. By the mid-19th century, the Jewish population had doubled, but still stood at around only 10,000. Jerusalem itself, however, was becoming a centre of international activity, due to the arrival of an increasing number of missionaries of various faiths.[5] These groups, to some degree, were encouraged to settle in Palestine by national governments that were seeking a pretext to gain a foothold in the city and the surrounding area. The British, for example, sought to protect the Protestants, the Russians the Greek and Russian Orthodox, and the French the Roman Catholics.[6] The Jews, however, had no national patron – either in Jerusalem or for the small pockets of Jewish communities outside the city. As a result, individuals came to play a more prominent role in the development and protection of the Jewish community in Palestine. One of the first to intervene in support of the Jews was Sir Moses Montefiore. During 1838, Montefiore tried – and failed – to negotiate a charter for land in Palestine where Jews would be able to live without interference. Unfortunately for Montefiore, his negotiating partner Muhammed Ali, the Viceroy of Egypt (and Palestine and Syria), was overthrown in 1841, and this helped put an end to the possibility of securing such a charter.

During the second half of the 19th century, the movement for national revival and independence of the Jewish people in Eretz Yisrael – Zionism – was born. The Jewish writer Nathan Birnbaum first used the actual term 'Zionism' in 1892.[7] A religious desire to return to the land of Eretz Yisrael had existed ever since the unsuccessful revolt against the Romans. This yearning was closely linked to the notions of messianic beliefs. The new Zionist movement, however, differed from the previous desire to return to Zion in its mainly secular content. Zionism did not develop in a laboratory.[8] The fierce anti-Semitism that swept through Europe at the time helped to shape Zionism's intellectual and political development. European nationalist and socialist doctrines influenced Jewish thinkers. In other words, the original Zionist thinkers were very much a product of their age.

The first major Zionist thinkers were actually predated by several of what can be termed pre-Zionist thinkers. Three figures warrant attention: Moses Hess, Rabbi Kalischer and Rabbi Alkalai. Moses Hess (1812–75), a German Jewish socialist, in his book *Rome and Jerusalem* – published in 1862 – argued that the establishment of a state by the Jews, based on socialist principles, would lead to a social and economic normalisation of the Jewish people. Central to the thinking of Rabbi Kalischer (1795–1874) was that the Messiah would come only after a large number of Jews had settled in Eretz Yisrael. Rabbi Alkalai (1798–1878) published a work in 1839 entitled *Pleasant Paths*, in which he also argued the need for Jewish colonies to be set up in the Holy Land as a condition for the return of the Messiah. There is also evidence of some basic Jewish nationalist thinking in the works of

Alkalai. Before his death in 1878, Alkalai had organised several groups of followers and had moved to Palestine himself to help with the development of Jewish settlement.

The first major Zionist thinkers were Yehuda Leib Pinsker (1821–91) and Theodor Herzl (1860–1904). In 1882, Pinsker published his book *Auto-Emancipation*, which argued in short that the emancipation granted by others would not solve the problems of the Jewish people. Only territorial concentration and sovereignty would lead to normalisation for the Jews. The most significant figure in the growth of Zionism during the 19th century, however, was Theodor Herzl. Born in Budapest, he was brought up in a liberal (reform) Jewish family. It was, however, not until he attended the University of Vienna, where he studied law, that his interest in Jewish affairs – and in particular the growing number of anti-Semitic incidents in Europe – took root. In 1896, he published his book *The Jewish State: an Attempt at a Modern Solution to the Jewish Question*. The basic central argument of the book was the contention that Europe's hatred of the Jews was unavoidable. The Jews, as a result, would be victimised and persecuted as long as they remained a vulnerable and unassimilated minority. The only solution, Herzl concluded, was the creation of a Jewish homeland.

In the following year the development of Zionism took a significant step forward from theory to reality when the World Zionist Organisation was created. In August 1897, it held its first congress in Basle, Switzerland. Following the Basle Congress it was clear that Zionism as a national movement had two inter-related aims. The first was the return of the Jews to the land by means of developing agricultural activities, and the revival of a national 'Jewish' life including social, cultural, economic and political elements. The second was to secure a national homeland for the Jews. More specifically, the Basle Programme stated that the aim of the Zionist movement was to create a homeland in Palestine for the Jewish people that was secured by public law. At Basle, Herzl stated that they were there to lay the foundation stone of the house that was to shelter the Jewish nation. In addition to holding its congress, the organisation started to lobby the relevant powers – the Ottoman Empire and Germany – for support for a Jewish homeland.

The second Zionist Congress meeting in 1898 passed a resolution that sanctioned efforts to gain a legal charter for Jewish settlement in Palestine. Herzl and the Zionist leaders initially approached Kaiser Wilhelm II, as Germany held some influence with the Ottoman Empire which controlled Palestine at the time. However, the Ottoman Sultan was against the idea, and the Kaiser was said not to wish to support the Zionists over his ally.

In 1903, Herzl's attention shifted to what became known as the Ugandan option. Central to this was the question of whether only Palestine (Eretz Yisrael) should be considered as the homeland for the Jews, or whether other areas should be discussed. The then British Colonial Secretary, Neville Chamberlain, suggested that there was a chance that the Zionists might be granted a homeland for the Jews in British East Africa. Herzl, although preferring Palestine, argued that some territory was better than none.

At the sixth Zionist Congress meeting in 1903, a map of East Africa – not Palestine – hung for all to see. After a stormy debate, Herzl won the day when a proposal to consider Uganda as a possible Jewish homeland was passed by 295 votes to 177, with 100 abstentions. Herzl, however, died in 1904, at the relatively young age of 44, robbing Zionism of one of its most important early leaders. One year after his death, the seventh Zionist Congress finally rejected the so-called 'Uganda Plan'. This vote caused a split in the movement, with some Zionists leaving the World Zionist Organisation. Some of these dissenters argued that the Jewish people needed an uninhabited territory, and that sadly Palestine did not meet this requirement. Others argued that the need for a homeland was so pressing that any land offered should be accepted. For the vast majority of Zionism, the vote in 1905 marked the end of the consideration of any land but Palestine for the Jewish homeland.

At the time of Herzl's death it was clear that two distinct groupings had emerged within the Zionist movement. The first of these, the cultural Zionists, were more interested in the development of Hebrew and Jewish culture such as language, arts identity and religion, than with the potential establishment of a state. They, in effect, saw Zionism as a solution to the problems of Judaism and they were associated with the thinking of the writer Asher Ginsberg (1856–1927). The second grouping, the political Zionists, argued that the need for territory was the most important requirement of the Zionist movement. Indeed, Herzl's pragmatic reaction to the proposals for the Ugandan option was a clear illustration of the aim of the political Zionists. As the Zionist movement as a whole grew, so more and more people started to emigrate to Palestine. These new immigrants expanded existing Jewish colonies and founded new ones. In 1909, the first Kibbutz was started by the Sea of Galilee, called 'Kibbutz Degania', and in the same year Tel Aviv was founded along the shoreline from Jaffa.

These settlement activities in Palestine represented the practical approach to Zionism, and this combined with political Zionism to form what was termed 'synthetic Zionism', which became closely associated with Chaim Weizman (1874–1952). Born in Russia, Weizman played a central role in the development of the Zionist movement and was to become Israel's first president. In 1904, Weizman emigrated from Russia to Britain, where he lobbied for the Zionist cause and played an influential role in winning some degree of British recognition for a Jewish homeland in Palestine. Along with David Ben-Gurion, Weizman became one of the central figures of the pre-state Zionist movement, serving as President of the World Zionist Organisation during 1921–31 and 1935–46.

In historical terms, the period of population change in Palestine was quite short, starting only in the 1880s. Perhaps the greatest myth surrounding the arrival of the various waves of Jewish immigration to Palestine during this time (Aliyah) was the question of their motives for coming in the first place. The majority of the immigrants who came to Palestine did not do so for Zionist reasons. Rather, they came for a variety of reasons that involved both persecution in their country of origin and a lack of third country option. The latter became an increasingly important factor when the United States closed its doors to Jewish immigration. Many who came to Palestine found life there to be too harsh and left. Emigration has been a constant problem for the Zionist movement, both in Palestine and subsequently in Israel. In both the Yishuv* and the subsequent state of Israel, there is clear linkage between immigration and security. In short, as much of the land as possible had to be settled in order to control it, and the only means of achieving this was by having a larger population to distribute around it.[9] This concept in modern terms is known as 'putting facts on the ground'.

In the early days of the first and second Aliyahs, the immigrants, most of whom came from Eastern European urban backgrounds, struggled with having to make the land fertile. It is here that one of the great dilemmas of the Zionist movement became apparent. Who should farm the land? The first immigrants took the view that local Arab labour was both better equipped to undertake this arduous task and also very cheap. The second wave of immigrants took the view that the state for the Jews would be built using Hebrew labour, and they clashed with the veteran immigrants over this question. Eventually, the second group carried the day, but the debate about using Arab or foreign labour never really went away. The fallout of the failed Camp David Summit of 2000 did not mean an end to the debate, only the replacement of the cheap Palestinian labour in Israel with foreign workers from Eastern Europe and Asia.

So how were the various waves of immigrants, with their different backgrounds and motivations for being in Palestine, shaped into a nation in waiting with a distinct political culture?

Here money talks. The majority, but by no means all, of the immigrants arrived in Palestine between 1880 and the mid-1960s with little in the way of capital and worldly possessions. Many had been forced to flee their country of origin at short notice,

* See Glossary on p. 232.

others – such as the Jews who escaped Germany under the Nazi regime – had seen their assets frozen or stolen. Upon entering Palestine they found a well-oiled and financed Zionist immigration absorption machine run by the Labour Zionist movement. The immigrants became highly dependent on this machine, run by the veteran immigrants and financed by world Jewry, for their everyday needs ranging from health care to education. Social and economic advancement was to be found through contacts with the Zionist organisations.

The leaders of the Zionist movement in Palestine were of course acutely aware of the dependency ties and used them effectively to ensure their leadership positions and support for their various political agendas. These strong dependency ties have played a pivotal role in Israeli society, with nearly all the newly arriving immigrants up to and including those who came from the ex-Soviet Union during the 1990s being heavily reliant on the immigrant absorption machine for their welfare. What is perhaps slightly different with the more recent immigrants is that their expectations of the absorption and integration process into Israel appear to be much greater than those of earlier immigrants. This has led to rapid disenchantment with Israeli governments from both sides of the political spectrum. The immigrants charge that governments prefer to protect the economic position of the veteran immigrants at the expense of the new ones.

The dependency ties meant that the vast majority of new immigrants accepted the rule of the leadership of the veteran immigrants. This leadership, which included such figures as David Ben-Gurion (Israel's first Prime Minister), was thus largely able to shape the newly arriving immigrants into its existing ideological and organisational structures. Dissent was not tolerated. Immigrants were expected to accept the existing social and economic structures. The increasing threat of Arab violence tended to reinforce these structures, with dissent being portrayed as close to treason. Consequently, even before the state of Israel was created, a strong, highly centralised élite had been formed that was transferred to the state of Israel in 1948 and came to characterise the first decades of Israel's existence.

To a large extent, external factors dictated the pace of development of Zionism in Palestine. Central to this was the attitude of the British authorities who ruled Palestine following the demise of the Ottoman Empire and the end of the First World War.[10]

What factors contributed to the developing British attitude towards Palestine, and how did it try to resolve the growing conflict between the Zionists and Arab populations?

The guiding light for British policy in Palestine was always national self-interest, defined here as shoring up British economic and political interests and checking those of perceived enemies – or as Gabriel Sheffer succinctly put it: 'the maintenance of British rule over Palestine at minimal cost and for an indefinite period.'[11] British policy in Palestine was not unique – as some claim – but rather consistent with the overall goal of British policy in the era of Empire. This was characterised by an identification of key areas of strategic importance to Britain and a divide-and-rule policy with the 'locals'. From this it is clear that there were instances where the British authorities clearly aimed to play Arab off against Zionist in order to avoid the British nightmare of both sides fighting together to remove Britain from Palestine.

More importantly, British policy was dominated by the question of which group was most useful to British interests at any given time. The Balfour Declaration, which gave support to the establishment of a Jewish homeland in Palestine, needs to be seen in this light, as do the various British proposals for resolving the conflict that as time went on came to reflect the British need to keep the Arabs on board. Charges of anti-Semitism in the British Colonial Office – and tales of the 'Lawrence of Arabia complex' (the alleged homosexual love affair between ex-public schoolboys and the Arabs) – may well hold some truth. Neither, however, was the main driving force in the formation of British policy towards Palestine.

At the start of the First World War in 1914 there were around 15,000 Jews living in Palestine. The war itself made the Suez

Canal and the area around it strategically important to the British, who had acquired it in 1875. This importance was increased by the fact that Turkey was part of the German–Austro-Hungarian Alliance – and the British did not want an ally of Germany to get too close to the canal. From this period on, the Arabs' strategic importance to the British was clear. The British encouraged an Arab revolt against the Turks in 1916 with promises of recognition and support for Arab independence in all the regions, and while the Arabs and British fought the Turks, the representatives of the British and French governments met, in effect, to divide up the Middle East at the conclusion of the First World War. The resulting Sykes–Picot agreement of 1916 was reached with only minimal consultation with local leaders, and was eventually modified as, during the final years of the war, the British position was strengthened and the French position weakened. The British Prime Minister, David Lloyd George, notified the French that they would have to accept a British protectorate over Palestine, as it was a strategic buffer to Egypt. The original agreement had called for much of Palestine to be ruled by a joint Allied condominium for political and religious reasons.

The First World War saw the British and Allied armies liberate Palestine from the Ottoman Empire and the period of the British Mandate (direct British rule) over Palestine commence. The initial signs for the Zionists were encouraging. In 1917, the British hoped that the support of world Jewry would help the war effort. There was also a fear that if the British did not attract the Jews, then the Germans would. Indeed, there is evidence that Kaiser Wilhelm II was preparing such a gesture to the Zionists with this very intention. It was against this background that on 2 November 1917 the British Foreign Secretary, James Balfour, wrote a letter to the President of the British Zionist Federation, Lord Rothschild. The letter contained so-called British support for the creation of a national home in Palestine for the Jews. In retrospect, the document reflected the penchant of the British civil service for framing proposals with a high degree of creative ambiguity that allowed for varying interpretations by each party.

The modern-day fictional head of the service, Sir Humphrey Appleby, would no doubt have been extremely satisfied with its wording.

The ambiguity of the Balfour Declaration, and subsequent failures of the Zionist movement to get the British to agree upon an interpretation of it or a redraft, led some Zionists to attempt to deal with the Arab leaders in Palestine directly. The concept of direct negotiations as providing the best opportunity to reach accommodation has been a consistent one in the conflict, and even the Oslo Accords for all their failings at least reflected a modern attempt at direct negotiations. Traditionally the problem has lain in finding a partner for negotiations. Ignoring the modern-day sound-bite culture of phrases like 'partner for peace', this nevertheless has always proved to be extremely difficult for the Zionists. Either their partner has been assassinated by opponents of a deal, or has deliberately reneged on the deal, or has been unable for a variety of reasons to keep their side of the bargain. Whatever the cause, the result is the same. Back in January 1919 we see an early example of this when Chaim Weizman, later to be the first President of Israel, signed a formal pact with Emir Feisal, who had been the leader of the 1916 Arab revolt against the Turks. The most important part of the agreement, signed on 3 January, concerned the guaranteeing to the Jews of the right of free immigration to Palestine and legal settlement of the land.[12] Conversely, it contained assurances that Arab tenant farmers would retain their own plots of land and be assisted in economic development. Opposition, however, from Arab nationalists and backtracking on what was agreed by Feisal doomed the chances of successfully implementing the agreement.[13] Another precedent was set here: the difficulty of implementing agreements (often in the face of hostile opponents of the pact) is often greater than that of reaching the agreement in the first place. One wonders if, when left alone to think, President Clinton could have come to the same conclusion a little more quickly during the mid 1990s.

As British control over Palestine deepened, so resentment of the British presence grew. Between 1920 and 1922, tensions between

ws and Arabs increased. On the Jewish side, these frustra-
tions were exacerbated by the publication of the White Paper
in 1922 by Winston Churchill, the Colonial Secretary, which
offered a more restrictive version of the Balfour Declaration. The
central feature of the White Paper was that the whole of Palestine
would not become the Jewish homeland. Worse was to follow for
the Zionists. In 1922, the League of Nations awarded the British
mandatory powers, which they had had, in effect, since the end of
the First World War. The Mandate itself contained the text of the
Balfour Declaration. This point was important, as it amounted to
formal recognition by the British of the Zionist claims and the
Zionist movement. Showing its true colours, however, as soon as
Britain was formally awarded the mandatory powers, it parti-
tioned Palestine into two territories: Palestine and TransJordan.
The River Jordan divided these two new states. Jews were not
allowed to settle to the east of the river. So from 1922 we start to
talk about a partition of an already divided land.

Throughout the 1920s and 30s, Palestine was run along the
lines of a British colony. The British High Commissioner, Sir
Herbert Samuel, had to deal with increasing anger from Arab
residents over the continuing Jewish immigration. Hostility
between the local Arab population and the Jews grew stronger
with the resulting outbreaks of violence and general civil unrest.
The British position reflected these difficulties, and as a result the
British established a framework policy for limiting Jewish
immigration to Palestine. Initially, the formula that was adopted
in 1922 was based on an economic criterion. This allowed
economically self-sufficient Jews, dependants of residents, and
those with religious occupations to enter Palestine. On top of
this, only what were termed as 'subsidised immigrants' were
allowed to enter. The World Zionist Organisation had to guarantee the maintenance of these immigrants for at least one year, and
this was later redefined as those who had a real prospect of
finding employment. Even then, these immigrants were allowed
to enter only up to a quota set by the authorities. The key to
immigration lay in the award of labour certificates that were
drawn up first by the Jewish Agency and agreed with the British

High Commissioner in Palestine. They were distributed along party lines, with each of the political parties receiving certificates in proportion to their political strength in the country. This fact further increased the dependency ties between the newly arriving immigrants and the Labour movement led by immigrants of the Second and Third Aliyah.

This pattern continued. As Arab hostility to the increasing pace of Jewish immigration grew even deeper, so the British reacted by severely limiting the numbers of Jews allowed to enter Palestine. For example, the Jewish Agency asked for 60,000 labour certificates in 1933 and 1934, but the British granted fewer than 18,000. In 1936, 10,695 were requested, but the British approved only 1,800. The British attempted to cap Jewish immigration, imposing an upper level set at 12,000 Jews per year. It was against the backdrop of spiralling violence that a Royal Commission of Inquiry led by the Earl of Peel was dispatched to Palestine on a fact-finding mission in November 1936. In July 1937, the Peel Commission published its report, which concluded that the competing claims of the Arabs and Jews over Palestine were irreconcilable. The situation, it argued in beautifully moralistic tones, was a fundamental conflict of right with right, and the only solution was to partition the land of Palestine into two states. This concept of right versus right here is important as it implies, correctly, that legitimate claims on the lands can be made by both sides. The solution to partition the land appears therefore logical. The proposal argued that the best solution was a Jewish state in one part of Palestine and an Arab state comprising the other part of Palestine and TransJordan, with the British continuing to control the city of Jerusalem and the areas surrounding it (see map 3). In truth, the Peel Report divided Zionists. Some argued that at least it represented a concrete proposal for a real state, while others opposed such a small geographic state. The Arabs rejected the plan and every subsequent proposal that would have led to the establishment of a Jewish state.

In 1938, the pattern of appeasing Arab violence continued when another Royal Commission – this time led by Sir John Woodhead – was dispatched to Palestine to examine partition plans. The Woodhead Report was published on 9 November 1938. Its findings dealt a severe blow to the aspirations of the Zionists. The report argued that the recommendations of the Peel Report were unrealistic and its proposed lines of partition unreasonable. In its place, the Woodhead Report recommended a new partition plan that would create a much larger Arab state – and conversely a smaller Jewish state (see map 4). The new plan allowed the Jews a state that would comprise only around 5 per cent of West Palestine and less than 1 per cent of the original Mandate territory. The Zionist movement reacted angrily to such a plan, while the Arabs once more rejected any plan that would have created a Jewish state.

As the Second World War approached, the British were forced to openly concede that the Middle East was an area of great strategic importance to it, and in February 1939 the British Colonial Secretary Malcolm MacDonald met with both Arab and Zionist leaders. His conclusion said much about British thinking at the time. He argued that it was the priority of the British government to ensure that the Arab governments were not tempted to accept possible support from hostile powers (Germany). In effect, if the British had to make a choice between the Arabs and the Jews, the British needed Arab help more than Jewish support. In short, the Arabs were more strategically important to the British than the Jews. This position became clearer still with the publication of another White Paper in May 1939, which declared that the authors of the Mandate could not have intended Palestine to be converted into a Jewish state against the will of the Arab population. As a result, within a period of ten years the British would set up an independent Palestinian state (in addition to TransJordan).

This was not the only sweetener to the Arabs. The White Paper called for a limit to Jewish immigration to Palestine of 75,000 for the following five-year period, which would make the Jews a third of the total population of Palestine. Following this five-year period, Jewish immigration was to be stopped. Just as thousands of Jews were attempting to escape the growing horror of Europe, so the British were closing their major avenue of escape. Illegal immigration, which existed throughout the period of the British Mandate, increased as the crisis in Europe worsened; the British imposed tighter controls, and as the Second World War approached these efforts were stepped up. The resulting bill from the White Paper was passed in the House of Commons by 268 to 179 votes, with 110 abstentions. Among those who condemned the actions of the British government was Winston Churchill, who argued that the bill broke a pledge to the Jews outside Palestine who sought a homeland. Opposition to the bill was not confined to Britain. The League of Nations Mandates Commission argued that the bill meant that Britain had reneged on its commitment to the League and the Zionist movement to support the principles of the Balfour Declaration. Events, however, overtook the League's criticisms as war loomed and the question of the future status of Palestine was no longer at the top of the agenda.

It is worth pointing out that though the proportion of Jews among the total population of Palestine increased steadily during the period of the British Mandate, the Arabs, by far, remained in the majority. For example, in 1930, Arabs accounted for 80 per cent of the total population of Palestine, and even in 1940 the figure was still as high as 70 per cent.[14] During the period of the Mandate the Arab population, contrary to some propaganda, did grow, but did so at a slower rate than within the Jewish communities in Palestine. From this it is important to dispel any notion that there were dramatic shifts in the demographic balance of Palestine. The changes were in reality much slower, and reflected the efforts of the British to restrict the entry of Jewish immigrants into the country.

The Second World War and the Holocaust are two events that go beyond the scope of this book. The effects on the Zionist movement and the subsequent state of Israel were of both a practical and a more profound nature. On a practical level, as details of the Holocaust started to emerge there was an intensification of the efforts of the Zionist movement to convince the British to re-open Palestine to Jewish immigration. The Holocaust led to a weakening, and in some cases an ending, of opposition to Zionism in most non-Arab countries. On the more profound level, the Holocaust had two effects on the Zionist leadership and on the subsequent state of Israel. First, the realisation that nothing was too horrible to happen, the shattering of the myth that these things just don't happen in a modern civilised world. As we shall see later, this fact affected Israeli foreign policy-making and Israeli national identity. Second, the development of the notion that the Jews must always be prepared to protect themselves – they could not rely upon others to do this for them. The European Jewry had been dependent upon someone else for their protection – the United States, Great Britain and others – and had perished as a result of the failure of that other party to defend them. The notion of self-sufficiency in defence was a cornerstone of Israeli defence doctrine, and played a role in the decision at the start of the 1970s to develop a military industrial complex (MIC) in Israel that would arm the Israeli military.

While the world was horrified by the Holocaust, most Western governments did little to increase Jewish settlement to their respective countries. This lack of an alternative host country made Jewish immigration to Palestine all the more important. The first post-war government in Britain led by Clement Attlee steadfastly refused to alter the policy on immigration to Palestine that had been laid out in the 1939 White Paper. Once more, despite the moral outrage in the international community over the Holocaust, the formation of British policy towards Palestine and the Middle East continued to be determined by British strategic interests. Indeed, as the war ended the British stepped up their efforts to stop illegal immigration to Palestine. They persuaded other governments not to sell boats or offer other forms of assistance to Jewish refugees. However, despite the best efforts of the British, some illegal immigrants did arrive in Palestine and were successfully absorbed by the Zionist movement.

During the Second World War, violence in Palestine had increased as the Jewish military forces became more active. In 1946 the violence escalated following the British decision to set up relocation camps in Cyprus for the Jewish refugees who had survived the Holocaust. To make matters worse, all Jewish illegal immigration ships that were intercepted on the high seas or even when within sight of Palestine were taken to Cyprus and the immigrants detained in camps surrounded by barbed wire and guards. The British took this a stage further with the interception of the ship *Exodus*, which was carrying nearly 4,000 immigrants to Palestine. The ship arrived and was able to dock in the port of Haifa in northern Palestine, but the British would not let the passengers disembark, and insisted upon the ship returning to its French port of origin. When the Jews refused to disembark in France, the British government sent the ship back to Germany – the country that so many of the immigrants were attempting to flee.

The then Leader of the Opposition, Winston Churchill, speaking in the House of Commons on 1 August 1946, supported the case that the Holocaust survivors should not be resettled in Palestine. 'No one can imagine that there is room in Palestine for the great masses of Jews who wish to leave Europe, or that they could be absorbed in any period which it is now useful to contemplate. The idea that the Jewish problem could be solved or even helped by a vast dumping of the Jews of Europe into Palestine is really too silly to consume our time in the House this afternoon.'[15] Such speeches, and the actions of the new Labour government, brought little credit on the British, and international pressure continued to increase on the Attlee government to do something for the Jews. On top of this, the British garrison stationed in Palestine was coming under increasing pressure following a series of attacks from Jewish forces that ranged from hit-and-run guerrilla operations to bombings, and this low-intensity war showed little sign of being resolved.

It was against this backdrop that in 1946 an Anglo-American Commission of Inquiry was established to investigate the refugee crisis. In May 1946 it published its recommendations, at the centre of which was the call for 100,000 Jewish immigrants to be allowed to enter Palestine immediately. The British government subsequently proposed the Morrison Plan, which would have led to the British Mandate in Palestine becoming a trusteeship, the country being divided into Arab and Jewish provinces with separate zones created for Jerusalem and the Negev Desert. Law and order, defence, foreign relations and the ports and airports were to remain under British control. The Morrison Plan accepted the one-off arrival of 100,000 Jewish immigrants, but from that point on, the old formula of immigrants having to prove their economic worth to the county was to be reinstated.

An illustration of the new political and economic realities in the post-Second World War period was that the United States was to finance the implementation of the immigration plan. Rather unsurprisingly, both the Zionist movement and the Arabs rejected the plan. Arab rejection was consistent with their previous hostility to any plan that allowed Jewish immigration, and Zionist opposition was predictable as the plan fell a long way short of realising their aspirations. The Morrison Plan marked the last major attempt of the British government to settle the Palestine question. Following the plan's rejection, the British handed over the problem to the newly created United Nations, which convened a special session on 2 April 1947 to discuss Palestine's future.[16]

Britain washed its hands of Palestine because the cost of maintaining a presence in the country, both financially and in terms of lives lost, was no longer outweighed by the strategic benefits of remaining. The withdrawal from Palestine should also be viewed as part of the process of de-colonisation that many British colonies underwent (for that was what Palestine had really become). As Britain departed, its forces left a country in chaos, on the verge of all-out war and with little chance of living in peaceful co-existence. Over 30 years of British rule had done little for Palestine except leave the traditional trappings of empire, such as an organised bureaucracy and legal system, much of which was adopted by Israel. This was not Britain's finest hour. From a Zionist perspective, Naomi Shepherd offers a more charitable summary of the period of the British Mandate. She argues that the Mandate offered protection to the Zionist beach-head in Palestine during its most insecure and vulnerable period during the 1920s and 30s. This, she goes on to suggest, was the fundamental political legacy of the Mandate, and was achieved in spite of the hostility of so many British officials to Zionism and despite the armed confrontations with Jewish groups in the twilight period of the Mandate.[17] There is some merit in Shepherd's conclusions, but to suggest that the Zionists survived as the result of British policy is overstating the argument. The Zionists survived, and indeed flourished, despite the actions and intentions of the British by, in effect, learning both how to co-operate with the authorities and how to circumvent them.

CHAPTER TWO

The Birth of the State

*How was Israel created, and are there any parallels
with the creation of a Palestinian state?*

Israel was created in 1948 by a combination of military might
and economic and diplomatic efforts. The three are closely
related. The Zionists' diplomatic hand would have been considerably weakened had they not had the required military force
to defend the infant state against the attempts of the Arabs to
destroy it. A state that was unsustainable in economic terms
would have had the same negative impact on the efforts of the
Zionist leadership to win international recognition for the
declaration of statehood. The absence of any of these pre-
conditions would render the creation of a state a meaningless and
self-indulgent act. There are of course obvious parallels with the
recent debate surrounding the creation of a Palestinian state in
the West Bank and Gaza Strip. Any similarities, however, are
confined to the area of nationalist aspirations.

The leadership of the Zionist movement in Palestine effectively
developed a state within a state during the period of the British
Mandate. This is sometimes referred to as a state in waiting. All
the trappings of statehood were present: armies, economic,
political and bureaucratic structures. The leadership of the
Labour Zionist movement, however, did not enjoy a total control
over the instruments of violence – an important pre-requisite for
statehood. Armed groups such as the Irgun and the Stern Gang
were closely related to the Revisionist Zionist movement that

contained such figures as Ze'ev Jabotinksy and Menachem Begin. It was only during the first ceasefire of Israel's War of Independence that the armed wing of the Labour Zionist movement struck a decisive blow against the Revisionist forces, when a ship carrying arms for Revisionist fighters was scuppered off the coast of Tel Aviv on 22 June 1948 by the Israeli Defence Forces (IDF) which were loyal to the provisional government of Israel led by David Ben-Gurion. The Altalena Affair as it became known (after the name of the ship) was a defining moment for the infant state, and the bitterness from the events in which several men lost their lives helped define the early bitterness between Ben-Gurion and Begin. Today, the Palestinian leadership faces similar problems, but here the forces that will be expected to enforce the law in a Palestinian state enjoy far less of a monopoly over the means of violence than the Labour Zionist movement did some 50 years earlier.

Back in 1948 (even after the UN had voted in favour of the partition of Palestine into a Jewish and an Arab state in 1947), there was still a feeling that a Jewish state might not be a realistic prospect, surrounded as it was by hostile Arab states and with lines of partition not particularly favourable to the Jews. The narrow coastal strip and the Jerusalem corridor looked vulnerable. The Jewish institutions in the British Mandate, while impressive, did not amount to the economy needed to drive a state. Yes, there was a degree of territorial continuity, but the size of the state fell far short of what even the moderate Zionists had hoped to obtain. Still, the pressing need for a homeland – confirmed so starkly by the Holocaust in Europe – meant that the Zionists had little alternative to taking a calculated risk and declaring statehood.

So on 14 May 1948, the state of Israel was created and the Declaration of Independence signed by the leading Zionist figures. As with any new state, the winning of international recognition was vital to its long-term survival. The prolonged debate in the United States over this question was an illustration of the complex set of issues and agendas that went into making the decision to ratify. In truth, the debate in Washington reflected the power struggle between the White House and the State Department over the formation of Middle East policy.

President Truman's commitment to a Jewish state was not only a product of his strongly held Christian views which manifested themselves in the form of guilt about the Holocaust, but also extensive lobbying by Zionist leaders, most notably Chaim Weizman, and political expediency – fear of alienating the US Jewish voters.[1] Secretary of State George Marshall led a department that was staffed by American Arabists who were in general much less keen on a Jewish state than the White House. Marshall, in furious arguments with President Truman, argued that to support the creation of a Jewish state (code for recognition) would lead to a marked increase in the already frequent Arab–Israeli violence and directly draw the United States into the conflict. Only after much debate, and after attempts to win support for a trusteeship for Palestine failed, was the decision of the US clear. It would support the creation of a Jewish state.

As Bill Clinton sat in his log cabin with Arafat and Barak some 50 years later, his mind must have strayed to the arguments put forward by Secretary of State Marshall in 1948. In 2000, the United States was drawn into the Arab–Israeli conflict to a much greater extent than it really wished. Not only was the President the major mediator between the parties, he was also judge, jury and executioner in terms of blaming one side or the other for the failure of the talks. On top of all this, there was a growing feeling in Washington that the US would eventually have to impose a deal on the parties as the only viable way of ending the conflict. There was also a belief that US forces would have to be stationed on the Golan Heights as part of an Israeli–Syrian peace deal. Clearly, Marshall was right on intellectual and strategic grounds that the creation of Israel would greatly destabilise the region and draw the United States deeply into solving the conflict.

The central factor in assessing our perspective on Israel is much related to the Marshall criteria. Is Israel the root cause of the violence in the Middle East or is it the front line against terrorism? President Truman and all his successors have been kind to Israel (even President Bush Sr) for various reasons ranging from strategic needs during the Cold War to more cultural explanations. All have taken the view that Israel was very much the front line, first in the fight against communism and the Soviet infiltration of the Arab states, secondly in the fight against international terrorism, and post-September 11 the war against militant Islam. This US support has been vital in securing Israel's existence at key junctures in its history.

It would not be until the Kennedy era of the early 1960s, however, that the United States translated this support for Israel into arms sales. Back in 1948, despite the support from President Truman, Israel was very much alone in terms of much needed help in the battlefield. Today, of course, the picture is very different, with Israel receiving around $1.5 billion of military aid from the US each year. In reality, this aid is self-serving for the United States, as the Israeli government invests heavily in the US military industrial complex, much of which is based in California. In recent years, there have been countless examples of Israel and the US co-operating on joint research and development projects, many of which are funded with the aid that America provides to Israel. At the start of the 21st century there is no closer ally of the United States in terms of military co-operation than Israel.

In retrospect it appears almost criminal that there was no real, serious discussion by both the Palestinians and the wider Arab world to strike a deal with the Jews. The partition plan presented by the United Nations Special Committee on Palestine (UNSCOP) in 1947 was more than fair to the Palestinians. The division of the land would have left the Palestinians with East Jerusalem as their capital and a viable state in terms of continuity of land. Indeed, it was the Jewish state that would have been more vulnerable, being little more than twelve miles wide in places and with a very narrow corridor linking West Jerusalem with the rest of the state.

Rational politics would seem to dictate that it would be the Jews who would object to such a state, one that fell far short of their minimum demands. And it is true to say that not all the Zionist leadership accepted the plan in good faith. Others rejected the partition as not giving enough land for a viable

Jewish state. The mainstream Zionist leadership, however, accepted the plan and the rest, as they say, is history. In recent years, some revisionist historians such as Avi Shlaim have claimed that there was in effect a plot – or collusion as he terms it – between the Zionist leadership and King Abdullah, the leader of TransJordan, to carve up the area earmarked to be the Palestinian state between their two countries. This would appear to be a little far-fetched, but it is true that since 1948 it has been in the interests of both Israel and TransJordan's successor, Jordan, to work to prevent the creation of a Palestinian state, which both countries believe to be a dangerous destabilising force on their respective borders.

The Palestinian rejection of the partition plan is the single biggest disaster in the history of the Palestinian people.

So why did it happen, and what was the rationale behind it?

The lack of a well-organised and politically astute leadership is central to the failure. Palestine was hierarchical: a few select families set and controlled the political agenda. This group believed that by not co-operating on any negotiations with the Zionists they could prevent the birth of a Jewish state. When this strategy failed spectacularly at the United Nations in 1947 they resorted almost exclusively to the military strategy of force, believing that they, along with their Arab brothers, could drive the Zionists out of Palestine – thereby allowing the creation of a Palestinian state in all the lands of the British Mandate of Palestine.

On paper, such a rejectionist strategy was both foolhardy and reckless. Despite a massive numerical superiority in both manpower and weapons, the Arab armies were untested in battle. Among the Egyptian army there was little war experience, even among the officer class. Indeed, Egypt had decided to send troops to Palestine to fight the newly created state of Israel only at the last minute, and did so when it became clear that if it had remained indifferent to the call to arms its dominant position within the Arab League would have been threatened.[2] The rationale behind this decision revealed a characteristic that has been central to the Arab–Israeli conflict since 1948, namely the importance of inter-Arab politics in dictating the responses of the various Arabs towards Israel at any given time. It was also unclear at the time how motivated the armies would prove in fighting for a land that – with the exception of the local Palestinian fighters – was not their own. Jewish forces even prior to 1948 had proved tenacious – if somewhat badly led – and knew that they were fighting for their very existence in Palestine, and after 14 May 1948 for the survival of the infant state of Israel.

The reality of the 1948 Israeli War of Independence confirmed the Arab military over-confidence. It was at leadership level, however, that the Arab armies were most handicapped. Little trust existed between the various Arab war leaders. King Abdullah of TransJordan was placed in charge of the joint Arab high command, mainly so his actions were transparent to sceptical Arab leaders who suspected that he was not totally committed to the Palestinian cause. In essence, and ignoring the Israeli myths that have grown up surrounding the 1948 war, the Arabs lost it mainly through their own failings rather than Israel winning it.

Within eight hours of its Declaration of Independence, Israel was attacked by seven Arab armies. By the end of the war, Israel had not only survived, but had conquered more land that was outside its control in the original UN Partition Plan. It paid a high price, however, for its survival, with over 6,000 dead – around 1 per cent of the total Jewish population in Palestine. This figure transferred into US proportions would have meant 2,500,000 lost in battle, and in UK terms some 500,000 killed. These comparisons illustrate the level of self-sacrifice and determination of the Jewish people to fight for their homeland. There is no accurate number of Arab war dead. If precise records of the figure were kept – and Arab bureaucracy is traditionally comprehensive – then the statistics remain locked away in Arab state archives, whose collections of documents have never been made available for public consumption.

On the battlefront, the Egyptian army attacked in the south. They quickly succeeded in reaching Gaza and carried on to the town of Ashdod, only twenty miles south of Tel Aviv. After heavy fighting, the Egyptians managed to cut off the Negev Desert from the rest of Israel. In the north, the Syrians attacked the Kibbutzim and settlements in the Galilee using their strategic positions in the hills overlooking these areas. In the east, the Jordanian army advanced towards Jerusalem. On top of fighting the regular Arab armies, the newly created Israeli Defence Forces (IDF) had to deal with continued attacks from the Palestinian Arabs. During the initial stages of the war the IDF was ill prepared, badly armed, and heavily outnumbered by the Arab forces. As a result, the Arabs made many early gains. These gains, however, were short-term. The IDF was getting stronger by the day, both in terms of manpower and armaments. As soon as the state of Israel was declared, it had opened its doors to the Jews that had been kept out by the British. Holocaust survivors and illegal immigrants held by the British in Cyprus were the first to arrive, many going straight into the front line. Israeli officials searched the world for arms and were successful in acquiring new weapons from Czechoslovakia and other countries.

The IDF went on the offensive. The Syrians in the north were pushed back, though the Jordanian army under its British Commander, General Sir John Glubb, succeeded in capturing the Old City in Jerusalem, the siege in Jewish western Jerusalem was finally broken, and operations were undertaken to widen control of the approaches to the west of the city. Not all Israeli operations proved successful, but the general tide of the war had turned in Israel's favour. It was during this time that the Israeli Air Force (IAF) became operational. Using three recently acquired second-hand B-17 Flying Fortresses, the IAF bombed Cairo and Damascus. In future Arab–Israeli wars the role of the IAF, and control of the skies, became a central strategic necessity for Israel.

International pressure to broker an end to the conflict was an ever-present factor in the war. During the initial stages, Israel had been keen for a ceasefire in order to buy some time, but as the war turned Israel became increasingly concerned about the prospect of the international community imposing a solution before it had time to retake key strategic areas from the Arabs. Count Bernadotte, the UN Special Mediator, had formulated a proposal that would have led to the Negev being removed from Israel in return for Israeli control of Western Galilee, returning Lod and Ramle to Arab control and placing Jerusalem and the international airport at Lod (today, Ben-Gurion airport) under UN control. Despite obvious Israeli concern over Bernadotte's proposals, he was cordially received by Ben-Gurion and other Israeli leaders on several occasions. On 17 September 1948, however, while driving through Jerusalem on his way to Government House in a demilitarised part of the city, Bernadotte was gunned down along with his French assistant. The three assailants – who were presumed to be Jewish – escaped and were never captured. Ben-Gurion decided that this was the time to act swiftly and forcibly. The Irgun, which in places had continued to exist outside the IDF chain of command, was given one day to hand over its arms to the IDF, and some 200 members of another Revisionist group, Lehi, including its leaders, were detained. By the end of the crisis, all Jewish forces came under the command structure of the IDF, and have remained so to the present day.

Only after protracted and heavy fighting in the south did the IDF led by General Yigal Allon succeed in driving the Egyptian forces out of the Negev and back into the Sinai Desert. The battles in the Negev did not end until the close of January 1949, nearly eight months after Israel's declaration of statehood. By this stage, the international community was becoming increasingly concerned about Israeli actions in the area. International pressure against Israel mounted as Israeli forces penetrated into Egyptian territory. The British delivered an ultimatum to the Israelis on 1 January 1949, that they would be forced to come to the aid of the Egyptians. Ben-Gurion, concerned over a possible total collapse of the Egyptian regime, and keen to avoid taking undue risks, ordered Israeli forces to be withdrawn from the Sinai by the following day. The Israeli actions in the south were the final part in securing control of all the territory that had been proposed to the Jews in the UNSCOP Partition Plan. Israel gained some 2,500 square miles of territory in addition to that proposed in the original plan. Egypt and Jordan divided up the remaining land between themselves.

Over-confidence and poor and divided military and political leadership were not the only causes of 'the disaster' that befell the Palestinian people in 1948. It was also caused to some degree by the lack of mass communications at that time. Information was in the hands of a select few whose own agendas often interfered with merely presenting the facts. One such case was Deir Yassin. Unquestionably, and for reasons that still remain disputed by both sides, a massacre took place in this Palestinian village in the hills around Jerusalem. Members of the Stern Gang – a Zionist Revisionist paramilitary force – killed many of the inhabitants of this village. Word soon spread by mouth, and the Palestinian leadership told local Palestinian journalists covering the events to exaggerate the massacre to include such charges that the Jewish fighters raped the local women. Such accusations contributed to the climate of fear that prevailed among Palestinian communities at this time.

Today, in the age of 24/7 news networks – and high numbers of domestic and foreign journalists in the Disputed Territories – there is a new set of problems of news manipulation for public relations purposes. Take the infamous example of the alleged massacre that Palestinian leaders claim took place in the Jenin refugee camp in 2002. The Palestinians were quick to link the imagery of Jenin to Deir Yassin, recalling the horrors of Israeli aggression. Even when the truth became known that no massacre had taken place, and that, to the contrary, the Israeli army had acted with professional restraint during military operations in the camp, the damage to Israel's standing in the world had already been done.

Israeli leaders have traditionally shown themselves to be less astute at playing this game than their Palestinian counterparts. To a certain extent this can be attributed to the fact that the Palestinians are generally perceived as the victims and Israel as the aggressors. Even with the bodies of Israeli citizens scattered on the street, foreign journalists can be heard doing their pieces to camera talking in terms of the Israeli occupation of Palestinian lands. Much of this victim culture or perception stems from what is known as the Palestinian refugee tragedy, which happened as a result of the fighting around the 1948 war.

There can be few more emotive aspects of the Israeli–Palestinian conflict than the issue of refugees. The Palestinian refugees are divided into two groups: those that fled in 1948, and a second group that left after Israel conquered the West Bank in 1967. The question of the return of the 1948 refugees is really Palestinian code for the destruction of Israel, as it would mean the Palestinians returning to lands that are now lived in by Israelis. In simple terms, the refugee issue remains an important political weapon which the Palestinians use to publicise their cause, gain world sympathy and damage Israel's standing among the international community. A seemingly endless stream of pressure groups, left-wing commentators and intellectuals (such as Benny Morris – see below) ensures that the refugee issue and Israel's complicity in its cause is never far from the headlines. It is important to state from the start that the conditions in which the 1948 refugees exist is deplorable. A lack of political sympathy for their plight should not be confused with a lack of feeling about the humanitarian issue, which at the start of the 21st century is wholly unacceptable.

So who caused the Palestinian refugee exodus? And who is to blame for the appalling conditions that some refugees have lived in for generations?

Currently in Israeli and Arab academic circles there is a hotly contested debate over who was to blame for the exodus. A group of scholars collectively known as the 'new historians' claim that the Zionist leadership was heavily involved in forcing the Palestinians out of the new state of Israel. Traditional Israeli historians argue that this is nonsense and that the 'new historians' have in effect doctored documents from the Israeli archive to distort the truth. A third group of historians take a much more pragmatic line, arguing that the Zionist leadership, and David

Ben-Gurion in particular, were no saints, but to suggest that in a premeditated plan of effective ethnic cleansing Israeli leaders drove large segments of the Palestinian population from their homes and into exile is sheer folly. In truth, the evidence suggests a complex set of reasons for the exodus, ranging from fear, to decisions taken by the Palestinian leadership to evacuate parts of the population with the aim of returning when the war against the Zionists was won. The 'new historian' Benny Morris concedes that the documentary evidence of events up to 1 June 1948 suggests a complex set of explanations for the exodus that falls somewhere between 'pre-planned outright IDF expulsion and Arab-engineered Machiavellian flight'.[3] Conflicts, of course, have a nasty habit of not going to plan, and what was meant to be a temporary period in exile for the refugees turned out to be a permanent one, with Israelis taking over the deserted homes of Palestinians and building new infrastructure on the site of Palestinian villages.

To be sure, there were areas where for strategic reasons the Israelis cleared villages. The major example of this was the clearing of some Arab villages that bordered the Tel Aviv–Jerusalem road.[4] The road, which became a vital artery for supplying West Jerusalem during the 1948 war, came under heavy Arab attack, with Israeli convoys struggling to get through with vitally needed supplies. The task of clearing the villages was assigned to Yitzhak Rabin – who later described it as unpleasant, but necessary. Charges that Ben-Gurion had ordered Rabin to 'drive them out' are hotly disputed. Even if Ben-Gurion did utter the phrase, it does not amount to a call to drive the Palestinians out of Israel.

The ultimate blame for the Palestinian refugee exodus must lie with the Arab leadership, who rejected the UN Partition Plan that would have ensured that the majority of Palestinians would live in their own sovereignty in a state that was internationally recognised. The failure to agree to a political solution meant that the Palestinian population was exposed to the uncertainties and risks that war brings. One wonders what would have happened to the Jews living under Palestinian sovereignty if Israel had been defeated in its War of Independence. One can only imagine the horrors that they would have faced, and the risk that they would have been expelled.

The question of blame remains a very salient issue today, as it deeply impacts on the negotiations over how to resolve the refugee question. The Palestinian negotiators demand the right of return for all refugees as a cornerstone of any peace agreement with Israel, as well as financial compensation for the refugees and their descendants. For its part, Israel rejects the right of return, but privately accepts that some form of compensation may be given, provided that it does not amount to an admission of Israeli complicity in causing the problem, and that someone foots the bill – code for the American taxpayer. Also, any financial compensation must come as part of an overall and compre-hensive deal for resolving the Israeli–Palestinian dispute. Just as the refugee issue retains huge symbolic importance for the Palestinian people, so it strikes a nerve with the Israeli popu-lation. Israelis view the right of return as an attempt to kick them out of their houses, and as a major and real threat to the state of Israel.

To some extent, all wars produce a victor and a loser, and in brutal terms the Arab leadership gambled on being able to overrun Israel and the Palestinian people paid the price. But what in many ways remains even more difficult to comprehend is the reaction of the Arab world to the exodus of Palestinians. Images of Palestinian refugee camps are regularly shown on Western television. The blame for the appalling conditions of some camps is placed squarely on Israel's soldiers. In reality, the Arab states that host the refugees have much to answer for. Collectively, the Arabs took the decision not to let these camps develop the infrastructure that would indicate a degree of permanence. The refugees were here only for a short time until the Zionist enemy could be overrun in a second war.

To some degree, there was also the fear that had already weak Arab regimes integrated the refugees, the destabilising effect of this would have led to the overthrow of the regime. King Hussein of Jordan was all too acutely aware of these dangers after Palestinians living in Jordan attempted to undermine the

Hashemite Kingdom, events that led to Black September in 1970, when the King finally lost patience and moved to expel the PLO from Jordan. The Lebanese – the PLO's next port of call – fared little better, with the Palestinians creating a state within a state in the south of the country and using Lebanese territory to mount attacks into northern Israel. Just as attacks from camps in Jordan had led to widespread retaliation from Israel, so the same cycle of violence developed in Lebanon, culminating in Israel's invasion of the country in June 1982.

It was during this war, which took place in the political chaos following the Lebanese civil war, that the massacres at the Palestinian refugee camps at Sabra and Shatilla in Beirut occurred in September 1982. Though the massacre was actually carried out by a local Lebanese Christian Phalangist militia, the Arab world and much of the international community blamed Israel, which at the time was occupying Beirut. Events at Sabra and Shatilla shocked most Israelis and led to the largest demonstration in Israel's history. The Israeli commission of inquiry called for the Minister of Defence, Ariel Sharon, to be removed from his position, and censured several heads of the army.

In terms of the Palestinian refugees, it reinforced their victim status and the image of Israel as a ruthless aggressive state. As a result, the key names in the Palestinian annals of refugee history are Deir Yassin, Sabra and Shatilla, and Jenin. The Palestinian leadership, to help create the victim culture, has ruthlessly exploited all three massacres – or alleged massacres. The downside of this for the Palestinian leadership has been that, by talking up the importance of the refugee, they have made it harder for themselves to effectively compromise on the issue during negotiations. During the recent aborted Oslo peace process, Yasser Arafat was effectively asked to cut a deal for the majority of Palestinians that would leave out the minority of Palestinians who live in exile in the refugee camps. Despite the political rationality of cutting a deal that would have led to a Palestinian state in the vast majority of the West Bank and Gaza Strip, Arafat felt compelled to hold out for a deal for the refugees – one which was not forthcoming from Israel.

An overlooked area of the refugee crisis caused by the 1948 war is the question of the Jewish refugees who were expelled from their Arab countries of origin following the creation of Israel. As with the Palestinian refugees, it is difficult to say for sure just how many Jewish refugees there were, though even the lowest estimates put the figure at around 750,000. So what did the cash-strapped Israeli state do with these Jewish refugees, most of whom arrived with very little? They did not leave them in camps to rot and to remind the world of the harsh treatment that they had received in their Arab country of origin. In contrast to the Arab leaderships with the Palestinian refugees, the Israeli leadership moved to integrate them fully within the state. To be fair, Israel had a vested interest in absorbing the immigrants to boost the demographic balance in the country in favour of Jews. That said, however, it still meant major short-term sacrifices for the infant state.

At the end of 1948, Israel had been established and successfully defended. The precedent of Israel winning the war and being unable to turn its military victory into a political one had also been set. For Israel, a political victory has always been defined as being able to agree peace with the Arab states on its own terms – in effect, to force the Arabs to the negotiating table when they realise that they can't defeat Israel on the battleground. Back in 1949, there was a sense of optimism among some Israeli leaders that the Arab states would accept their defeat in the war and look to forge a peace with Israel. The armistice talks on the Greek island of Rhodes that took place at the conclusion of the war were intended to serve as the springboard for meaningful peace negotiations and agreements within six months. Such an aim proved over-ambitious and, in retrospect, extremely naïve. Though the talks did produce armistice agreements between Israel and Egypt, Jordan, Lebanon and Syria, there were no meaningful peace negotiations.

A young Yitzhak Rabin, who had been dispatched by Ben-Gurion as a member of the Israeli delegation to the talks, thought that the agreements were very bad for Israel, and begged not to have to sign the documents. Rabin sensed at the talks that the agreements would lead to another round of hostilities in the near future. Another young officer who was part of the Egyptian delegation, Gamal Abdul Nasser, and who met Rabin during the talks, was to play a major role in proving Rabin correct.

So why was there no peace following the 1948 war? And who is to blame?

Within the Arab leadership there was a sense of shock and dismay that, after a positive start, the war had gone so badly. Many of the regimes that had been unstable before the war started to crumble, to be replaced by military juntas and coup followed by counter-coup. Arab strategists picked over the running of the war and argued that the greatest Arab deficiencies had been in the lack of co-ordinated planning between the various armies, which had meant they had not maximised their manpower and fire-power superiority over the Israelis. In short, the war planners looked to learn the military lessons to ensure that the Arabs would be victorious in the second round of hostilities.

The 'Arab street' remained extremely hostile to Israel, and this in turn tended to reinforce the rhetoric used by Arab leaders hopeful of scoring populist points and avoiding talking about other more difficult areas, such as the transition of many Arab economies from agricultural-based ones to manufacturing. Arab leaders have always used the Arab–Israeli conflict not only as a means of ensuring the legitimacy of their rule, but also as a convenient excuse for the shortcomings of their regime. Everything from unemployment to the price of bread was put down to the Zionists. Sadly, this strategy was shown to work, and Arab leaders have refined it and fine-tuned it over the years, and it remains largely in place today.

Israel was no innocent party either. Any formal peace deal with the Arabs following the war would have meant Israel making concessions on the issue of the Palestinian refugees and returning to the original UN Partition Plan by handing back the land they had conquered during the war. If the war had taught the Israeli leadership one thing, it was that the original partition plan left parts of Israel – such as Jerusalem – highly vulnerable to Arab attack. The debate in Israel over peace opened up divisions between its political élite, but Ben-Gurion, who favoured the *status quo* of no war and no peace, was the dominant figure.[5] Michael Oren has astutely summarised the reasons why there were no formal peace agreements prior to the Suez War of 1956: 'Nasser could not agree to a settlement that would undermine his status in the Arab world, while Ben-Gurion would not make major territorial and financial sacrifices to achieve a mere non belligerency pact with a single Arab state.'[6] In reality, Israel would not acquire the bargaining chips it felt it needed to trade until the Six Day War of 1967. From then onwards, the debate centred on returning the West Bank, Golan Heights and Gaza Strip, which Israel conquered during the war, to the Arabs.

Israel was to remain isolated both politically and economically in the Middle East until the first real cracks in the Arab wall of rejection started to show with the visit of President Anwar Sadat to Jerusalem in 1977. Had King Abdullah of Jordan not been assassinated by a Palestinian as he entered the al-Aqsa mosque in Jerusalem in July 1951, then he might have been the first Arab leader to make peace with the Jewish state, though he faced considerable opposition from his subjects to any deal with Israel.

In many ways, King Abdullah's difficulties in his peace-making attempts mirrored the difficulties of the Camp David Summit in 2000. Leaders with little or no mandate from their respective constituencies, negotiating with one eye on their own political legacy, do not make good ingredients for successful peace-making. Just as King Abdullah was not in a strong enough position to be able to force a deal through, so Ehud Barak and Yasser Arafat were in a similar boat.

Georg Hegel, the 19th-century German philosopher, famously wrote that experience and history teach that nations and governments have never learnt anything from history, nor acted upon any lessons that might have been drawn from it. Looking at the history of the Israeli–Palestinian conflict, there would appear to be a strong case to support this theory. President Clinton ignored the warning signs that lit up the road to Camp David: the political weakness of Ehud Barak, who was elected in Israel on a deliberately vague platform of peace and security; and Yasser Arafat, who an increasingly large segment of the Palestinian population were – in private – beginning to view as an obstacle to their nationalist aspirations, and whose rating in Palestinian opinion polls was declining.

If President Clinton had understood the setting and language of the Arab–Israeli conflict, he would not have set up the three-men-in-a-lifeboat scenario, which is what the summit really amounted to. The President, no matter how unwittingly, pushed Barak and Arafat overboard to try to save his own skin. Barak shared some of the responsibility for his own demise. According to Secretary of State Madeline Albright, he had pressurised Clinton into convening a summit (Barak wrongly believed that a pressure-cooker atmosphere would produce results).[7] A true American statesman would not have listened to him. Clinton by this stage, however, had abandoned political judgement in favour of 'win or bust' on one last hand of blackjack. For their part, the Palestinians went public in their criticism of the President, complaining that he had pushed the date for the summit on a Palestinian delegation that was hardly ready.[8] According to Abu Mazen, President Clinton, in pressurising Arafat, argued that if the Palestinians had declined the opportunity to take part in the talks they would have been blamed for the failure of the process.[9]

With typical predictability, within a year Barak was banished from the political arena, thrashed by the veteran hard-liner Ariel Sharon in Israel's election for Prime Minister. Arafat, blamed by even his European allies for the collapse of the talks, took the only road he knows and understands, a return to tactical armed struggle against Israel – not in the name of Palestinian national-ism, but more by way of saving his own skin. So when President Clinton pointed his finger, he should have done so at himself. As a leading Republican and astute foreign policy observer, Senator John McCain noted in 2001 that he could not help but feel that the President's foreign policy had laid the seeds of 25 years of war for America to deal with.

CHAPTER THREE

Searching For a Place Among Nations: The Old World Versus the New

It seems hard to believe now, but when Israel was created, the intention of its founding fathers was for the Jewish state to be a non-aligned country – looking neither east nor west.[1] So what changed? Why is it today so closely associated with the United States that joint flag-burning of the Stars and Stripes and Star of David has become the norm among militant Islamic groups in the region? Such is the perceived closeness of the relationship that frequently used phrases for Israel in the Arab media include 'American Zionist entity' and 'the junior Satan'. Politically, Israel is viewed by some in the Arab world as the American regional puppet, and as the 51st state. Some more anti-Semitic groups stress the importance of the Jewish lobby in the United States in controlling US policy towards Israel, while others talk openly about the 'Jews' in the White House. Regarding the latter, the current Bush administration – which is generally viewed as the most pro-Israel administration in history – must disappoint those conspiracy theorists with its lack of Jews serving in senior positions.

What led Israel to the United States and vice versa was a combination of strategic, political and cultural factors. It was not, however, until the Suez War of 1956 starkly revealed the new Cold War regional order of its day that Israel's relations with the United States took on heightened significance. The war illustrated to the most recent imperial powers in the region, France and the United Kingdom – who less than half a century previously had carved up the bulk of the Middle East between them with the Sykes–Picot Agreement of 1916 – that they were no longer the major external powers in the region. The new external power-brokers were the United States and the Soviet Union, and the Middle East was to become a major theatre of conflict in the Cold War right up until the collapse of the Soviet Union at the start of the 1990s.

Some – such as the British parliamentarian and writer Enoch Powell – query Suez as the cut-off point for 'the British empires in the sand'.[2] Surely the British must have realised that their days as a regional power were over at the end of the Second World War and the handing over of the British Mandate to the United States? British and French policy-makers, however, were slow to grasp the new post-Second World War realities and the decline of empire and rise of de-colonisation. The Labour government in Britain led by Clement Attlee had continued to believe that it had a role to play in bringing peace between Israel and the Arabs. For a variety of domestic and foreign policy reasons, the Attlee government was very anti-Israeli. Proposals such as calling on Israel to return the Negev in exchange for peace with Egypt did not go down well in Jerusalem. David Ben-Gurion was particularly distrustful of the British, viewing them as pro-Arab and as perceiving Israel as a country that could be bullied into reaching accords with the Arab states on the terms, and serving the interests, of the British only. The Foreign and Commonwealth Office (FCO) was singled out for special criticism, staffed as it was – and remains today – by Arabists whose aim is to preserve the pro-Arab nature of British foreign policy-making. The FCO as an institution reflects the consensus within Whitehall that the UK's national interest is often best served by developing and maintaining close links with Arab states, and that Israel is little more than a nuisance. As a result, the FCO is often quick to condemn Israeli actions, and even its research wing has a tendency to exclude people whose opinions do not match the institutional consensus.

In the period between its creation in 1948 and the Suez War of 1956, Israel found itself suffering from similar problems with the State Department in the United States, which is largely staffed by

Arabists who owe their career development to time spent serving in Arab capitals.[3] Again, the collective policy-making output of the State Department at the time was aimed at ensuring the maintenance of US interests in the Middle East region which were, in their view, best served by developing alliances with Arab states. The actions of the State Department and Secretary of State Marshall in opposing the creation of Israel back in 1948 reflected the start of this policy. To a certain extent, the Middle East was less strategically important for the United States than for the UK or France at this time, simply because the US was less reliant on the region for its oil supplies.

For Israel, Suez marked an important turning point in both domestic and foreign policy.[4] Henry Kissinger's famous quip that in Israel there is no such thing as foreign policy, only domestic policy, appears to be borne out by events here. In short, Suez reflected the victory for Israel's first leader, David Ben-Gurion and his supporters, over its second Prime Minister, Moshe Sharett, who was more open than Ben-Gurion to agreeing to make meaningful concessions to the Arabs in return for peace. Like everything in Israeli politics, it was not that simple. Ben-Gurion wanted to promote some of his young supporters over and above the generation of the Third Aliyah, whom the 'old man' saw as unsuitable for high office. Among Ben-Gurion's 'young turks' were Moshe Dayan and Shimon Peres, who in the ensuing decades both went on to hold almost every high office in Israel.

In strategic terms, Ben-Gurion's and his allies' argument was that the military balance of the Middle East was changing fast, and not in Israel's favour. If Israel did not act immediately to check this shift, then it might be too late. The threat was both real and perceived. President Gamal Nasser had been busy re-arming Egypt's armed forces since coming to power. In truth, however, it is unclear what Nasser's short-term intentions were regarding Israel. In his first major speech as President he outlined what was then in the Arab world a radical programme of social and economic reform, at the centre of which was the desire to rid Egypt of what he saw as the economic colonialism that had existed even after the country had become independent. No mention was made during the speech of the Arab–Israeli conflict. This led some to conclude that Nasser would devote his time and energies to domestic policy. His major overseas adversary appeared to be the United Kingdom, which still controlled the Suez Canal, a vital artery for the oil supply route from the Middle East. Hopes were raised when Nasser appeared to give the green light to secret talks between Egyptian and Israeli officials in Paris. The talks, sadly, were aborted after a rogue Israeli spy ring operating in Egypt was caught attempting to place bombs in Cairo cinemas. Despite private messages sent by the then Israeli Prime Minister, Moshe Sharett, to Nasser stating that he had not authorised the actions, Nasser concluded that even if what Sharett claimed were true, the 'hard-liners' in Israel were in control and were sending him a clear message. In Israel, the political fallout from what became known as the Lavon Affair (after Pinhas Lavon, the Minister of Defence) rumbled on for over a decade.

If this was a brief window of opportunity, it did not re-open for many years, as the Egyptian leader adopted increasingly hard-line positions towards Israel. He started to re-arm Egyptian forces with modem weapons for, as he put it, 'the decisive battle for the destruction of Israel' that was to follow. On 27 September 1955, Egypt signed a massive arms deal with Czechoslovakia that transformed the Egyptian forces into a fully-fledged modern army and provided the Soviet bloc with its first major foothold in the region. The arms agreement gave Nasser a major political boost and helped to establish him as the leading anti-Western-imperialist in the region.

Among his many mischief-making activities, Nasser backed the cross-border fedayeen raids by Palestinian guerrillas on Israel and supplied weapons to the FLN (Front de Libération Nationale) in Algeria who were fighting against French rule. Unwittingly, he had given Israel and France a common cause that Israel was to exploit. Egypt had taken two decisions that appeared to provide a clear insight into its intentions: the establishment of a joint military command between Egypt and Syria in 1955

(Jordan joined in 1956), which was perceived as an indication that Nasser was organising the Arab world for a second war against Israel; and the nationalisation of the Suez Canal on 27 July 1956. The latter was seen as a threat to British and French strategic interests, notably the oil supply routes through the canal, and mobilised the two European powers to make contingency plans for dealing with Egypt. British and French forces were moved into the Mediterranean in order to prepare for a potential seizing of the canal zone. Though this aspect of the crisis was independent of the Arab–Israeli conflict, it had an effect on the Israeli decision-making process and the planning of the campaign against Egypt.

On 1 September 1956, the Israeli Military Attaché in Paris cabled Moshe Dayan, the Israeli Chief of Staff, informing him of the Anglo-French military plan against the Suez Canal, and that the French military were keen for Israel to participate in the operation. Ben-Gurion replied that he was 'in principle' in favour of Israel co-operating in such an operation. A series of initial meetings followed, before a secret summit was held in Sèvres, at which Ben-Gurion (Dayan and Peres), the French Prime Minister Guy Mollet and the British Foreign Secretary Selwyn Lloyd worked out the details of the military plan. An atmosphere of mistrust remained between Ben-Gurion and the British government, left over from the twilight period of the British Mandate in Palestine – and also as a result of British governments' attempts at intervention in the Arab–Israeli conflict between 1948 and 1956. Consequently, the plan was devised so that Israel's first moves would not be interpreted as an invasion, so that its forces could be withdrawn should the British and French not keep their side of the bargain. Eventually, the Sèvres Protocol was signed on 24 October 1956, and only three copies of the document were created. The British Prime Minister, Anthony Eden, probably fearing the damage if the document was leaked, ordered the British copy to be destroyed.

The fighting started rather quietly on 29 October 1956. During the first 24 hours, the Egyptians were not sure if the operation was an invasion or just another reprisal raid. The Israeli military planners had got it right and had used a classic strategy of the decoy – in this case, moving troops towards the Jordanian border where tensions were running high due to a series of incursions and retaliatory raids by Israeli forces. Israeli paratroops were dropped into the central Sinai at the eastern entrance to the Mitia Pass, some 145 miles from Israel and only 45 miles from the Suez Canal. There is little doubt that such a daring opening added to the element of surprise and Egyptian confusion at the true intentions of the 395 paratroopers who took part in the drop. Strategically, this area was vital, as it cut the southern Sinai from the northern sector and gave the Israeli forces an early advantage that they did not lose. The key to the Israeli plan was time. The Israeli General Staff (military high command) argued that international pressure would soon build for a ceasefire – and it was vital for Israeli forces to achieve their war aims as quickly as possible.

The major Israeli war aims were threefold: to destroy the Palestinian fedayeen infrastructure in the El Arish and Gaza areas; to end the threat posed by Egyptian forces in the Sinai; and to capture the strategically important Red Sea port of Sharm el Sheikh. In just over one week, Israel had reached its objectives. Israeli predictions, however, of the growing international pressures proved to be well founded. President Eisenhower was furious about the outbreak of the war, coming as it did only a few days before the US Presidential elections. On 30 October, the US convened the UN Security Council and called for Israeli forces to withdraw to the 1949 armistice lines. Britain and France vetoed the motion. From a British perspective, this was the first time that it had used its power of veto: doing so in favour of Israel must have seemed a little ironic, given its aforementioned hostility to Israel.

On 31 October, against a backdrop of British and French bombing of Egyptian airfields, the UN General Assembly met to add further pressure to intensive diplomatic efforts from the USA and the Soviet Union to end hostilities. At the same time, Anglo-French forces were sailing across the Mediterranean, but it was a battle against time before international pressure for a ceasefire became too strong. Increasingly hostile public opinion at home meant that additional limitations were imposed on British operations by the political masters. On 6 November, British troops landed at Port Said and the French at Port Fouad, but before the forces could break out, the British government – under intense foreign and domestic pressures – agreed to a ceasefire for midnight on 6/7 November. The French had no real alternative but to follow the British, and so the 1956 Suez crisis came to an end.

In military terms, Israel emerged from the Suez War having achieved its military aims. It occupied the Sinai, the Gaza Strip and the port of Sharm el Sheikh. In political terms, its gains on the ground proved to be short-lived. Under intense pressure from the United States – acting both directly and through the United Nations – Israel was quickly forced to return all these lands to Egypt. Worse still for Israel was the fact that President Nasser not only remained in power, but was perceived by the majority of the Arab population as having stood up to Western imperialism; and that the UK and France were perceived as having come to Israel's rescue (this of course was far removed from the true picture).[5]

The United States, which viewed Nasser as a nuisance and the Suez crisis not sufficient to merit the use of force[6] (there is an interesting irony here with Saddam Hussein), effectively made Israel pay a heavy price for the war. Despite this setback, US–Israeli relations were becoming closer. The bi-polar Cold War international system was already developing, with Egypt being re-armed by the Soviet Union, and Israel coming to be seen as a strategic ally of the United States. Britain and France, meanwhile, all but disappeared as regional players. It was not until the EEC was born, and its successor the EU, that Europe would attempt to play a major role in the Middle East.[7] Israeli suspicions of Europe, which were put on temporary hold during Suez, returned, and to this day Israeli governments argue that there is little role for Europe to play in the region until it adopts a more balanced approach (code for less pro-Arab) to the affairs of the region.

In recent years, tensions between Israel and Europe have become even more profound. While Israel enjoys a healthy trading relationship with member states of the EU, on a political level the EU has been extremely critical of Israel's actions in the West Bank and Gaza Strip, which Israel has controlled since the Six Day War of 1967. Tensions exist at both the EU institutional level and between Israel and specific member states. European leaders have tended to take a more pro-Palestinian line than their American counterparts, and there has always been a feeling in Jerusalem that some European leaders wish to impose an agreement on the Arab–Israeli conflict that does not fully take into account Israel's security needs.

From time to time, a European leader will put himself forward and attempt to sell himself as 'Israel's friend'. The current British Prime Minister, Tony Blair, is one such figure. He informs Israeli PMs that he defends Israel's interests in the EU, while at the same time making speeches in the House of Commons calling on Israel to make the kind of concessions than many Israelis regard as a collective form of national suicide. His wife oversteps the mark of decency by condoning the motives for suicide bombers. In truth, Israel's only recent friend in the UK has been Margaret Thatcher, who placed Israel very much in the category of the front line against terrorism, and not the cause of it.[8] Blair thinks that Israel is both, and this inconsistency makes the relationship Israel has with the UK insecure and problematic. Though in private he is uneasy dealing with Yasser Arafat and all his baggage, and prefers to talk to other Palestinian leaders, he still insists that Arafat is relevant to the process.[9] What he fails to comprehend is that Arafat remains, to a certain degree, relevant through the actions of himself and other European leaders.

Israel's post-Suez relationship with the United States developed into what many commentators describe as the 'special relationship'. Strategically, as the Cold War developed and the Soviet Union formed patron–client ties with the Arab world – which included substantial transfer of weapons to the Arabs – so Israel became an important ally of the United States in its quest to stop the spread of Soviet influence in the Middle East. During the 1960s this strategic relationship was translated into arms sales by the US to Israel, and the development of the concept of 'qualitative edge' of equipment. The thinking behind this is that Israel needs to make up for its manpower deficiency in respect to the Arab armies by having a better-equipped army in terms of planes, tanks, missiles etc. This doctrine has become central to Israeli military planning needs, and it takes a great deal of capital to maintain the advantage.

Closely related to this is the concept of Israeli deterrence systems that are aimed at preventing a war from starting in the first place. It was in this area that the major bone of contention arose between Israel, the United States and the Arab world during the 1960s, namely the building of Israel's nuclear reactor at Dimona and the revelation that Israel had become a nuclear power. Ben-Gurion had taken the first steps towards turning Israel into a nuclear power in 1957–8. At first, there was little debate among the Israeli élite on the issue, and any reservations that were raised were in the areas of the cost of the programme and technical issues. It was only in the 1960s that debates on Israel's nuclear choices and the effects of these on Israeli deterrents and military systems started taking place among the élite, and these were kept away or disguised from the public.[10] Even today, Israel refuses to publicly acknowledge that it has a nuclear bomb, to avoid being forced into signing non-nuclear-proliferation treaties. A leading Israeli scientist who attempted to expose the truth to the *Sunday Times* in the UK remains in jail, held in solitary confinement (so he cannot pass on secrets to fellow inmates) after being kidnapped by Israeli agents and flown back to Israel. Though to outsiders his treatment appears harsh, most countries, including the United Kingdom, would likely have taken such action if a scientist sought to reveal nuclear secrets in times of war.

The Arab states have consistently argued that there is no justification for Israel to hold nuclear powers. This argument seems rather strange, given the fact that the Arab states still actively seek the destruction of Israel. Israel's nuclear programme raises the question of double standards, as Samuel Huntington has outlined: 'non-westerners do not hesitate to point out the gaps between Western principle and Western action. Hypocrisy, double standards, and but nots are the price of universalist pretensions ... non-proliferation is preached for Iran and Iraq but not for Israel'.[11] The concept of Western (code for US) double standards is used in the Arab world as a rallying point for often militant opposition to Israeli and US actions in the region.

The United States had two major fears about Israel's nuclear weapons: they would lead to nuclear proliferation in the Middle East; and whether Israel could be trusted with command and control. Israel was not alone in attempting to build nuclear weapons. President Nasser of Egypt had a nuclear programme staffed mainly by ex-Nazi scientists. Israeli intelligence targeted these scientists in an assassination campaign, and for this and a number of technical reasons, Egypt gave up its quest for an independent nuclear capability and instead came to rely on the Soviet Union for a nuclear umbrella.

What remains unclear is under what circumstances Israel would be prepared to use its nuclear weapons. On only two occasions was the issue raised at leadership level, and even here the seriousness of the threat to use the weapons is uncertain. During the early stages of the Yom Kippur War of 1973, when it looked a distinct possibility that Israeli forces might be overrun by Egyptian and Syrian forces, Moshe Dayan, the then Minister of Defence, is said to have raised the issue of the use of a tactical nuclear strike as a last resort. The idea appears to have been quickly dismissed, and there is no published record of any serious discussion having taken place about using such weapons.

In the lead-up to the Persian Gulf War of 1991, the Israeli Prime Minister, Yitzhak Shamir, sent a message through diplomatic and intelligence channels to Saddam Hussein marking out the red lines for the coming war. Shamir stated that if Iraq used chemical warheads in any missiles that were launched against Israel, then Israel would respond with a tactical nuclear strike on Iraq. Again, the seriousness of Shamir's threat was never tested, as Iraq refrained from using weapons that contained chemical or biological warheads, and indeed one warhead was made of cement.[12] On this occasion, Israeli deterrence worked. One can only speculate what Saddam Hussein would have done if Israel did not have its nuclear deterrent, but it surely would have tempted him to use more deadly weapons than the conventional SCUDs he employed against Israel.

Saddam Hussein was no stranger to nuclear technology. Back in the late 1970s and early 80s, Iraq undertook a programme to build a bomb. The Israeli government led by Menachem Begin monitored developments closely, and eventually took the decision in 1981 to launch a daring air raid on Iraq's nuclear reactor near Baghdad, which resulted in its destruction. At the time, Israel was widely condemned by the international community for its actions, and the raid caused some tension for a period between the Begin government and the new administration in the United States led by President Ronald Reagan. In retrospect, however, the prospect of Saddam having nuclear weapons is terrifying. Unlike Israel, his record indicates that he would have been partial to using them in the Gulf War against Iran, and even against his own people. The removal of Saddam from Kuwait in 1991 would have been greatly complicated by Iraqi nuclear weapons, and whether he would have used them against Israel.

In recent years, the nuclear question has focused on Iran and its attempts to build a nuclear reactor and gather the necessary materials to have the capability of building a nuclear bomb. Before September 11, Israel was a lonely voice in warning the world of the dangers of Iran acquiring nuclear weapons. To be sure, the US was closely monitoring events, but it was left to Israel to threaten military action. Plans were drawn up in Tel Aviv to attack Iran's nuclear reactors, but as yet had not been given the political green light. Since September 11, the United States has pursued a much more aggressive campaign against Iran and its quest for nuclear weapons.

The complexities of the Israeli–US relationship have certainly been compounded by Israel's decision in effect to develop its own fully independent nuclear umbrella. It is, to some degree, understandable given Israel's history and the basic fact that at crucial times it has had to stand alone in a hostile neighbourhood. Nobody talks about nuclear weapons in these terms, but when it comes down to it they really are Israel's way of ensuring that there can never be a Holocaust of the Jews in the Middle East as there was with the European Jewry. The notion of self-sufficiency in terms of defence and deterrence is therefore a central pillar of Israel's security doctrine. The recent US efforts at counter-proliferation, with its implication for America not to use nuclear weapons first, has a profound impact on Israel's need to maintain its own weapons.[13] In short, Israel can't rely on a US nuclear umbrella – especially with American interests in the Arab world.

So what about the $3 billion that the United States gives to Israel each year? Does this not make Israel a puppet state of the US and damage its independence?

The simple answer is no and yes. Critics of Israel such as Edward Said take great exception to its reliance on US aid, which Said breaks down to around $1,000 per Israeli man, woman and child each year.[14] The aid, which is divided roughly equally between military and economic, has a complicated history that dates back to the Yom Kippur War. During the war, the United States transported large plane-loads of arms to Israel to help replace the weapons that had been lost during the initial Egyptian and Syrian thrust of the war. Israel sustained heavy casualties during this period of the fighting and much of its front-line equipment was destroyed, particularly tanks. This airlift helped Israel secure victory more quickly than would otherwise have been the case. It did not, however, alter the course of a war that had already turned in Israel's favour. After the conflict, Israel became increasingly dependent on the US for aid to address the cost of paying for the war and the subsequent rebuilding, together with the international recession of the 1970s.

In recent years, there have been calls from some Israeli leaders for the country to start weaning itself off the economic aid.[15] Leaders such as Yossi Beilin argue, correctly, that Israel has to stand on its own two feet, and that the aid acts as a form of subsidy that distorts the true nature of the Israeli economy and helps postpone difficult decisions from being taken on economic reform and liberalisation. With the recent wave of Palestinian violence and the subsequent damage that this has done to the Israeli economy, it looks probable that Israel will not be able to address this question before the Arab–Israeli conflict is resolved.

It is worth pointing out that Israel is not the only Middle Eastern country to benefit from aid from the United States. Since signing the Camp David Accords in 1978, Egypt has received $2 billion of aid from the US each year. The award of this aid was central in the late President Sadat's decision to sign a peace treaty with Israel. Jordan also receives generous benefits in the form of direct aid or the writing off of debts, as did the Palestinian Authority (PA) before it resorted to tactical violence to achieve its political aims.

With Israel's relatively low credit rating for a developed nation, it has on two occasions in the recent past had to ask the US to act as guarantor in order for it to borrow money. In 1991, the issue of the Shamir government's request for $10 billion of loan guarantees became a major hot potato as the US administration led by President Bush Sr attempted to link the issue of the granting of the guarantees, which were badly needed by Israel to help alleviate the effects of a recession and to successfully absorb the influx of immigrants from the Soviet Union who were arriving in Israel, to a freeze on settlement building. The dispute over the granting of the loan guarantees epitomised the tensions and bad blood between the Bush and Shamir administrations. It is probably fair to say that the period between 1990 and 1992 marked the lowest point in US–Israeli relations. This despite the fact that Shamir had taken the highly unpopular decision among his Cabinet colleagues not to respond to Iraqi SCUD missile attacks during the Persian Gulf War in case it damaged the US-led coalition.

Shamir, incorrectly, saw the dispute as a one-off that would soon be resolved, and thought that normal service would soon be resumed.[16] In reality, it reflected changes in the strategic use of Israel to the US in light of the demise of the Soviet Union, and self-imposed US pressure to move forward the peace process between the Israelis and Arabs. The aim of the latter was to help alleviate the charge of double standards over the enforcement of UN Resolutions regarding an Iraqi withdrawal from Kuwait and similar resolutions calling for an Israeli withdrawal from the Disputed Territories. In short, it appeared that Israel was no longer as necessary a partner in the region for the US as it had been since Suez. The Bush administration seemed intent on developing ties with the Gulf States in the hope of winning big military and civilian contracts from these countries, as well as developing closer ties with moderate Arab states as part of the US policy of dual containment of Iraq and Iran.

Few were more acutely aware of these changes than Yitzhak Rabin, who had just defeated his old rival Shimon Peres to become leader of the Israeli Labour Party, some fifteen years after he had been forced to resign over his wife's failure to close a bank account during his tenure as Ambassador in Washington. Rabin understood the relative weakness of Israel, and after winning the general election in June 1992, attempted to seek an accommodation with the Arabs using a 'land for peace' formula because he viewed peace as imperative to Israel's continued existence.

Central to Rabin's thinking was the fear that the outside world led by the United States would eventually force Israel to accept a deal with the Arab states on terms that were far from favourable for the Jewish state. Better to exploit the demise of the Soviet Union, and the emergence of the United States as the sole superpower in the region, to agree a deal with as many Arab states as possible, and with the Palestinians. Rabin viewed such agreements as strengthening Israel, not weakening it, by firmly establishing Israel's position in the new world order. Rabin also foresaw a second round of hostilities against Saddam Hussein that in his opinion would further erode Israel's position, and would lead to the United States coming under strong pressure from Arab states to deal with the question of the perceived case of double standards. What Rabin did not predict, however, was that Great Britain, which had stood side by side with the Americans in Iraq, would lead the campaign to pressurise Israel into making concessions while Palestinian violence continued unabated.

Back in 1992, Rabin proved just the tonic the American

administration needed. His acceptance of land for peace, and clever definition of settlement freeze, meant that Israel was soon granted the loan guarantees and Rabin found himself the man of the hour in Washington, both with President Bush who invited him to the US, and with his successor President Clinton. Rabin placed a great deal of importance on, and spent much time developing, good personal relations with both Bush and Clinton. Contrary to the public's impression of him, Rabin is an extremely charismatic and charming man when on a one-to-one with someone he clearly accepts to be above him in the pecking order.

In all special relationships, the ties that bind allies together exist even without the added ingredient of personal chemistry between the leaders, but the latter can help forge even greater understandings. In the early days of the state, Ben-Gurion preferred not to visit the United States and instead Chaim Weizman, Israel's first President, and Golda Meir did much of the meeting and greeting. Later, President Nixon was a great admirer of Golda Meir and Yitzhak Rabin. Conversely, Menachem Begin viewed President Carter with great suspicion yet still managed to help secure the Camp David Accords, Israel's first treaty with an Arab state.

It was President Clinton, however, who took the importance of personal chemistry to new heights. His relationship with Yitzhak Rabin was extremely close, almost father and son. Both men shared similar visions of peace-making – the land for peace formula. To a certain extent, Rabin may have duped Clinton into thinking that he was willing to go much further than in reality he wanted – or was able – in offering concessions. Near the end of his life, Rabin was becoming more contractually committed to the Clinton-sponsored process with the Palestinians, signing additional agreements with Arafat, while at the same time his reservations were increasing about the failure of the Palestinian Authority to prevent an increasing number of terrorist attacks on Israelis. Clinton spoke movingly at Rabin's funeral in November 1995, and promised that the search for peace would continue – code for expecting more Israeli concessions within the land for peace framework. The election of Benjamin Netanyahu in May of the following year led to one of the most difficult periods in Israeli–US relations. For a start there was a clear lack of personal chemistry between the two leaders. They did not share a political, social and economic vision, as Rabin and Clinton had enjoyed. In the area of peace-making, there were major differences of both style and substance in their approaches that caused tensions almost immediately.

In short, Clinton expected Israel to continue to make concessions to the Palestinians in order to attempt to keep the Oslo peace process on track. Netanyahu, who had rejected the Oslo Accords during his time as Leader of the Opposition, had only accepted them during the election campaign. Israeli cynics – and many Arabs – suggested that he had accepted the accords only to get himself elected in Israel's first direct elections for Prime Minister. This was unfair, but Netanyahu was keen to re-negotiate some of the accords and, put simply, Clinton was not. The old quip of Napoleon, who stated that a man may be a good general, but asked: is he a lucky one?, is also extremely relevant to politics. Netanyahu was certainly not blessed with good fortune. As he assumed office, the implementation of the Oslo Accords – which had already been dogged by crisis after crisis – was entering an even more complex and dangerous phase. Netanyahu was faced with a series of conflicting pressures. Most of his own Cabinet opposed – or at best were lukewarm towards – Oslo, but the US administration was pressuring him to make additional Israeli troop withdrawals from the West Bank.

To deal with the problem of the growing US pressure, Netanyahu employed a tactic that, while not completely revolutionary in US–Israeli relations, was nonetheless considered a radical departure from the norm. Netanyahu understood that while a Democrat occupied the White House, the Republicans were strong in both the House and Senate. There was a sense among Netanyahu's key advisors that a) Congress was much more sympathetic to Netanyahu's vision of peace and b) that it was keen to exert a growing independence from the White House, particularly after the Lewinsky affair. Such political tactics of going over the President's head and appealing directly to

Congress enraged Clinton, who in typical behaviour responded by attempting to talk directly to Israelis over Netanyahu's head.

This clearly difficult period of the special relationship ended with the election of Ehud Barak in May 1999. Clinton viewed Barak as sharing his vision, and soon the new Israeli PM received the stamp of approval from the President – an invitation to visit the White House as soon as possible. White House photo opportunities – for that was the major purpose of a trip to meet the President – make for good TV back home, so Barak duly trotted off for a meeting of minds. Such an invitation had been denied to Netanyahu during Israel's long election campaign – a sure sign of Presidential disapproval.

It is not enough to merely outline – as some writers such as Abraham Ben Zvi do – the strategic factors that formulated the relationship. Nor does it suffice to focus solely on the personal chemistry in the special relationship – or to examine the role of Jewish lobby groups such as AIPAC (America Israel Public Affairs Committee) in developing and fostering the ties.[17] Clearly, then, shared cultural factors between two sets of people play an important role as well. Both Israel and the United States are immigrant societies in which peoples from sometimes very different backgrounds and experiences are assimilated into one state. The great 'melting pot' is a phrase that can be applied equally to Jerusalem and New York. Both societies are fairly new, the majority of immigrants coming to the United States in the last 100 to 150 years, and even more recently to Israel. To some extent, there is a shared sense of the frontier spirit, overcoming physical obstacles to build new societies in the wilderness and facing the respective local native American and Arab populations – many of whom were none too keen to see the new arrivals.

Any read of a textbook of American history and a similar book on Israeli history reveals the shared symbols and myths that go into creating the culture of a state. In Israel it was the all-conquering Sabra (native born Jew), tanned and wearing an open shirt, farming the land or serving in the great Israeli assimilator, the Israeli Defence Forces (IDF). In the United States the corresponding frontier image is of the cowboy settling new lands, driving the cattle from state to state, and building new communities in the wilderness. It is through these shared symbols and more that the two countries are bound.

Of course, it is impossible to ignore the large number of Jews living in the United States, many of whom have either direct personal or business links with Israel. Others have an emotional linkage that manifests itself through participation in Jewish group activity, much of which is directed at raising funds for the state of Israel. When the Jews left their European countries of origin, most came to the United States – while the US allowed Jewish immigration – rather than going to Palestine. It was only really when the US closed its borders to Jewish immigration that Palestine became the only alternative to remaining in the country of origin. It is also important to remember that the Jewish world is a small one. Attend a Jewish dinner and you will likely hear conversations about mutual friends. Someone always knows someone else's grandchild who is studying in Jerusalem, or who made Aliyah to Israel.

Until the recent wave of violence, many Americans, both Jews and non-Jews, took advantage of increasingly cheap and fast air travel to visit Israel. The United States has long been the desired destination for the majority of Israelis holidaying, visiting relatives, or on business. Similarly, exchange programmes involving American students going to the Hebrew University in Jerusalem or Tel Aviv University were commonplace. Though the majority of students undertaking such programmes were Jewish, by no means all of them were. Many were simply American students who had chosen Israel for their Junior Year Abroad programme.

Perhaps the greatest cultural linkage lies in political culture. It is here that both Israel and the United States retain a healthy respect and deference for democracy and democratic values. And not in some rather cynical British way, where the majority of the population take democracy for granted and where there is an absence of debate on its form, but rather in a way that says we owe our existence and way of life to democracy. Here there has been much scholarly debate about the moral value of Israeli democracy. Bernard Lewis argues that Israeli democracy is something of a variation on the norm in the region, and in little ways helps alert some in the Arab world to the benefits of a democratic polity and liberalised economy. In short, it sets Israel apart from other states in the region.[18] Critics of Israel place less emphasis on the value of Israeli democracy, arguing that it ignores the Emergency Defence Regulations that Israel uses to rule the Palestinians in the Disputed Territories – or indeed the preventative detention of Arabs in Israel.[19] It is, in effect, democracy for the Jews. This charge needs, however, to be viewed within the context of the permanent state of hostilities that Israel has found itself in. One wonders what other countries would have done if faced with similar threats.

Though it is often stated in coffee-table discussions that Israel is a democracy and that the other regimes in the neighbourhood fall far short of being termed democratic states, little is made of what this actually means. On the negative side, Israel draws too much of its short democratic traditions from the British system of democracy which evolved over centuries, and which relies too heavily on convention rather than formal orders such as written constitutions and Bills of Rights. This said, it is a wonderful testament to Israeli democracy that despite the absence of these pre-requisites for modern democracy, the treatment of minorities in the state remains good, particularly given the context of the ongoing conflict with the wider Arab world.

The treatment of Israel's Arabs is, however, by no means perfect. They are not allowed to serve in the IDF, although they can vote and have their representatives serve in the Israeli Knesset. Such a state of affairs remains much better than the treatment of minorities in many Western democracies. Unfortunately, in recent years tensions between Israeli Arabs and Jews have increased. To a large extent, this has been caused by the 'Palestinianisation' of the Israeli Arabs through the efforts of Arafat and the PA to mobilise support within that community. Evidence of this transformation can be seen in the voting patterns of Israeli Arabs in Israeli elections, and the more overt role that Arafat now plays in encouraging these patterns. At the start of the current round of violence between Israelis and Palestinians, Israeli Arabs took part in the unrest (unlike during the original Intifada of 1987–92), and some thirteen of them were shot dead by Israeli police during riots in northern Israel in October 2000. The resulting Or Commission, which reported at the start of September 2003, concluded that a number of police officers and political leaders should not be allowed to serve in similar positions in the future.

Israel terms itself a parliamentary democracy, and in recent years has toyed, unsuccessfully, with the notion of shifting to a system which falls somewhere between the British system and the American executive-led government. It is in the judiciary, however, that the Israeli–American systems share similarities. Both countries have fiercely independent supreme courts whose integrity is shown in the number of rulings that they make against the government and in upholding the rights of the individual citizen. Today, with the growing number of challenges to Knesset and government decisions in areas such as human rights, the role of the Supreme Court is becoming even more central.[20]

Since the start of the 1990s, Israeli politics has taken on a very distinctive American flavour. Today, all the major parties in Israel conduct American-style primary elections to select and order their party lists that are put forward at each election. The conventions that are held to announce the results come with balloons and all the razzmatazz of similar events in the States.

Television has overtaken the party institutions as the point of reference for politicians. For many years, Israel had only one state-controlled television channel. It is only in recent years that Israelis have been offered a wider choice, which has expanded further with the arrival of cable television. Today in Israel, just as in America, there is a wealth of political and news programming which offers the viewer choice, and the politician the opportunity to get his face on television. The down-side to this is that producers are, of course, interested in people who disagree with the government on the chosen topic of the day. This has tended to help foster levels of dissent within the major political parties which make their macro-management all the harder. There is a suspicion that at least some of this dissent is inspired by opportunism rather than any ideological objections to government or party policy.

The social and political cultural linkage between Israel and America is so important that when an event or person challenges the linkage, the potential for lasting damage is much greater than, say, differences over the speed and direction of the peace process. Take, for example, President Reagan's visit to the cemetery in Bitburg that contained the graves of former SS officers.[21] There were few greater friends of Israel than Ronald Reagan. The period of the Reagan administration (January 1981–January 1989) was characterised as one of the most productive in Israeli–US relations. As a man, Reagan's affinity for Israel went well beyond the strategic and vote-gathering rationales. He was fully committed to the Israelis' image as pioneers, and the linkage of the pursuit of the American dream and the Israeli dream of peace was startlingly clear to him. In Reagan's somewhat simplistic world of 'cowboys and Indians', it was clear where he placed Israel. Returning to the defining opinion-maker about Israel, Reagan saw Israel very much as the front line against terrorism, communism and the spread of Islamic fundamentalism.

So why visit Bitburg? And how did this damage US–Israeli relations?

Reagan's visit to the cemetery was certainly ill judged and insensitive, but no more than this. His advisers allowed a situation to develop that they should have prevented at an early stage. In the end Reagan was placed in an impossible position, and despite heavy lobbying from Jewish groups and individuals he had little diplomatic room for manoeuvre. His visit to Bitburg did not amount to a change of US policy towards Israel, the Holocaust or Germany's Nazi past. Many Israelis, however, found it difficult to comprehend how this President of all Presidents could visit such a place that contained the bodies of the murderers of Jews. Though the Israeli government and US administration worked hard to defuse the political fallout from the visit – which in reality was extremely short-term – the lasting impression that Reagan's visit left with Israelis was of a President who was willing to draw a line under Germany's past, and this was simply not acceptable to most of them.

Reagan's visit triggered something in Israelis that we can loosely call the 'old world–new world' syndrome. Israelis of all ages – but particularly among the MTV generation – tend to view the United States as the brave new world. This manifests itself in the import not only of American political culture, but general American culture ranging from literature to pop music, Levi jeans, and even American slang. Anyone who takes a walk through Tel Aviv's thoroughfares can't fail to notice just how far American culture has encroached into Israel. Israel is not unique in this, of course. A similar stroll through the centre of London, Paris or Rome would create a similar impression. What is unique to Israel is the extent to which this culture is openly embraced at the expense of an Israeli cultural identity. To put it in youth speak, what is in fashion in New York will soon be in vogue in Tel Aviv.

During the recent build-up to the war in Iraq, US Secretary of Defense Donald Rumsfeld, when replying to a reporter's question, remarked that he considered France and Germany to be part of the 'old Europe'. Though this was said in the heat of the diplomatic struggle that was taking place in the United Nations Security Council over a proposed second resolution for the war in Iraq, its importance still resonates today, particularly in Israel. Rumsfeld was of course referring to old Europe as the German–Franco axis that has driven political and economic developments in Western Europe since the 1950s. Many Israelis refer to all of Europe as old Europe or the 'old world'. One must remember that for many Israelis there is little sympathy for the European plight. Among the remaining veteran Israeli Jews of Ashkenazi (European or North American) origin, there linger painful memories – either of persecution experienced directly or tales passed down through the generations in families.

Most of the founding fathers came from Eastern Europe, and in a strange way Israeli leaders have always had a difficult relationship with the whole of Europe. Europe is the continent of the modern-day persecution of the Jews. Though few Israeli leaders have the courage to say it in public – for fear of damaging Israel's largest export market – there is currently in Jerusalem a sense of unease at the limited response of European governments to the wave of anti-Semitism that is sweeping through Europe, and is at its worst in France and Germany. Even in the so-called racially tolerant England, Jews are regularly attacked in the major cities simply for wearing kippas, graves are desecrated and synagogues experience strange fires.

Israelis view current events in Europe as part as a continuing pattern of anti-Semitism and not as a series of one-offs, as many commentators from the liberal left-of-centre-dominated European media suggest. There is a sense that old attitudes have not really changed, and that Israel provides a good target for this anti-Semitism. In short, many members of the Israeli intelligentsia regard the current pro-Palestinian, or in a general sense pro-Arab, bias within the policy élites in Europe as being based not on rational politics – or even on notions of David and Goliath – but rather on the institutionalised anti-Semitism which remains present in many European states. They cite the lack of action by governments against the desecration of Jewish synagogues and other Jewish symbols, and a lack of concerted action on the increasing number of physical and verbal attacks on Jews, particularly in countries such as France. Recent comments by a French diplomat referring to Israel as that 'shitty little country' have added to this belief.

The collective institutions of Europe (currently in the guise of the European Union, and formerly the EEC) are seen by Israel as the key political root of the problem. The general bias in these institutions – which are becoming all the more powerful, not in creating a comprehensive European foreign policy but certainly in drawing up the guidelines of policy – is viewed as pro-Arab and anti-Israeli. Even the language that EU officials use reveals their difficulties. They talk of 'cycles of violence' and the need for Israel to make concessions in order to prevent additional violence. Just as Reagan and America view Israel as the front line against terrorism and radical Islam, so most of Europe views it as the root cause of the problem. And it is this starting point, together with the institutionalised anti-Semitism, that makes Israeli governments extremely nervous about allowing the EU, or individual member states, to act as a mediator in the Arab–Israeli conflict.

Does Israel stand alone in the Middle East?

Isolation has been an important concept in the Arab–Israeli conflict, and has had a profound effect on the development of Israel since 1948. Arab leaders, in decision-making that was wholly compatible with their historic total rejection of Israel, moved to isolate Israel economically and politically. The introduction of a primary and secondary economic boycott of Israel was intended to help destroy the economic viability of the Jewish state. In modern times we have not witnessed a boycott that was so strong and so vindictive. The secondary boycott promised that any third party companies that trade with Israel would find their goods boycotted by the Arab world. Hence Pepsi Cola, for example, did not sell their products in Israel for many years, with Israelis reliant on Coca Cola instead. In recent years the secondary boycott has to a certain extent broken down, but Israelis have long memories. Many refuse to drink Pepsi today, even though it is widely available in Israel and cheaper than its rivals, preferring to stick with Coke, which in the past refused to capitulate to Arab pressure and kept exporting to Israel.

The Arab boycott helped condition two important aspects of Israel's relationship with the outside world: a need to find economic markets outside the region – traditionally Europe and America, but in recent years the Far East and Africa as well – and to develop strategic ties with the non-Arab states in the Middle East. Regarding the latter, Israeli policy-makers have looked to form ties with both the Iran of the Shah and, since the early 1990s, with Turkey.

The reaction of the Arab states to the Palestinian Al-Aqsa Intifada (or, more correctly, war of attrition) from October 2000 onwards demonstrated the increasing complexity of Middle East politics, and in particular Israel's place in the region. Put succinctly, Israel is no longer totally isolated in the region, but nor is it by any measure fully integrated. The Arab–Israeli conflict is no longer the only one in the Middle East: the increasingly large numbers of inter-Arab disputes have become equally important. In times of crisis, however, such as the violence in Israel and the Territories in October 2000, popular pressures grow on even those Arab regimes that have ties with Israel to isolate it.

Since October 2000, the more pragmatic Arab countries such as Egypt and Jordan have moved to prevent an escalation of the Israeli–Palestinian conflict for two reasons. First, in order to diminish the threat of the conflict turning into a full-scale regional war, and second, to prevent the unrest spreading into their countries. In the case of Jordan, this was particularly important given the fact that a large proportion of its population is of Palestinian origin. However, for Egypt this was also a factor in a country that has in the past seen mass popular rallies against Israel. It was these domestic pressures that led Egypt to recall its ambassador from Israel in November 2000.

The more radical Arab countries, led by Iraq and Libya, called for a regional war against Israel in order to defend their Palestinian brothers. Syria, under its new leader President Bashir Asad, attempted to position itself between the pragmatics and the radicals. It allowed Hezbollah to mount operations against Israel, notably the kidnapping of four Israeli soldiers on 10 October 2000, as well as attacks by Palestinian groups opposed to the peace process. At a specially convened Arab summit, Syria fell short of demanding a regional war, fearful that it would be drawn into a direct conflict with Israel. The *status quo* of no war, no peace that existed between Israel and Syria during the end of the reign of Bashir's father remained intact. The favoured Syrian position is to work to diplomatically isolate Israel in the region and to tighten the Arab economic boycott of Israeli goods. In effect, Syria aims to dislocate Israel from the Middle East and force it to seek links and trading partners elsewhere.

In order to counter such strategies, Israeli policy-makers have for many years sought to find suitable partners with which to construct a coalition of minority states in the Middle East, or simply a partner with which to develop a strong bilateral alliance. The period following the Madrid Peace Conference (1991) and, to a larger extent, the Oslo era (1993) in the Middle East offered new possibilities for Israel to become an attractive ally to non-Arab states in the region, and potentially in the long term to ruling élites in moderate Arab states. Furthermore, Israel's high level of military sophistication and its willingness and need to develop arms sales with allies makes this attractiveness even greater to the military establishments of these countries. Among the wider Arab masses, however, Israel remains the Zionist enemy, and this domestic restraint has prevented many of the more pragmatic Arab leaders from developing ties with Israel or deepening existing ones.

In the past, Israel's choice of strategic partners has been dominated by short-term needs over a longer-term view. This is hardly surprising, given the nature of the threat that Israel has faced over the last 50-plus years, but nonetheless is a reflection of the systematic concentration on the present – or near future – over longer-term planning that still dominates Israeli decision-making today.

During the 1990s, Turkey, however, emerged as the natural choice of ally for Israel. It is a secular, non-Arab state with close ties to the United States through its participation in NATO. Though not a member of the European Union, it enjoys close political and trade links with many European governments, and was seen as a gateway to the newly created Central Asian republics. In geographic terms, Turkey shares a border with Syria, along which there had been an increasing number of incidents involving Turkish and Syrian forces. As a result, in the realm of mutual interests it was difficult to see two better-suited countries in the region for fostering closer ties. The speed and scale of the development of ties between Israel and Turkey from 1995 onwards meant that the relationship became as important as any peace agreement that Israel signed with the Arabs.[22]

Israeli political and military planners aimed at developing an alliance between Israel, Turkey and Jordan to counteract the threats against the Jewish state in the region. On the political side, ties between Israel and Turkey flourished, with close co-operation in developing economic ties. The Turkish military, which is central to the political system, was pleased by the sale of high-quality Israeli military hardware to the Turkish army. Israeli anti-terrorist training and intelligence skills have been useful to the Turks, who spent the decade in a low-intensity war with the PKK Kurdish guerrilla group. For the increasingly cash-strapped Israeli military industrial complex (MIC), the sales were a welcome boost. By the end of the 1990s, it appeared that Israel was selling its top-of-the-range new weapons to the Turks, thus illustrating the Israeli sense of security in the relationship.

On the military front, throughout the 1990s there were a growing number of joint military manoeuvres involving the armed forces of the two countries. Though these exercises were often dressed up as simple search-and-rescue operations, Arab states such as Syria saw them as war games. Jordan, though not directly taking part in the exercises, sent observers and talked about long-term plans to become more actively involved in such events. With the state of near permanent crisis in the peace process between the Israelis and the PA during the late 1990s, the Jordanian leadership was careful not to be seen publicly as an additional part of the Israeli–Turkish alliance. In November 2000, Turkey offered to mediate between Israel and the PA. Such a move was an illustration of the close ties that Turkey has developed not only with Israel but also with the PA.

In recent years, Turkey has become a very popular tourist resort for Israelis who enjoy relatively cheap package-deal holidays with the added bonus of being able to purchase cheap Turkish leather goods. At one point in the 1990s, Israel was so awash with people – including ministers – sporting their cheap Turkish leather jackets that it was obvious where individuals had spent their holidays. It remains to be seen, however, if the ties that bind Turkey and Israel together will last the test of time.

Central to recent Israeli decision-making in strategic matters has been the desire for Israel to find a new use of itself for the United States. It was hoped, for example, that Israel could serve via its links with Turkey as an introduction service for US companies in Central Asia, but this never fully materialised, many US companies finding it easier to deal direct with these new states and all the old-style Soviet bureaucracy that remained in place in many of them. Conversely, when Israel has attempted to go it alone and develop strategic ties with countries that do not reflect the foreign policy objectives of the United States, it has been forced to eventually back down if any conflict of interest has arisen. The most recent example has been Israel's attempt to sell high-tech weapons to China against the wishes of the Bush administration, which has shifted US interests away from China towards Russia and what they see as its reformist leader, Vladimir Putin.

It has been fascinating to watch the Bush administration's interaction with Israel and the wider Middle East peace process develop. While nobody knows the exact origins of the phrase 'peace process', William Quandt suggests that it was first used in the US State Department in the early 1970s to suggest an on-going process of negotiations between Israel and the Arab states.[23] At times, however, it has come to be employed to disguise a lack of substantive progress in the negotiations. The media appear hooked on the term, with phrases loosely bandied around such as 'another nail in the coffin of the peace process' or 'the peace process is back on track'. Initially, it looked like the Bush administration was keen to enter one of those periods of inertia and devote little time or few resources to the Israeli–Arab conflict. President Bush appeared to concur with the view that the Clinton administration had pursued peace too avidly and that this had helped start the war.[24] As the President's Press Secretary Ari Fleischer put it in March 2002: 'by pushing the parties beyond where they were willing to go … it led to expectations that were raised to such a high level that it turned to violence.'[25]

So how did we get from this starting point to the smiling face of President Bush at yet another Middle East summit shaking the hands of Ariel Sharon and the then Palestinian PM, Abu Mazen?

One of George W. Bush's rare overseas trips before becoming President had been to Israel at the end of 1990s. Here he was entertained on what is affectionately known as the 'Sharon sandwiches and settlement tour of the West Bank'. Bush was said to be amazed at how narrow Israel was within parts of the Green Line, commenting that in places Israel was narrower than his ranch in Texas. At the time of the visit, neither Sharon nor Bush was in power, but both formed a friendship or understanding that was to serve them well after Bush's election in November 2000 and Sharon's in early 2001.

Initially, the Middle East went to plan for Bush, who refrained from becoming over-involved in the process to end the Palestinian violence. Bush came increasingly to support in private Sharon's view that Arafat was an unreliable partner for peace, or incapable or uninterested in stopping the progressively more violent Palestinian attacks on Israelis. More and more, Bush came to view Arafat – the man – as simply evil.[26] To be fair, he did allow the State Department to appoint a new Special Envoy to the Middle East, with Colin Powell's old friend and army colleague Anthony Zinni assuming the role. Sadly, Zinni was no expert – as Bush well knew – and his only achievement was getting both sides in the conflict to agree on one point. He was not up to the job and was hopelessly out of his depth.

There is a strong belief among American experts that American foreign policy began on September 11 2001, and certainly US policy towards the Middle East was heavily affected by the events in New York and Washington. Slowly but surely, the Bush administration was forced to become more engaged in events. In President Bush, Israelis found a leader who clearly not only believed in the strategic use of Israel to the US – and who saw Israel as the front line in America's 'war on terror' – but crucially who also shared the cultural factors that had linked Ronald Reagan emotionally to Israel. Bush sees no contradiction in his pro-Israel sentiment and his openly held belief that the two-state solution (Israeli and Palestinian states existing side by side) is the only way to resolve the Israeli–Palestinian conflict. Bush has effectively been willing to stand up and fight the Palestinian corner – with the proviso that a Palestinian state is both democratic and not led by Yasser Arafat, with whom Bush's patience finally ran out in 2002.

Some Israelis would be quick to point out that this is not the only grey area in Bush's mind-set. To date, President Bush has authorised two major wars since declaring the start of America's war on terror (and countless other actions), yet his administration has at times been openly sceptical or even hostile to Israel's policy of extra-judicial killings (targeted killings) of Palestinian militants, nearly all of whom were involved in the planning and execution of attacks on Israeli cities and the civilian population.

The publication of the 'road map' peace proposals, first in the summer of 2002 and then officially in May 2003, led the United States to an unprecedented commitment to the Israeli–Palestinian peace-making. The irony of this is clear for all to see, but it remains to be seen if this heightened intervention will bring any substantive results. President Bush has followed the pattern of the recent Presidents, in that it is impossible to ignore the Middle East.

Arab suspicion of US intentions in the region has intensified since the war in Iraq. The two basic theories are, firstly, that the US wishes to create a new empire in the sand – ruling the Middle East either directly or through economic control over Arab markets and oil production. This reflects the usual chant of American liberal academics such as Noam Chomsky, that everything revolves around control of the oil supply. If this charge were made against European powers that remain heavily dependent on Middle East oil supplies, it would be more compelling. Indeed, European countries such as France did very well out of the oil for food and medicine programme during the rule of Saddam Hussein in Iraq. The United States' oil supplies, however, are much more diverse than during the early 1970s when Arab regimes used oil as a political weapon. The US, as well as developing its own supplies, has looked increasingly to non-Middle Eastern countries to cover any shortfall caused by Arab political actions. Today, while the US still needs Arab oil, it is not the critical factor in defining American foreign policy. Since September 11, that policy has clearly been dominated by the need to shift the war against terrorism away from American soil towards distant shores, and to cut such international terrorist organisations off at source. For American leaders, the nightmare scenario is that Washington DC and New York become commonplace war zones just as Haifa, Tel Aviv and Jerusalem have become for Israelis.

The second Arab conspiracy theory is that everything is the fault of the Jews and that what we are seeing is an attempt by Israel and its US ally to force the Arabs into peaceful co-existence so that Israel can exploit cheap Arab labour in the form of economic colonialism, thus transferring Israel into the regional superpower able to dictate the economic and political agenda of the Middle East. While such cheap labour clearly benefits the Palestinian economy in that the earnings of the labourers help stimulate growth, the political argument is that Arabs should not be doing the 'black work' for the Jews. Indeed, following the Iraqi invasion of Kuwait in 1990 and the resulting Persian Gulf War of 1991, when Palestinian workers were forced to flee Kuwait for their support of Saddam Hussein, the Israeli labour market has become even more important to the Palestinians.

Whatever the reality, Israel has a problem with the perception that its relationship with America has created in the Arab world. As the West's war with radical Islam intensifies in the coming decades, as scholars such as Samuel Huntington suggest it will, and the number of disenchanted Muslims grows as oil wealth declines and eventually dries up, so resentment against the US and Israel will intensify. Assuming that the United States remains the economic powerhouse of the modern world, this will make Israel a legitimate target in the eyes of many in the Arab world. Oil is not the only natural resource that has a limited life-span in the region. We are likely to see an increase in the numbers of conflicts in the region over the lack of other natural resources. Perhaps the most pressing case here is water. If conflict in the 20th century was over the division of lands in the region, then it is likely to be over water in the 21st century. Even Israel, with its modern technology, and image of making the desert fertile, has in recent years started to import water from Turkey.

If, as appears likely, the population in the region continues to increase and the gap between rich and poor widens, then it does not take too much crystal-ball-gazing to suggest that many Arab regimes looking for an outlet for popular frustration and fear will cite Israel as the cause of all ills. Arab leaders will no doubt stoke the embers of Arab nationalism into life, that will in all likelihood lead to additional rounds of conflict between Israel and the Arabs – regardless of whether Israel has signed peace deals with the various regimes. This doomsday scenario could, however, be largely avoided if we see a process of modernisation of the Arab world and its embrace of democratic values. To date, however, attempts at modernising such areas as political institutions and the economy through programmes of economic liberalisation have proved to be far from successful.

For Israel, the prospects of regional integration into the Middle East appear bleak for the foreseeable future. Accepting the assumption that whatever Israel offers to make peace will not stem the tide of anti-Israel rhetoric in the Arab world, then it is difficult to foresee any end to the Arab–Israeli conflict. This is very bad news indeed for Israel, as its economic prospects depend, to some extent, on peace – a point that Arab leaders know well and in the past have been only too quick to exploit. As a result, we are likely to see the Israeli economy become even more dependent on the United States. The calls from some Israeli leaders to – as I put it – wean Israel off at least the economic aid look at this juncture to be a little far-fetched – a long-term aim, perhaps, rather than a prudent economic policy. This in turn will create the vicious circle of Israel becoming ever more seen as an American puppet in the region – a state that fails to meet one of the very basic criteria for statehood: namely, independent economic viability.

One of the major concerns for Israel remains the fear of the old world – or rather that the anti-Semitism that led to a Holocaust will be transferred into the Middle East. Israel's missiles and nuclear deterrents would appear to have removed any possibility of such a catastrophe in the short term. The increase in anti-Semitism, however, is not unique to Europe. In the Middle East, Palestinian children continue to learn that Jews are pigs, and children's cartoons continue to incite and indoctrinate children from primary school age upwards. The Syrian press still routinely makes comparisons between Zionism and Nazism. One hopes that, if the United States is intent on spreading democratic values in the region, anti-Semitism can be checked through the advent of new education programmes. If this does not happen, then, sadly, the pre-conditions that led to the election of the Nazis in Germany and all the horrors that followed will also be present in the Middle East.

As Ariel Sharon was sitting down with President Bush, all these factors must have weighed heavily on him. He, more than most, knows that if Israel is to have a long-term future, then its reliance on the United States is likely to increase and not decrease as many Israelis had hoped. At the same time as not wishing to bite the hand that feeds, Sharon is also aware of the dangerous concessions that the United States asks Israel to make, which will in the long term weaken it if, as I outlined, the Arab–Israeli conflict continues beyond the near future or peace agreements signed by Israel and various Arab regimes. This decision-making dilemma for Sharon and his successors appears difficult to solve. That said, Israeli–US relations have been shown to be extremely robust and able to withstand periods of disagreement between the two. Israel, however, in being no longer a valuable asset to America in purely strategic terms – the two wars against Iraq confirm that it can be a strategic liability – needs to proceed with caution before it risks a full-scale political row with any future American administration.

CHAPTER FOUR

The Second Republic:
Waiting for Peace

Arab historiography charges that Israel was the aggressor in the Six Day War of June 1967. Both Israel's use of the pre-emptive strike and the outcome of the war, which left Israel in control of areas over three times its pre-1967 size, are highlighted as evidence to suggest that the war was part of an Israeli plot to grab Arab lands and to establish control over the Old City in Jerusalem. The actions of President Nasser in mobilising the Arab armies towards war with Israel are described as Nasser indulging in diplomatic brinkmanship, the bottom line being that Egypt had no intention of actually going to war with Israel. Such arguments, as we shall see, are sheer folly. To a certain extent, theories surrounding Nasser's true intentions are somewhat superfluous for – as all Arab governments understand – Israel has only a small full-time or professional army, and relies heavily on its ability to mobilise its reserves quickly. Such mobilisations cost money and damage the economy – soldiers have to be away from their offices – and Israel, once mobilised, simply cannot afford to stay so for long periods. Nasser must have realised that Israel could not afford to play his games. It is inconceivable that once he had bullied King Hussein of Jordan to join the Arab Axis of Egypt and Syria, that this would not be viewed as a declaration of war by Israel.

The major problem with Arab accounts of the war is that they confuse Israel's geo-political position after the fighting stopped with its standing prior to the outbreak of the war. Israel's ultimate conclusive victory masks the picture of the country in the weeks and months prior to the outbreak of hostilities, which was characterised by anxiety and fear that Egyptian war fever and celebrations in advance of expected victories were well founded. Israelis, in short, were living under threat of attack. There has been much debate about the legitimacy of Israel's pre-emptive strike which effectively ensured an Israeli victory. Here it is difficult to disagree with Michael Walzer's assessment that 'states may use military force in the face of threats of war, whenever the failure to do so would seriously risk their territorial integrity or political independence'.[1] Under such circumstances, it can be said that they have been forced to fight and that they are the victims of aggression. Or to put it another way, they do not have to wait to be attacked if the threat of aggression is real and is likely to result in an attack at some point in the near future. On this basis, the grounds for Israel's strike would appear to have been legitimate and not a conspiracy to grab as much Arab land as possible.

The 1960s in Israel were a time of great change that in many ways marked the start of the transition of the state to a new Israel. Just as the images of the bombed-out bus and the Israeli soldier firing at Palestinian protestors characterise the start of the 21st century, so two striking images symbolise the changes that took place in Israel during the 60s. The first is of Adolf Eichmann, the Nazi architect of the Holocaust, sitting in the dock of an Israeli courtroom in Jerusalem listening intently to translations of the proceedings through headphones. The second is the footage shot by Israeli planes during their pre-emptive raid on the Egyptian Air Force that all but secured an Israeli victory on the opening day of the Six Day War of 1967. Below, the outlines of Egyptian planes can be seen burning on the ground. Today, such images of aerial bombing have become the norm, but back in the late 1960s in the era of black and white television their impact was made all the greater.

A cliché analysis of these two events would suggest that one represents the Jew as the victim, the other the Jew as the warrior. This is of course highly simplistic, but these labels have stuck to the present day. The two images, however, do remain important symbols of the changes that took place within Israel during this period, and how the notion of the Jews as warriors became somewhat overstated until the 1973 Yom Kippur War punctured it. To talk – as many still insist upon – of the Six Day War of 1967 in terms of creating a new Israel is also a little simplistic: other social and cultural and political changes contributed to the birth of a new republic. Nonetheless, the changes that war brought to Israel and the Middle East proved to be extremely lasting and significant.[2] In order to understand the impact of the war, it is important to look back at the 1960s in Israel.

Israel was largely oblivious to the 'swinging sixties' exemplified by music, fashion and a new sexual openness that was prevalent in cities such as London and New York. Two events largely characterised the sombre mood that prevailed in Israel in the pre-Six Day War period: the trial of Nazi architect of the Holocaust Adolf Eichmann, and concern that Egypt's increasingly hostile propaganda against Israel would lead to a third Arab–Israeli war – one in which the very existence of the state would become threatened once more. The capture of Eichmann by agents from the Israeli secret service Mossad in May 1960 in Buenos Aires led to a trial that brought back memories of the Holocaust to its survivors, many of whom lived in Israel. To some extent, the trial helped educate a generation of Israelis to the full horrors of what happened. Previously, some Israelis regarded Holocaust survivors as a morbid curiosity. Many were unable to fully comprehend the scale of the events that had taken place in Europe, and the self-image of the Jew as a victim conflicted with their education that stressed the traditional image of the Sabra (Israeli-born Jew).

Once Eichmann had been captured and interrogated, he was drugged and brought back to Israel. On 23 May 1960, Ben-Gurion informed a stunned Knesset of the capture of one of the leading figures of the Nazi movement to remain alive. The trial of Eichmann opened in Jerusalem on 11 April 1961 and lasted until December. The proceedings were conducted in a sombre manner: Eichmann sat behind a protective screen listening to the translation of the proceedings. The trial was open to the public, and over this period thousands heard the horrifying details of the atrocities. On 15 December 1961, Eichmann was sentenced to death by the court on fifteen counts of crimes against the Jewish people. Eichmann's appeals to the Israeli Supreme Court and the President on the grounds that he was obeying orders were rejected. At midnight on 31 May 1963, he was hanged; to this day he remains the only man to have been executed in Israel. The effect of the trial on the Israeli national psyche cannot be over-estimated. The trial came at a time when Nasser and Egypt were making threats through Radio Cairo of driving the Jews into the sea, and that Israel would be destroyed. Taken together, these created a very serious mood in Israel during the early 1960s.

This mood was further compounded by Israel's perceived international isolation, which came at the same time that the Soviet Union was becoming deeply immersed in the Arab world, both politically and in terms of supplying large quantities of weapons to Egypt, Syria and Iraq. The United States was much less committed to selling arms to its client state in the region. Yes, Israel did buy weapons, but not on the same scale as the Arab states. During the 1950s, Israel had bought arms from France among others, and had gone to war against Egypt with both France and Great Britain on its side. But with De Gaulle in power in France, Israeli–Franco relations had cooled. In short, Israel stood very much alone during this period, while the Arab world enjoyed the growing military and economic patronage of the Soviet Union.

There were two other dangerous factors for Israel at this time. Following the Suez War of 1956, the Arab world had fallen under the influence of President Nasser. This was due to a number of reasons: his charisma and charm, his anti-imperialist credentials, and his Arab nationalist ideology of Pan-Arabism – although regarding the latter, Nasser's definition remained somewhat vague about the nature of the Pan-Arabist state.[3] Ironically, while Nasser was at his strongest – exporting his curious brand of Nasserism to the wider Arab world, enjoying the respect and adulation of the Arab masses – Israel was relatively safe from attack. It was only when the tide appeared to be turning that

Israel became more vulnerable. Nasser's programme of modern-isation of the Egyptian economy failed to deliver the expected results, his army was bogged down in a war in Yemen that it appeared incapable of winning, and his experiment in Pan-Arabism had clearly come off the rails. Once more, an Arab leader who was experiencing difficult times at home used Israel to transform his standing. In Nasser's case, this transformation was immediate, as his tanks rolled into the Sinai and he forced the hand of the United Nations to withdraw its peace-keepers who had played a vital role in keeping the Israeli–Egyptian border quiet since 1956.

If Israel's major fear is a weakened Arab leader looking for a way out of domestic difficulties, then its ultimate fear is an Arab leader who has the potential to persuade or coerce the Arab front-line states into mounting a joint attack on Israel. It should be remembered that with Israel's consistent manpower deficiency, it has to devote the majority of resources to one theatre of conflict before moving them to deal with a second threat. A well-organised surprise attack on more than one front will cause the greatest difficulty to Israel.

Sadly, for all the Middle East, Nasser became intoxicated with his popularity among the Arab masses and appeared to lose his ability to rationally think through where events would eventually lead. Somewhere in the back of his mind he must have known that he could not win a war against Israel. Did he think that the Soviets would intervene and play, and perhaps that the United States, which was fighting its own war in Vietnam, would be keen to settle any war on Arab terms? Put succinctly, Nasser gambled on being carried to victory on a wave of popular Arab support and favourable international conditions created by the increased penetration of the Soviet Union in the Arab world. The Soviets also helped create the pretext – or excuse – for war with false intelligence reports of tank exercises in Northern Israel, which they used to suggest that Israel was preparing for a surprise attack on Syria.[4]

Pretext and motivation remain the two most potent ingredients for starting a war, and both were clearly present here, along with the absence of logical military thought. A conversation that Nasser had while persuading King Hussein of Jordan to join the fight against Israel in the coming war says much about his state of mind at the time. Though it should be remembered that Nasser was trying to convince the King that an Arab victory was assured, his comments are nonetheless enlightening. The King warned that Israel might start the war by launching a surprise attack, and suggested that the Egyptian Air Force would be the target of Israel's first assault. Nasser replied: 'That's obvious. We expect it.' He went on to lecture the King on the Egyptian military's placing particular emphasis on his air force, which he now believed represented a formidable challenge to the Israelis.[5]

On the morning of 5 June 1967, Israeli planes attacked Egyptian airbases and, achieving near total surprise, proceeded to destroy the majority of the Egyptian Air Force on the ground. In the main attack some 309 Egyptian aircraft were destroyed. Following the raids, unaware of the catastrophe that had befallen the Egyptian Air Force, the Jordanian, Iraqi and Syrian Air Forces joined the battle. The Israeli Air Force (IAF), freed from action in the south, turned its attentions to these planes and by the end of the first day the Jordanian Air Force had all been wiped out. By nightfall on the second day the IAF had achieved near complete superiority in the air. These two days marked the finest hour of the IAF and one of the darkest periods for the Arab states, which had seen their mainly Soviet-supplied aircraft removed from the war barely after it had started. The successful outcome of the war for Israel was assured, but the extent of the victory was largely determined by the efforts of its ground forces.

In the battles that followed, Israel first defeated the Egyptian forces in the Sinai and then, after some debate, moved against the Syrian positions in the Golan Heights. The IDF was also successful in defeating the Jordanian forces in the West Bank. The most symbolic and emotive victory, however, for Israel was the conquering of East Jerusalem, and in particular the Old City. Paratroopers led by Motta Gur succeeded in capturing the Old City only after fierce battles in its narrow streets, and secured Jews access to their holy sites within the walls of the city. The final stage of the war came on 10 June when Syrian forces broke and gave up their positions following intensive IAF attacks. IDF personnel were airlifted to seize key strategic positions such as Mount Hermon in time for Israel to accept a UN-brokered ceasefire that came into effect at 6.30 pm.[6]

The Six Day War crushed Nasser as a leader, and as a man. On 9 June 1967, Nasser resigned. He returned to office only after large demonstrations of support for his leadership from Egyptians, and remained there until his death in 1970. At the time of the popular demonstrations, however, the Egyptian public did not know the magnitude of the Egyptian defeat in the war. When it did become known, there was widespread social unrest at the lenient sentences imposed at the trials of the so-called culprits of the war. In short, Nasser's regime was in trouble, and this was compounded by an economic crisis that left Egypt more reliant on the Arab world for survival. As a result, Nasser had no option but to fall into line with Arab thought towards Israel, which was characterised by continued hostility. Towards the end of his days there were signs that he was looking for a possible political reconciliation with the United States, and this policy impacted upon his calls for a more circumspect Arab political stance towards Israel. At the same time, on the military front, Nasser actively waged a war of attrition against Israel that escalated into major artillery exchanges and heavy retaliatory Israeli air raids.

Central to Nasser's thinking was the deeply held Arab belief that Israel must not be allowed to turn its military victory into a political one in which the Arabs would be forced to negotiate on Israel's terms to get back the lands they had lost during the war. On the military side, Nasser concluded a secret agreement with President al-Atasi of Syria on 15 August 1969 which he hoped would ensure that Israel faced a difficult dilemma in a couple of years' time, when it would be forced to fight any future war on two fronts simultaneously.[7] Though neither the Syrian President nor indeed Nasser remained in power long enough to see such an agreement implemented, it is revealing evidence of forward planning for the next major Arab–Israeli war. Nasser also concluded at the meeting the need to strengthen air defences using Soviet equipment and advisers. The lessons of 1967 had been learnt. In the short term, Nasser and the Arabs developed a new military strategy for dealing with Israel.

If from the Six Day War onwards the aim of the Arab states was primarily to recover the lands they had lost during the war (the Golan Heights for Syria, the Sinai for Egypt, and the West Bank and East Jerusalem for Jordan),[8] why was the Arab–Israeli conflict not simply resolved using a land for peace formula?

In order to answer this question it is important first to understand how the Six Day War impacted upon Israel, as well as the other social and cultural changes that were taking place in the country, changes that proved to be just as important as the consequences of the war itself.

In simple terms, the war created a situation whereby Israel became an occupying power, ruling over some one million Palestinians for the first time. New phrases were introduced to the Arab–Israeli conflict such as 'demographic time bomb', 'functionalist solution' (return of some of the lands), and 'annexation'. On the positive side, the war had provided Israel with the bargaining chips it had always lacked. Initially, the belief of the majority of the ruling Israeli élite was that some – or indeed all – of the lands would be traded for peace, thus allowing Israel to live behind secure and permanent borders. Those that called for some of the lands to be retained and annexed did so for security reasons. Areas such as the Jerusalem corridor were to be expanded, and Israel was, in effect, redressing some of the imbalances that the end of the 1948 war left. According to all the mainstream Zionist parties, Jerusalem was to remain the eternal and undivided capital of the Jewish state.

On the down-side, the debate over what do with the spoils of victory was set against a backdrop of generational change in the political leadership, mixed together with the start of the demise of the Israeli Labour Party, which under various labels had ruled not only Israel since its creation but much of Jewish life in Palestine during the period of the British Mandate. As a result of both, there were growing divisions among the senior Israeli political élite as to what to do about the West Bank in particular. Golda Meir, who succeeded Levi Eshkol when the latter became Israel's first PM to die in office, adopted a hawkish line, making her infamous statement that there was no such people as the Palestinians. In short, there was a sense of political inertia in Israel in the period following the war, which was reflected in the lack of dynamic peace-making initiatives on the part of the Israeli government.

It is important to remember that Golda Meir was the last of the Jews of the Second and Third Aliyah – the founding fathers and mothers of the state – and that the battle to succeed this generation was extremely bitter, being governed by both person-ality clashes and differences on policy that centred on the issue of the future status of the lands captured during the war. Such was the paranoia about causing a public split at the crucial juncture in Israel that – unbelievably as it may appear today – the debate was suppressed by the party leadership. For many years following the war, the party adopted no formal policy document on the status of the Disputed Territories. So much for Israeli democracy!

There were two other factors that helped precipitate Israel's inertia. The first was the fact that, while the Israeli élite did not expect Arab leaders to fall in love with Israel after the war, they at the very least expected the Arab political and military élites to understand that they would never be able to defeat Israel in a war. Israel's Chief of Staff during the Six Day War, Yitzhak Rabin, defined this in greater detail, arguing that the Arab élites must understand that they would stand no chance of defeating Israel until they (the Arabs) enjoyed air superiority – either through sheer numbers of planes, or the ability to shoot down Israeli aircraft using surface-to-air missiles (SAMs). Accepting this premise, then a *status quo* of no war, no peace was accept-able to Israel in the short term.

The second was the blatantly hard-line position that the Arab states adopted towards Israel following the war. Political confirmation of this appeared at the Khartoum Summit on 1 September 1967. It laid down the 'three noes' resolution: no recognition of Israel, no negotiations with Israel, and no peace with Israel. Under pressure at home and within the Arab world, President Nasser publicly flexed his Arab nationalist credentials by adding an additional 'no' to the Khartoum resolution: no concessions on the legitimate rights of the Palestinian people.

On the military front, Nasser moved quickly to attempt to rebuild morale among the Egyptian armed forces. In doing this, he developed a new military strategy for the continued struggle against Israel based on three phases: defensive rehabilitation, offensive, and finally liberation. Nasser, in short, was in no mood for what would be seen as surrender, and though he would live long enough to see the implementation of only the first two phases of his plan, he pursued its aims with increasing vigour. Though not as dramatic as other wars in the history of the Arab–Israeli conflict, the resulting war of attrition was nonetheless highly significant from a military and tactical point of view. Its direct impact could be seen in the development of weapons by both the US and the Soviet Union, with the superpowers' apparent use of the Middle East theatre, in part, as a testing ground for missile technology and air defence systems.

The period between the Six Day War of 1967 and the 1973 Arab–Israel War, as a result, saw superpower involvement in the area rise to higher levels than previously witnessed. This was particularly true in Egypt and Syria, where the use of Soviet advisers was increased. Soviet personnel piloted MiG jets with Egyptian markings and manned the surface-to-air missile batteries. The period following the Six Day War was therefore dominated not by peace talks but by a deepening internationalisation of the Arab–Israeli conflict – and a near-constant low-intensity war that reached various levels of violence. With the hindsight of history, it is clear that much of the military activity during this period was directed at research and development for the next Arab–Israeli conflict.

To what extent did the Palestinian issue complicate the situation in the post-Six Day War period?

A similar war of attrition took place on the Israeli–Jordanian front, mainly in the north Jordan Valley area where the PLO, acting at times with tacit Jordanian support, launched attacks against Israeli targets in the West Bank and into Israel itself. The Israelis mounted large-scale retaliatory operations against PLO bases in the area, and to a degree succeeded in pushing the PLO units out of the West Bank and into the East Bank in Jordan.

The military situation, however, changed dramatically from September 1970 onwards, following a failed PLO assassination attempt on the life of King Hussein of Jordan. The King came to realise that the PLO had effectively created a state within a state in Jordan, and was operating to such a degree of independence that the existence of the Hashemite Kingdom was at stake. He moved quickly and decisively, launching an all-out attack against the Palestinians during August and September 1970. At this stage, Syrian armoured units invaded Jordan and were met with heavy resistance from the Jordanian army.

During the tense days following the Syrian invasion, Israel and the United States made it clear that they would not be able to stand back and allow a Syrian take-over of Jordan. Israel let it be known that it might be forced to use the IAF to defend Jordan, and plans were even drawn up to use Israeli ground forces. For its part, the US moved its Sixth Fleet to the Levant Coast and started to plan for major troop movements from Europe to the Middle East. The Soviets clearly got the message, and advised the Syrians to pull back. By the end of the crisis, the PLO had been eliminated as a fighting force in Jordan, and its remnants moved to Lebanon to continue operations against Israel from its new host country. These attacks and reprisal raids by Israel continued until the 1982 Israeli invasion, when the PLO was once more forced to seek new headquarters, this time in the Tunisian capital, Tunis. Following the departure of the PLO from Jordan, the war of attrition on the Jordanian front came to an end.

In retrospect, the idea of Israel helping an Arab state, which only just over three years earlier had been part of the Arab axis against Israel, would appear to be like something out of a Fellini film. In truth, Israel sought to maintain the Hashemite rule over Jordan in order to help create a stable eastern Israeli border, and conversely to prevent the creation of a Palestinian state in Jordan under the control of Yasser Arafat. King Hussein met inter-mittently with Israeli leaders during his long period of rule. Indeed, on the eve of the Yom Kippur War in 1973, the King attempted to warn Golda Meir of the coming surprise attack by Egypt and Syria. Sadly for Israel, his warning fell on deaf ears. Meir thought the King's warning to be too imprecise, and it went against Israeli intelligence assessments that concluded that the Arabs were not preparing for another major war.

So why, if relations between Israel and Jordan from 1970 onwards were so cosy, did it take a further 24 years for the two countries to sign a formal peace agreement?

A number of factors have shaped Jordanian policy towards Israel: the limitations of Jordan's economic resources; its geographic position as a front-line state with Israel and the relative weakness of Jordan's army in comparison with Israel's; and the fact that a third of the Jordanian population is of Palestinian origin.[9] In political terms, the latter factor in particular meant that King Hussein felt unable to reach a public accord with Israel before an Israeli–Palestinian peace agreement was signed. Conversely, at inter-Arab level Jordan's policy towards Israel has largely been shaped by the desire to keep other Arab states – such as Nasser's Egypt in the 1960s and Syria in 1970 – from interfering in Jordan. This has meant that at different times Hussein has participated in Arab wars against Israel (1967) and at other junctures refrained from doing so (1973). In private, King Hussein hoped that any agreement between Israel and the Palestinians would fall short of creating a strong and viable Palestinian state that would threaten the rule of the Hashemite Kingdom over the lands on the East Bank of the River Jordan. The King's real nightmare, however, was a PLO-led Palestinian state that would destabilise the region.

This became more intense following the events of September 1970, and the PLO campaign of international terror that aimed to win publicity for their case and force Israel into agreeing to their radical demands. Not that there was much chance of Israel agreeing to its own destruction – the ideological cornerstone until Yasser Arafat's apparent embrace of the two-state solution in 1988 (code for accepting Israel's right to exist).

The question of Jerusalem was also of great concern to the King. Following the Six Day War, Israel gained control over the entire city, expelling Jordanian forces from East Jerusalem and the Old City. Israel, however, granted special status to Jordan in the Old City, with King Hussein given a role in the maintenance of the Islamic holy sites in that part of Jerusalem. Moreover, Hussein, who was afraid that any deal to create a Palestinian state would lead to Palestinian (PLO) control of the sites, jealously guarded this. It was this very fear that led to King Hussein all but publicly endorsing the candidature of Benjamin Netanyahu over Shimon Peres in Israel's 1996 elections for Prime Minister. At the time, the King's action raised a few eyebrows in the Arab world, as Netanyahu was a well-known critic of the Oslo Accords, while Shimon Peres was generally seen as the architect of the Accords which, if implemented, aimed at resolving the Israeli–Palestinian conflict through a two-state solution.

Of course there were periods of tension between Israel and Jordan, particularly after the political consequences of the birth of the new Israel – or the second republic, as it is often referred to. It took the King some time to grow accustomed to Menachem Begin after he became Prime Minister in 1977, though there was a sense of relief in Amman when the first Begin government (1977–81) turned out to be a much more pragmatic administration than Begin's ideologically-based rhetoric from his days in opposition would have suggested. The major crisis, however, arose during the period of Israel's second National Unity Government (1984–88), when in January 1987 the Labour Party leader and Minister of Foreign Affairs, Shimon Peres, negotiated with King Hussein what became known as the London Agreement (though the bulk of the negotiations took place in Ascot, a town some 25 miles west of London, where the King had an official residence).

The resulting plan included provision for Palestinian elections (no PLO participation was to be permitted) leading to an international conference, the results of which – according to Peres – were not to be binding to Israel. The King had a somewhat different interpretation of this part of the document. The Likud argued that, in typical Peres tradition, he had not consulted with Begin's successor as Israeli Prime Minister, Yitzhak Shamir, about the contents of the plan – or even told him that he was talking to the King. Peres denied the charge, arguing that Shamir had known and approved of his mission to London and that he (Peres) had informed him of the agreement as soon as he returned from England.[10] Whatever the truth, Shamir flew into a rage when presented with the details of the plan, and instructed his Likud colleagues in the Cabinet to block its path.

As a result, the London Agreement was consigned to the dustbin of history, and a furious King Hussein renounced Jordan's claim over the West Bank. This amounted to the King washing his hands of the Palestinian issue, and robbed Israel of its Jordanian option whereby the Palestinians would come under Jordanian sovereignty, or some form of Jordanian–Palestinian confederation would be created to resolve the Palestinian issue. From this point onwards there was only really one viable diplomatic solution to the Israeli–Palestinian conflict, the two-state solution: an Israeli state living side by side with a fully independent Palestinian state. Few in Israel – with the notable exception of the far left parties – were brave enough to admit this at the time. Israelis simply weren't ready to think the unthinkable at this stage.

Events in Kuwait in 1990 conspired to bring the King and Yitzhak Shamir together for the first time. Away from the media spotlight and the ongoing diplomatic efforts to avert war, Shamir held a secret meeting with King Hussein in London. The meeting took place on 4 and 5 January 1991 at the King's private residence, where he outlined his dilemma: why he was driven to publicly support Saddam, his lack of trust in the Iraqi leader, and his fears that a war would be a disaster for Jordan. In short, the King feared that if he did not support the Iraqi leader the Palestinians in Jordan might riot, and the resulting social unrest could endanger the Hashemite Kingdom. The King assured the Israelis that he would not let a third force (Iraq) use Jordanian territory to mount attacks against Israel. In return, Shamir promised the King that Israel would not use Jordanian sovereign territory to launch attacks against Iraq (both land and air space).[11] As any attack by the IAF on Iraq would have to fly over Jordan, Shamir was, in effect, severely limiting his hand to respond to Iraqi attacks on Israel. Shamir did not inform the US of the outcome of the meeting, a deliberate oversight aimed at ensuring that the US continued to lobby Israel to stay out of the war. The wily old PM wanted to extract the maximum political and economic price possible from the US for Israeli restraint.

Once the PLO had signed the Oslo Accords with Israel, King Hussein felt able in 1994 to start the process of normalisation with the Jewish state. The personal chemistry between the Israeli Prime Minister, Yitzhak Rabin, and the King clearly played an important role in securing a peace treaty. Problems that arose during the negotiations, such as border disputes and water rights, were imaginatively solved, usually with the direct intervention of the King and Rabin. Israel handed back sovereignty of key farming lands and was subsequently allowed to lease these lands back from Jordan. The question of Jordanian water demands was met by joint plans to develop increased water resources. King Hussein and Yitzhak Rabin signed the peace agreement between Israel and Jordan on 26 October 1994 on a mine-cleared site in no-man's-land on the Israeli–Jordanian border. President Clinton, always keen on a Middle East photo opportunity, attended the ceremony, despite the fact that once more the United States had not played a major role in the negotiations. The ceremony was a highly choreographed event which lacked the tension of the previous year's Israel–PLO signing ceremony in Washington. The King and Rabin tried not to look like two old friends who had known each other all their adult lives, but like elder statesmen ending nearly 50 years of conflict. Sitting among the many dignitaries was a beaming Yitzhak Shamir, telling anyone within earshot that it was his meetings with the King some four years earlier that had laid the foundations for the agreement.

From 1996 onwards, however, the Israeli–Jordanian relationship started to deteriorate. This was in part due to the increasing opposition in Jordan towards the peace treaty, particularly among the East Bankers and the Palestinians. The opposition grew as the anticipated economic peace dividend from the agreement did not materialise for Jordan. Paradoxically, one of the major reasons for this lack of an economic dividend was Jordanian domestic opposition to closer economic links with Israel. There was no sustained programme of US aid, as there had been for Egypt following its signing of a peace treaty with Israel. As the Palestinian track became deadlocked, so King Hussein came under increased pressure not to develop closer ties with the Netanyahu government and Israel.

The issue of water returned to the agenda when it became clear that the joint water projects had simply not emerged and that there was a water crisis in Jordan. Many Israeli leaders – including Peres – felt that Rabin had been too generous to Jordan in the articles on water rights, and this issue threatened to sour relations between the two countries even further. The personal chemistry that had been such a feature of the Rabin–King Hussein relationship was absent from Netanyahu's relationship with the King.

The relationship reached new lows when Israeli agents attempted to murder a political leader of Hamas, the radical Islamic Palestinian group, on 25 September 1997 by poisoning him in a street in central Amman. A furious King Hussein demanded that Netanyahu release the spiritual leader of Hamas, Yassin, from prison in Israel and allow him to return home to the Gaza Strip. This was a high price for an Israeli leader to pay, but Netanyahu obliged and today Yassin remains in Gaza, despite Israeli attempts to kill him.

Following the death of King Hussein and the coronation of King Abdullah II, there has been a marked public distance between Jordan and Israel. The Israeli–Jordanian peace, however, remains a stable one, but one that is becoming more closely based on the Israeli–Egyptian model of cold peace than any warm relationship. In essence, it remains as it always has been: a marriage of convenience that reflects the joint strategic interests of both Israel and the Hashemite Kingdom.

How did Egypt and Syria come together to launch a surprise military attack on Israel in October 1973?

The events of September 1970 inadvertently secured Israel's strategic relationship with the Hashemite Kingdom, but did not impact on the other two Arab states that lost lands during the Six Day War. The death of President Nasser, who despite all his apparent shortcomings remained the leader of the Arab world, marked a crucial turning point in the Arab–Israeli conflict. In many respects, Nasser had always remained a pragmatist, an unusual state of affairs – though not in the Middle East – for a leader who was so heavily reliant on the use of ideology to justify his actions. To his dying day, Nasser wished to remain leader of the Arab world and the most popular figure on the 'Arab street'. In this respect, when presented with the choice of making genuine peace with Israel – accepting the concept of co-existence or remaining head of the Arab world (the attainment of both was impossible) – he always chose the latter.[12] This pragmatic choice, however, should not be mistaken for ideology. Nasser was far too complex, wily and addicted to power to be shackled by the chains of ideological politics.

Both Egypt and Syria underwent political transformations at the start of the 1970s, with two new leaders attempting to develop their power-base and win popular Arab support. Though very different, President Anwar Sadat of Egypt and President Hafiz al-Asad of Syria each needed to be seen to secure at least an Israeli withdrawal from part, if not all, of the lands captured by Israel. It would be foolhardy to attach labels such as 'pragmatic' or 'ideologue' to either man, as this would prove to be extremely misleading without a careful definition of each term. What is clear is that, in the Arab political world of coup and counter-coup, each man needed tangible signs that the Arabs were going to regain the lands lost in 1967 in order to help mask growing economic and social problems in their respective countries.

In retrospect, those who claim that an opportunity for peace was missed between 1970 and 1973 appear over-optimistic. In truth, diplomatic efforts at bringing about peace came into a difficult regional and global environment. The internal dynamics in Israel and the Arab world were not conducive to peace-making. Similarly, the influence of the Cold War on the region's politics made it difficult for any initiative to succeed. Nasser's death came at a bad time, with a lack of a clearly identified natural successor. His eventual successor, President Sadat, was considered a stop-gap appointment at the time, something of a playboy with limited diplomatic or political abilities. Naturally, he lacked the legitimacy that Nasser had developed over the years, and therefore did not have – at this stage anyway – the degree of room to manoeuvre that Nasser had enjoyed.

For his part, Sadat came to realise that the deep internal divisions in the ruling élite in Israel over the future of the Territories – and the hawkish line of the Golda Meir government towards the Arabs in general – doomed any diplomatic efforts to eventual failure. Consequently, he prepared Egypt for war. He expelled the Soviet military personnel from Egypt in July 1973 in order to give himself a freer hand to manoeuvre, though he did not break off relations, and Egyptian armed forces continued to be supplied by the Russians. He sought US support, and was to some degree wooed by American officials who saw the strategic value of developing US–Egyptian ties. He attempted, with a good deal of success, to lull Israel into a false sense of security by strictly observing a ceasefire in the Suez Canal area. Israel viewed the calm as a sign of Arab military weakness, not as part of an overall war plan. In 1973, the Israeli élite was convinced that all was quiet on its southern front, and that there was little prospect of war.

How was the Israeli élite so willing to accept the belief that, in light of the persistent diplomatic failures, the Arabs would not turn to the war option?

Following the Six Day War a very new Israel emerged, though many of the changes can be attributed to factors other than the war itself. It is important to look at the characteristics, the outside perception and the political reality of this 'new Israeli republic'. The arrival in Israel of the Orientals – Jews from North Africa and the Middle East – helped transform the country from a relatively homogeneous society to a more diverse one. Such changes led to deep divisions in Israeli society that could be seen at economic, cultural and political levels. The arrival of the 'Oriental Aliyah' brought new challenges for a country that was struggling to finance the absorption machine. Many of the Orientals were forced to live in poor conditions upon their arrival in transit camps, and were eventually located in what became known as 'development towns' situated away from the established population centres. The conditions in the development towns were basic in terms of welfare provision, social conditions, employment prospects and education. The difficulties were compounded by the fact that the majority of Jews from North Africa and Asia came from poor backgrounds with minimal formal education. Within the Israeli jobs market they were usually employed in menial jobs.

In effect, the arrival of the Oriental Jews had created a two-tier Israel: a fact that the original Zionist thinkers had not foreseen or prepared for.[13] The concept of a two-tier society remains an uncomfortable one to those who aspired to ideas of egalitarianism for the Jewish state. Amos Oz, one of Israel's best-known writers, famously highlighted the difficulties in a chapter of his book *In the Land of Israel*. The book, which describes the author's travels around Israel and conversations with a broad section of Israeli society, contains a wonderful section on Oz's visit to Beit Shemesh, a town founded in the early 1950s that is predominantly inhabited by Oriental Jews. One participant in the dialogue Oz started in a local café sums up the difference between the Ashkenazi and Oriental Jew: 'Chaim Bar-Lev [leading member of Israeli Labour Party] has a pin in his leg, and David Levy [leading Oriental politician] has a pin in his leg, because they both fell and broke a leg. Where did Chaim Bar-Lev, the so-called leader of the Workers' Party fall? From his horse. Like some English Lord. But David Levy fell from a third-storey scaffold. That says it all.'[14]

In retrospect, the Israeli authorities did a remarkable job in absorbing such numbers with the limited finance and the continuing strains imposed upon the economy by the Arab–Israeli conflict. To all intents and purposes, these immigrants were refugees, and their plight is often forgotten or over-shadowed by the tragedy of the Palestinian exodus from Israel. The predominantly Ashkenazi élite attempted to shape a single Israeli national culture that was based on European thinking, rather than adopting Middle East influences that were more familiar to the Orientals. Many Israelis, despite the widely held view that Europe was the old world, argued the importance of keeping Israel 'European' in terms of identity and culture, and this set of beliefs largely shaped Israel's education system, its media, judiciary, industry and democracy. The leadership marginalised Arab or Middle Eastern culture, and this in the long term had a profound impact on the political and cultural alienation of the new immigrants.

At first, as these new immigrants were highly dependent on the state and Mapai, the forerunner to the current Israeli Labour Party, to meet their everyday needs, strong dependence ties emerged between the party and the Orientals. Over a period of time it became clear that the party was not able to meet the aspirations and demands of these groups, and so the process of crossing the political divide started, and by the 1970s the majority of this group were strong supporters of Menachem Begin and the Likud.

For his part, Begin had remained in opposition since the creation of the state.[15] Ben-Gurion had made it clear that he saw everyone as potential coalition partners, with the exception of Herut (the political party of the Revisionists) and the Communists.

In 1965, Herut merged with the Liberal Party to form Gahal, which marked the start of the shift to the political centre of the descendants of the Revisionist movements in Israel, confirmed with the formation of the Likud (Hebrew for Union) in 1973. By the time of the Six Day War in 1967, Mapai's support was being noticeably eroded as a result of this growing political and social alienation of the Orientals. This erosion of support came at the same time as the party faced growing internal problems involving disagreements over key issues of party organisation and the fallout from the Lavon Affair, compounded by the generational and ideological challenge of the young guard in the battle of succession to the élite of the Second Aliyah.

Israel's victory in the Six Day War brought benefits to the government, but in the long run led to an increasing split within Mapai – and, after 1968, the newly formed Israeli Labour Party. The National Unity Government that had been formed before the war remained in place until 1970. For the first time, Menachem Begin and Gahal (later to be the Likud) were included in the coalition, providing them with a degree of legitimacy they had not previously enjoyed. The outcome of the war brought a series of challenges in terms of what should be done about the territory that Israel had captured. This became the major divisive issue of Israeli politics, and remains so to the present day. For Gahal, the capture of these lands appeared to offer the prospect of the realisation of the Revisionist dream of 'Greater Israel' – a Jewish state on both banks of the River Jordan. In practical terms, in the first instance, this would have meant the annexation of the captured West Bank to Israel.

The Labour movement, unlike Gahal, was deeply divided over the future status of the territories, with no clear unity emerging among the senior leadership on the issue. Some favoured returning all the lands to the Arabs in exchange for peace, others exchanging some of the land for peace, and a third group hoped to integrate the territories economically into Israel without annexing the lands. The divisions not only reflected differing opinions over the issue but also deep personal animosity and the struggle for power within the movement.

In 1968, the Israeli Labour Party was formed against a backdrop of economic recession which had led to large-scale unemployment and a high rate of emigration. The merger between Mapai and Achdut Ha'avodah appeared perfectly natural; in the previous years they had become closely identified with each other, submitting joint lists in Knesset elections and working together in successive governments. The merger with the third party, Rafi, however, was much more problematic. The ill feeling caused by the Lavon scandal from the mid 1950s remained, particularly in David Ben-Gurion. Moshe Dayan, who had emerged as the leading figure in Rafi following the Six Day War, took a more pragmatic line. In truth, Rafi had little choice but to seek to join the new party. In the 1965 Knesset elections it had won only ten seats, a performance that had fallen well short of its own expectations. In terms of party organisation, Rafi had not developed the kind of local structures that are required to sustain a major political party, and therefore its long-term prospects appeared bleak. There were problems between Achdut Ha'avodah and Rafi, with the former regarding the latter as dangerously right-wing on socio-economic issues.

The formation of the Israeli Labour Party took place at the start of the race to succeed the ageing Levi Eshkol. Dayan, who regarded himself as the obvious candidate for the leadership of the new party, was keen to persuade his Rafi colleagues to join the new party in order to pursue his leadership claim. Rafi eventually consented to Dayan's wishes and joined the new party, but a small minority refused and formed another new party called the State List. There were two additional challengers to Dayan for the leadership of the Israeli Labour Party: Pinhas Sapir from Mapai and Yigal Allon from Achdut Ha'avodah. Sapir was the leader of the Gush, running the party both financially and organisationally. He was seen as the natural insider to succeed Eshkol. For his part, Allon was the undoubted leader of Achdut Ha'avodah, but there were questions as to his ability to win support from other factions in the party. It came as little surprise that the greatest rivalry was between Dayan and Sapir, and this was heightened by their differences over the future of the territories that Israel had captured during the Six Day War. Sapir favoured using them as a negotiating card and was not against the eventual return of them to the Arabs. Dayan favoured what became known as the economic integration approach.

Such was the extent of their rivalry, and that of their supporters, that it was impossible for the party to devise any public plan for the future of the territories for fear of splitting the new party. The importance of the succession battle in determining the actions of the key members of the élite during this period cannot be overstated. Throughout Israeli history up to this point, whoever had been leader of the party had also been PM. The consequence of Allon's, Sapir's and Dayan's actions was that there was little prospect of Israel being able to make any clear decisions about the future status of the territories and, as a result, any negotiations with the Arabs. This fact was to come back to haunt both the party and Israel.

In the event, Levi Eshkol died suddenly in February 1969. His death came too soon for the younger candidates to assume the premiership, so the torch passed to another of the elders, Golda Meir. Meir had previously been thought too old to succeed Eshkol, but his premature death meant that she took office as Israel's fourth Prime Minister, and was the last of Israel's founding fathers and mothers to lead the country. Meir came from Mapai and was supported by Sapir. Such was her stature that her attempt to take office went unchallenged. Dayan was biding his time while Sapir became Secretary-General of the party and worked at consolidating the position of the centrist elements within it. Meir governed Israel, with her close advisers and colleagues taking the major decisions, rather than the Cabinet. This small group was soon labelled Golda's 'Kitchen Cabinet' after the location of their meetings. Other ministers were generally excluded from the wider decision-making process and concentrated on running their respective ministries.

In Israeli society, the Six Day War had changed the national psyche to a much more confident one. The period between 1967 and 1973 saw a cultural boom, particularly in the cities. On Independence Day 1968, Israeli Television started transmission, and by the early 1970s almost every Jewish family had a TV set. It would be years before Israelis had the choice of more than one channel, but the existence of a national TV channel arrived at the right time for Israelis keen to be seen as a 'normal country'. The advent of TV increased the worldly knowledge of Israelis and started to transform the electoral process, just as TV had changed the face of US politics in the 1960 Presidential campaign.

Culturally, Israel changed. Fashion became an issue with the advent of long sideburns and bell-bottom jeans, Israeli modern rock and pop music was born, and in the spring of 1973 Israel competed in the Eurovision Song Contest for the first time, finishing a creditable fourth. In sport, the basketball team Maccabi Tel Aviv became increasingly successful and competed in the European championship. Indeed, during the 1970s Maccabi Tel Aviv won the championship and soon became one of the most recognised names in the world of basketball. The Ashkenazi population of Israel were keen to be competing within a European framework, as this strengthened the ties between Israel and Europe and reflected on the developing Israeli culture.

At the root of this new-found confidence was the widely held feeling that the Arabs would not be able to defeat Israel in war and would one day attempt to seek peace with the Jewish state. The War of Attrition that raged for much of this period was seen as a series of border incidents and not a direct threat to the survival of the state. In many respects, Golda Meir symbolised the country she led: strong, self-confident, but most of all underestimating the nature of the continued Arab threat to Israel.

On a political level, the biggest change brought about by the Six Day War was the advent of the Israeli settlers in the West Bank and Gaza Strip.

The stereotypical image of the 180,000-plus Israeli settlers who currently inhabit the West Bank and Gaza Strip is of machine-gun-toting, Arab-hating Jews. Politically, they are characterised by an increasingly hostile media as extremist, and the major Israeli obstacle to peace. According to elements of the European press, attacks on settlers by Palestinians are now deemed to be legitimate – settlers, it seems, are no longer classed as civilians. Mention the words 'Israeli settler' and two names are usually remembered: Baruch Goldstein (the perpetrator of the Hebron massacre in 1994) and Yigal Amir (the assassin of Yitzhak Rabin in 1995). The fact that the latter was not a settler at all illustrates the problems of misrepresentation that the settlers regularly face.

So who are these settlers? And are they a homogeneous group or are there major differences in outlook and rationale for living in the Disputed Territories?

Today, the settlements range from villages to large towns.[16] There are three basic types of settler in the West Bank, and even this is a simplification. The first group, which are the largest numerically, are deemed as economic settlers, and live primarily in the well established major settlement blocks that are likely to remain under Israeli sovereignty after a deal is struck on the partition of the land between Israel and a Palestinian state. This group were enticed to live in the West Bank primarily by the generous tax breaks offered by successive Israeli governments during the 1970s and 80s, and by seemingly good road communications into Jerusalem. Today, just as commuters trying to enter London spend much of their day bumper to bumper on entrance roads to the capital, many of this group do likewise on the limited access roads to the city at the top of the hill. Many are young couples that can't afford to set up home in the over-priced centre of Jerusalem. Israel claims that many of these settlements around Jerusalem are not settlements at all, but rather housing projects that reflect the demographic growth of Jerusalem. The Palestinians charge that they are political settlements and reflect a concerted Israeli attempt to encircle Jerusalem, thus ensuring Israeli control over the entire city.[17]

The second group of settlers live in more outlying settlements that have assumed the characteristics and infrastructure of small towns. This group have more of a religious tinge to them, and strongly believe that Judea and Samaria (the Israeli term for the West Bank) should be part of the Jewish state. Many within this group carry weapons and come under attack from local Palestinians. The location of some of these settlements can be viewed as provocative, as they sit near, or next to, Palestinian villages and towns. The political rationale for many of these settlements was security. For with every settlement this size comes a considerable IDF presence and permanent-looking security infrastructure such as watch-towers, good quality roads and army bases. There is currently a debate within Israel as to whether such security infrastructure actually helps in Israel's fight or diminishes Israel's security by leading to an increase in the number of attacks against it. It is envisaged that many of these settlements will be dismantled by Israel after a final status agreement is reached with the Palestinians.

While a small and vocal minority of this group is likely to resist any attempts to physically remove them, the vast majority – with the right financial inducements – can be convinced to relocate within the Green Line that divides Israel proper from the West Bank. The financial inducements are likely to prove extremely important, as some of the settlers within this group have moved into the area in order to make a quick buck through buying up lands that they know will be purchased off them at a generous price, allowing them to make a sizeable profit. Though the international media concentrates on examining the ideological agenda of the settlers, it largely ignores the economic agenda of some of them.

Numerically the smallest, the third group are the Zealots who live on the periphery – sometimes with the permission of the Israeli government, and other times illegally. These settlements are usually very small, and look very temporary, with settlers living in tents, caravans or prefab huts. These settlers tend to be the most militant and, with all the publicity they attract, are the group that does most to create the strong anti-settler feeling that many people hold. They strongly believe that they have a God-given right to settle in any part of the West Bank – and their aim is to create as many outposts as possible in order to make it as difficult as possible for any Israeli government to hand over the land to the Palestinians.

People from within this group have threatened civil dis-
obedience, and even violence, if any attempt is made to remove
their outposts or isolated settlements. The international media
tends to devote a disproportionate amount of time to this group,
with images of lonely hill-tops, caravans and Israeli flags making
good television. But the truth is that when the time comes for a
permanent agreement with the Palestinians, any potential Israeli
Prime Minister is likely to take strong action against this group.
At present the situation is complex, with radical Jewish philan-
thropists in the United States helping to fund some of these
settlements. In private, all recent Israeli Ministers of Defence
have taken action against this group. More action is needed, but
in Israel there is a sense among the mainstream political and
military élite that the dismantling of these settlements should
be offered as a concession in the political process with the
Palestinians. The Palestinians argue that such settlements are
illegal and provocative and should be dismantled now before any
political negotiations.

Perhaps the greatest significance of the start of the settlement
programme by the Labour-led government back in 1967 was that
it sent a message to the Arab states that Israel was attempting to
'put facts on the ground' that would make it difficult for future
governments to offer territorial compromises. A widely held
misconception is that the major settlement activity took place
under Likud-led governments. This simply is not the case. One
joke among the Likud is that when Labour is in power, settlement
expansion is referred to by the United States as natural expansion, and when the Likud is in power, similar expansion is termed
an obstacle to peace.

In the period following the Six Day War, the major charge
against Israel in Arab circles was that Israelis had become
extremely arrogant. Accounts of the war were full of tales of the
extraordinary prowess of the Sabra (native-born Jew), and conversely were used to reinforce the Israeli stereotypical image of
the Arab fighter as a coward. It would seem that the war transformed Israelis overnight from feeling very insecure and afraid
about the future of the state into the opposite – super-confident

that the Arabs would not attack when they knew they would be trounced on the battlefield. This, of course, is a simplification, but nonetheless it was a terrible miscalculation that most ordinary Israelis made, as did the collective political and military leadership of the country.

The simple truth is that the Arabs came to grips with the results and consequences of the Six Day War much quicker than the Israelis. On the military front, Arab and Soviet generals came to the rapid conclusion that any advance of Arab armies would have to take place under the cover of batteries of SAMs in order to dilute the threat posed by the Israeli Air Force. A degree of surprise was viewed as an important ingredient, though total surprise was not deemed necessary, as it was widely presumed that the United States would not accommodate any Israeli request for a pre-emptive strike – even if there were overwhelming evidence of an imminent Arab attack. On the political front, there was an understanding that such an attack by the Arabs should be of a limited nature, with the intention of re-taking the lands lost in 1967 and then hoping for a superpower-sponsored ceasefire so as to hold on to the gains made on the ground. Mention was rarely made of the Palestinians, outside of the usual lip service paid by Arab leaders, with phrases like 'there will be no stopping until the liberation of Jerusalem is complete and all the Zionist infidels are removed from the city'.

Just as the most striking image of the Six Day War had been the pictures of IAF jets destroying the EAF on the ground, so the most striking images of the Yom Kippur War were of exhausted Israeli soldiers attempting to prevent the initial wave of Arab attacks from breaking through Israeli front lines. But perhaps the image that best characterised Israeli fears during the early days of the war was that of Moshe Dayan, who at this time was serving as Minister of Defence. Dayan appeared on Israeli television on the second evening of the war with the aim of reassuring Israelis. Dayan, looking tired and strained, could barely look at the camera. His face projected a sense of shock and dismay at events, and transmitted just how grave the situation had become for Israel. Dayan never really recovered from the shock of the war.[18]

The fact that this was Moshe Dayan, the all-conquering hero of the Suez War and the Minister of Defence during the Six Day War, added to this sense of shock.

Indeed, Dayan's greatest contribution to Israel's victory in 1967 was the fact that he had restored the Israeli army's confidence that it would win the war.[19] This was due in no small part to Dayan's drive and zeal, and his rejection of military help from the United States to help resolve the pre-war crisis.[20] In 1973 things were different, with probably the most recognisable face of the Israeli leadership (with the possible exception of Golda Meir) admitting that Israel was in deep trouble. And this time Israel would not be able to stand alone, but rather would have to ask the US to re-arm it in the middle of the war. In truth, away from all the bravado and womanising that defined his life, Dayan was a complex man. He was prone to periods of severe depression, but at a time when scrutiny of politicians was far less intense than it is today, he managed to mask much of the darker side of his character from the public.

The Yom Kippur War (War of Atonement) or, as it is known by its other names, the October War, Ramadan War, or simply the 1973 War, caused a trauma in Israel that has lasted to this day. Though Israel emerged from the fighting as the clear victor and, as Peter Mansfield puts it, 'had snatched a stunning victory from the initial defeat', it paid a heavy price with 2,521 Israelis killed and some 7,056 wounded. True, Arab losses were substantially higher, but were much less in terms of proportion of the total population.[21] In Israel, it seemed that at least one man from each town or village failed to return safely from the front.

In the short term, the war led to the shattering of the myth of Israeli invincibility that had developed since the 1967 war – and the security credentials of the political ruling élite from the Labour Alignment. The origins of the war itself, to a large degree, lie in the outcome of the Six Day War – and specifically the political and military lessons that the Arab leadership learnt from this defeat. President Sadat planned to recover the lands lost to Israel in 1967 by a mixture of political and military moves. He concluded, correctly, that any military action taken by Egypt would be met by a massive retaliation by Israel. Consequently, the Egyptian leader understood that there was little alternative but to launch as big an attack as possible.

In Israel, the general assessment was that the Arabs would not launch an attack until they had sufficient numbers of aircraft capable of knocking out Israeli airstrips and neutralising the IAF – the major determining factor in Israel's victory in 1967. Israeli intelligence concluded that this point would not be reached until 1975, and thus the threat of an attack in 1973 was minimal. Unbeknown to the Israelis, however, the Soviets had developed a new strategic missile defence system which included missile batteries that had been moved into the Suez Canal zone and new long-range SCUD missiles that could threaten Israeli population centres. The idea of the latter was to deter the IAF from operating deep in Egyptian territory. This plan was to prove highly successful, with the IAF largely ineffective in the opening days of the war.

Once it became clear to Sadat that there was a war option, he moved quickly to enlist the support of President Asad of Syria for a joint operation. Asad consented, and planning for a simultaneous assault on Israel began in earnest in January 1973. The first SCUD missiles arrived in Egypt. Their arrival proved to be the final determining factor in Sadat's decision to use the war option. Ironically, at the same time in Israel, AMAN, the intelligence wing of the Israeli army, concluded that any war was unlikely until 1975.[22] The Soviets also moved quickly to increase the air defence systems of Syria, particularly in the Damascus region.

Israeli intelligence was not blind to the Egyptians' preparations for war. In May 1973, they concluded that this was merely part of the Arab strategy of brinkmanship, but that nothing would come of it. The Israeli Chief of Staff, David Elazar, however, did not share the conclusions of the intelligence findings and ordered a partial mobilisation of Israeli reserves. Sadat decided for a number of both military and political reasons to postpone the war until September/October – the next time when the tides in the Suez Canal would be right for an Egyptian crossing. In Israel, the intelligence services were seen to have been proved right, and this was to have a profound effect on the decision-making process in the weeks leading up to the war.[23]

In September 1973, Israeli intelligence noted another major build-up on both the Egyptian and Syrian fronts, and made the assessment that these were routine large-scale exercises that had taken place several times before. The intelligence assessment was arrived at within the wider framework of the belief that the Arabs would not attack until they had superior air power to bomb Israeli cities, and against the backdrop of having been proved right in May 1973.[24] On this occasion, the assessment was wrong, and it went a long way to giving the Egyptians and Syrians the advantage in the early days of the war. On a political level, Minister of Defence Moshe Dayan was inclined to agree with the assessment, but Chief of Staff Elazar remained more sceptical. On the eve of the war, with the concentration of forces on Israel's northern and southern borders increasing, Elazar asked for a Cabinet meeting and the IDF was put on alert.

On the morning of 6 October – the Day of Atonement and one of the holiest days in the Jewish calendar – when intelligence information confirmed that the attack would be launched that day against Israel, a stormy meeting took place between Elazar and Dayan. During the course of the discussion, Elazar pleaded for permission to launch a pre-emptive strike against the Egyptian and Syrian forces and to issue the order for a general mobilisation of Israel's reserves. Dayan refused both requests, but did agree to a small mobilisation for defensive purposes.[25] Both men then took their case to the Prime Minister, Golda Meir, who supported Dayan that there be no pre-emptive strike. She was later to argue that the political damage that such a strike would have caused far outweighed the military gains from such an action. Patrick Seale emphasises the importance of this, arguing that perhaps the greatest Arab coup was the fact that they prevented Israel from striking first, a fact that allowed the Arab armies to dominate the first 48 hours of the battle.[26] On the mobilisation issue, Meir compromised between Dayan's and Elazar's positions and ordered the mobilisation of 100,000. Of the three key players at the time, only Elazar seemed to fully grasp the military seriousness of the situation.

On time, at 2 pm, the Egyptians and Syrians attacked, and the war that the vast majority of the Israeli political and military élite thought would not happen, had started. When the fighting stopped, the Arab leadership pointed to the massive US airlift of arms to Israel during the war that many felt helped turn its tide in Israel's favour. Much in the same way as the 1956 intervention of Britain and France was portrayed as a reason for the Egyptian military setbacks at the Suez war's conclusion, so the US airlift of arms was used as the explanation for the eventual rout of the Arab armies in 1973. Golda Meir never attempted to hide the importance of these shipments of arms, and used it to vindicate her decision not to launch a pre-emptive strike on 6 October. Her belief was that, had Israel done so, it would not have received the support of the US administration later in the war.

In the months and years following the end of the war, Israel signed disengagement agreements with the Egyptians and Syrians. An interim agreement on the Sinai was also signed between Israel and Egypt in September 1975. This agreement called for withdrawal of Israeli forces to the Mitla and Gidi Passes, the setting up of electronic surveillance in the Sinai – manned by US personnel – the return of the Abu Rudeis oil fields to Egypt and the opening of the Suez Canal to shipping bound to and from Israel. In many respects, this agreement proved to be the forerunner to the Camp David Agreements that were to follow.

Though Israel emerged as the clear military victor, on the political front the outcome was very different. President Sadat, the main initiator of the war, emerged, despite the undeniable defeat of his armies, with his domestic position greatly enhanced. His control over both Egypt and the Egyptian military were significantly stronger. He used Egypt's eventual military defeat as an excuse to purge the military of opponents to his rule. Clearly, the initial successes of the Arabs in the war and the accompanying return of national honour (so important in the Arab world) provided Sadat with the room to manoeuvre to start a political dialogue with Israel. This was to lead to his visit to Jerusalem and the eventual signing of a peace treaty with Israel. In Syria, the war enhanced the position of President Asad, but here, unlike in Egypt, he had little intention of negotiating with Israel. He came to use his increasingly important position within the wider Arab world to ensure that no such negotiations would take place for years to come.

Throughout his period of rule, President Asad viewed the Arab–Israeli dispute on two levels. The first was the simple Arab commitment to destroy the 'Zionist entity'. The second level was more strategic. Asad viewed Israel as the major regional power and sought to reach parity with it, either for the purpose of waging war with it or for reaching a political settlement between the Arab world and Israel. Regarding a potential political settlement, Asad was governed by the belief that peace is never established between the weak and the strong, but rather between equal partners.[27]

From time to time, Asad gave interviews to Western periodicals in which he appeared to accept the notion that Syria would one day sign a formal peace treaty with Israel, providing it agreed to withdraw from all the territories that it captured in 1967 and accepted the existence of a Palestinian state.[28] To a large extent, such talk was part of a complex diplomatic approach, with Asad trying to pressurise Israel into political concessions by making Syria appear reasonable to the United States. Perhaps the real proof of the pudding was to be found in the post-Oslo period, 1993–4, when the then Israeli Prime Minister, Yitzhak Rabin, offered to return all the Golan Heights to Syria in return for peace.[29]

Asad did not embrace the offer for a number of reasons, perhaps the most important being that a peace agreement with Israel would have endangered the future of Ba'ath rule in Syria, by leading to calls for a reduction in military spending and economic liberalisation. Strategically, Asad saw a Ba'ath-led Syria as too weak to make peace, and conversely – with the emergence of the United States as the sole superpower in the region following the collapse of the Soviet Union – Israel as too strong. Right up to his death, he continued to exploit Israel's

Achilles heel, Lebanon, by waging a proxy war through Hezbollah. Asad is rumoured to have passed away while on the phone discussing the proxy war in Lebanon with the Lebanese Prime Minister. For Asad, just as it had been for Nasser, the Arab–Israeli conflict brought a degree of legitimacy and popular support for Ba'ath rule in Syria. The difference between Asad and the other Arab leaders of his generation was the sophisticated way he exploited the conflict for his own ends under the cover of being the gatekeeper of Arab nationalism.

In Israel, few talk about the Yom Kippur War as a victory. The war had a number of important consequences for the country as a whole and its leadership. First, it led to the earliest set of negotiations with an Arab country over a permanent peace treaty. Second, it created a growing economic dependence on the US. As the war cost Israel the equivalent of a year's GNP, so its debt burden increased and levels of US aid were increased – and remain in place to the present. Finally, the war contributed to the decline of the Labour Party. It had ruled Israel since its creation in 1948, but lost power in 1977 to the Likud led by Menachem Begin. The trauma caused by the war – the high casualty figures in Israel (over 2,500 dead), the mistakes in the political and military leadership, and the shattering of the post-1967 euphoria – all played an important role in reshaping Israeli society. Israel took stock of the military lessons of the war and restructured its armed forces to meet the demands of the new high-tech warfare, but the shattering of confidence proved more difficult to rebuild. This was not made any easier by the increase in Palestinian terrorist attacks during this period, which was testing the resolve of the Israeli nation once more.

The Yom Kippur War had a traumatic effect both on the Israeli leadership and throughout Israeli society. In domestic terms, it speeded the decline of the Labour Party and hastened the arrival of Begin and the Likud in 1977. The 1973 Knesset elections that were held soon after the conclusion of the war saw the Alignment (comprising the Israeli Labour Party and the left-wing workers' party, Mapam) lose only five seats from the 1969 election (56 to 51). Gahal, and in 1973 its successor party the Likud, saw its number of seats increase from 26 in 1969 to 39 in 1973. This was an impressive gain, but it was not enough to bring down the Alignment.

Following Golda Meir's resignation due to ill health in 1974, Yitzhak Rabin took over as Prime Minister. Rabin had little political experience and in the domestic arena his administration was far from successful. In effect, Rabin was left to lead a party that after some twenty years in power was in deep decline, its natural voting constituencies shrinking in contrast to the increasing demographic importance of the Oriental voters, who by this stage were very much in the camp of the Likud. Rabin himself was not a party man, and decided to largely ignore it and concentrate on Cabinet government. Thus, at a time when the party needed to be reformed and revitalised, it received little attention. For much of his period in office the new PM concentrated on foreign policy issues, and in particular the negotiations with the Egyptians over disengagement agreements in the Sinai, whose attainment Rabin correctly saw as a vital stage in securing a more permanent peace with President Sadat and Egypt.[30]

At a time when unity within the party and the government were of paramount importance, new divisions dominated the headlines, especially the conflict between Rabin and his Minister of Defence, Shimon Peres. The rivalry between the two candidates was more of a personality or factional contest, in that there were no real ideological differences between them. In short, the rivalry between the two senior figures in the party and the government reflected simple power politics, in that since 1974 they had both sought the same office. Their backgrounds and experiences were very different. Rabin had been a career officer in the IDF, while Peres had enjoyed an equally successful career as a political technocrat. Though Peres had never served in the army, he was largely credited with having made a considerable contribution to Israel's defence via arms procurements in the 1950s and the development of its nuclear capability during the early 1960s. The political differences between them at this stage tended to be on questions of focus: Rabin favouring the USA and Peres Europe. In the past there had been a dispute between them over the purchase of military equipment for the IDF, Rabin preferring to buy foreign military equipment and Peres wanting to build up the Israeli defence industry. In understanding this crucial relationship, the personality differences between them cannot be stressed enough. Rabin was considered an introvert, largely distrustful of politicians and preferring to appear to be above politics, while Peres is an extrovert who enjoys political intrigues and party political games.

Two additional domestic problems contributed to the decline of the government and its eventual defeat in 1977. The first was the break-up of the historic partnership between the Labour Party (and its forerunner Mapai) and the religious parties. This ended in 1976, due largely to the political inexperience of Rabin. The PM organised an official government reception to welcome the arrival of some new F15 jet fighters from the USA on the eve of the Sabbath. Unfortunately, though the event was timetabled to finish before the start of the Sabbath, the planes were late in arriving and therefore technically the Sabbath had been broken. A religious party, Agudat Israel, tabled a motion of no confidence, claiming that a public desecration of the Sabbath had taken place, and in the subsequent vote some members of the National Religious Party (NRP) abstained. Afterwards, a furious Rabin dismissed the entire party from the coalition, thus rendering himself the head of a minority government, the first leader of the Labour Party to be in such a position. In truth, to be fair to Rabin, the split with the NRP had a degree of inevitability about it.

Since the Six Day War, the NRP had become more extreme in its policy towards the Territories, and was heavily involved in the settlers' movement. This shift to a more hawkish position was also the result of a generational change in the leadership, with the emerging new younger leaders pushing the party into the Likud bloc. Following the split with the Labour Party, it would be over twenty years before the NRP joined a Labour-led coalition. In the meantime, it proved increasingly difficult for the Labour Party to form coalitions, even after they secured more seats than the Likud in elections.

The second problem concerned the increasing number of

scandals involving leading Labour Party personnel, both in the government and in Labour-controlled institutions. The first major public scandal involved Asher Yadlin, the party's choice for the next Governor of the Bank of Israel. Yadlin was convicted of accepting bribes and making false tax declarations. During his trial, Yadlin had implicated two Cabinet ministers and several other prominent figures in the Labour Party in illegal fund-raising activities for the party. The crisis deepened when Avraham Ofer, the Minister of Housing, committed suicide after charges of corruption had been made against him. Just when it seemed that things could not get any worse for the Labour Party, a story was published in the Israeli press stating that the PM's wife, Leah Rabin, had not closed down a bank account in the USA which had been opened during her husband's tour of duty as Ambassador to Washington at the start of the 1970s. At the time in Israel there were strict foreign currency laws in place that prevented Israelis from holding bank accounts abroad.

In a rare move by a Sabra, Yitzhak Rabin stood by his wife, who was facing a possible jail sentence for her oversight, and decided that in light of the scandal he would resign as PM and leader of the party. It emerged that as leader in a minority caretaker government Rabin could not resign, so he had to take sick leave. He was replaced by his arch-rival Shimon Peres, both as PM and leader of the Labour Party. Coming so close to the 1977 election, the Rabin resignation had obvious ramifications for the party's chances of re-election.

The results of the 1977 election were labelled by Chaim Yavin, Israel TV's anchorman, as 'an upheaval or earthquake' when, for the first time, the Likud led by Menachem Begin emerged as the largest party and were able to put together a coalition government. Accepting the widely held view that governments lose elections rather than oppositions win them, there is a need to understand two factors: the reasons why the Labour Party lost in 1977 after 29 consecutive years in power; and the long-term reason for the decline in the party's fortunes.

Regarding the timing of the demise, it is clear that the scandals played a major role, as did the formation of a new party, the

Democratic Movement for Change (DASH), which had been created largely in response to the failings of the Labour Party, and which succeeded in winning fifteen seats in the election at their expense. In the period prior to the start of the campaign – and during it – the Labour Party leadership made a series of organisational errors and misjudgements that contributed to the party's poor showing at the polls. In one of his last decisions before resigning, Rabin had appointed an ex-general with minimal political experience, Chaim Bar-Lev, as campaign manager. Predictably, Bar-Lev did not have the necessary skills to direct a major campaign.

In addition, the Labour Party moved the Histadrut elections, which had previously taken place in advance of the Knesset elections, to after them. In the past, the Histadrut elections had been used as an opportunity for voters to cast a protest vote against the party, with many returning to support it in the subsequent national ballot. In 1977 such tactical voting was not possible. Finally, the failings of the leadership of the party in the period leading up to the start of the Yom Kippur War, and during the initial stages of the war, led many Israelis to vote for the first time for a party other than the Labour Party. The party had escaped punishment in the 1973 elections because the country was still too traumatised by the war. By 1977, the blame had been apportioned by both the official inquiry and by Israelis themselves.

Longer-term reasons for the decline of the party included institutionalised corruption among the party élite after nearly 30 years in power. Also of great importance was the changing demographic balance in Israel, whereby voters of Oriental origin were becoming increasingly numerically important; this group tended to vote for the Likud. Initially, upon their arrival in Israel, the Orientals – who were highly dependent on the state for their social and educational needs – threw in their lot with the dominant party, Mapai, just as previous immigrants had done. The Orientals, however, over a period of time developed their own distinctive constituency interests (they had little in the way of political leadership when they arrived in Israel), and came to the conclusion that Mapai and the Labour Zionist movement in general were putting the interests of the veteran immigrants over the Orientals. There was increasing criticism of the way their immigrant absorption process had been handled, and of attempts to force them to adopt the Ashkenazi-dominated national self-image.

Menachem Begin, while of Ashkenazi origin himself, appealed more to this group in cultural terms by giving the impression of being an observant Jew, and more conservative in the general sense. Herut and its successor the Likud's more hard-line position towards the Arabs also appealed to this group, many of whom had suffered discrimination in their countries of origin. To some degree, class and ethnic models of explanation can be applied here, with the Orientals' sense that the Ashkenazi élite wanted them to do the 'black work' in Israel. To this day, and despite attempts by Labour Party leaders such as Ehud Barak to apologise for the past, the way the party formerly treated the Orientals means that the relationship between them and the largely Ashkenazi-dominated Labour élite remains extremely difficult. The outcome of recent Israeli elections has in part been determined by how many voters of Oriental origin have been willing to cross over from the Likud and vote for Labour Party leaders.

The failure of the Labour Party to successfully deal with the central issue of the future status of the territories that Israel had captured in 1967 also played a role in its long-term decline. In effect, the party had failed for war-weary Israelis who were keen to chance returning land in exchange for peace. Nor did the party represent those Israelis who saw the lands as an opportunity to reinvigorate Zionism, to develop and cultivate them for the Jewish state. Finally, the party had failed to successfully manage the economy, and had delivered in economic terms only to its traditional supporters.[31] Of course all these factors are inter-related, and scholars attribute various degrees of significance to each of them. An understanding, however, of these long-term explanations is important in explaining why the Likud became the dominant force in Israeli politics for the subsequent fifteen years.

The election of Menachem Begin and the Likud in 1977 was perhaps the most visible sign of the creation of the new Israeli republic.[32] *The Times* of London portrayed the election as a contest between good and evil: if Labour was re-elected there would be peace in the region, but if the Likud was elected there would be another major war. Begin appeared to be from another age – just as, say, Donald Rumsfeld appears to have walked off the set of a 1950s detective movie. Begin's victory speech was shown on TV, and with his formal dress and heavily accented English he resembled a pre-Second World War European leader. He did not look Israeli at all – he didn't even appear to have a suntan, and he wore a tie. This was all new. Begin talked in the past tense, and when interviewed we noticed that he appeared to ignore the interviewer and look straight into the camera, as if he wanted to jump out of the TV set and into our living rooms.

Begin was a complex character. Any man who spends 29 years as the leader of the opposition must have special characteristics, both positive and negative. Begin's political background appeared to be very different from the pragmatic policies he was pursuing in office. Why did he cling to the ideology of a Greater Israel (a Jewish state on both banks of the River Jordan) during those long years in opposition? And why was this fixation so strong? Begin claimed that Israel had a biblical right to these lands. The work of the revisionist leader and thinker Ze'ev Jabotinsky reveals that Begin's attachment wasn't that simple, that there was another element to Greater Israel – the issue of Israeli security. The phrase 'the Iron Wall' was coined by Jabotinsky to describe what Israel would have to do in order to survive in a hostile environment. In effect, the Arabs would accept Israel only once they realised that they could not destroy it by military means.[33] Begin's desire to expand its borders was based therefore on a cocktail of religious legitimacy and security necessities.

If this was true, why did Begin suddenly change when he came to power, and not annex these lands as he had promised to do for his entire political career?

The answer lay in two areas: the insecurity of the Begin government, and the simple fact that the United States would have done all in its very considerable power to block any such move towards annexation. At the time, the Israeli press was full of stories about the imminent demise of Begin and the Likud. The Likud's election victory was described as a freak road accident, in other words one that would not be repeated. It seemed strange that, despite the fact that Begin had won the election with a clear majority, he should be discounted so easily. Surely, though, the real explanation of the government's position was that after all those years in opposition, Begin lacked experience in governing, and that was why there was a seeming series of mistakes and splits in the government. This didn't mean that one day they wouldn't be an effective government – just that it would take time to learn.

Likewise, another newcomer, Jimmy Carter, appeared to bring something different to American politics. Much was made about his Southern roots and peanut-farming background. He was clearly an outsider, just as Begin was in Israel. Anwar Sadat was a handsome man with a beautiful wife. Would this be the first Arab to break ranks and deal with Israel? The papers at the time indicated that this was unlikely, domestic opposition being cited as the principal reason. Sadat appeared to continue regardless. He was always on our television screens. Unlike Begin, Sadat was relaxed in front of the cameras, and gave many interviews dressed in casual clothes, usually polo shirts and slacks, sitting down on a sofa. He appeared awfully Western, almost American, and his Western-styled wife reinforced this impression. Sadat, like Carter, seemed to represent something new.

Just as Begin and Carter were outsiders, so was Sadat. Yes, he had been the deputy to his predecessor as Egyptian leader, the late President Gamal Nasser. As we have seen, however, he was considered something of a playboy (political code for a stupid prat) by his peers. Sadat was appointed as leader after Nasser's death in 1970 as a stop-gap. There were deep divisions in the Egyptian military, and Sadat appeared to threaten no one. How wrong they were. Soon after coming to power, Sadat started to purge the military and political élite of Nasser supporters. In historical terms, his shift from the Soviet camp to the American camp provided the last necessary ingredient for what was to follow at Camp David in the sizzling summer of 1977.

Prior to Camp David had come Sadat's visit to Israel. The visit was perhaps the most significant development in the Middle East for decades. Indeed, P.J. Vatikiotis suggests that Sadat's initiative 'constituted perhaps the first serious act of policy taken by an Arab ruler in the (then) thirty year conflict'.[34] Again, the images were black and white, and appeared surrealistic. Two, however, stood out. The first was the arrival of Sadat at Ben-Gurion and his smiling face as he was introduced to the line of Israeli dignitaries – which must have been akin to coming face to face with all your enemies in the space of five minutes. Sadat, the showman, pulled it off spectacularly. Surely an Oscar for best performance under duress should have been presented to him.

The second image was the frown on the face of Yitzhak Shamir, the then Speaker of the Knesset and later Prime Minister of Israel, as he listened to Sadat's speech through a pair of chunky headphones. Sadat had come in the name of peace, but would drive a hard bargain to give Israel what it most wanted. In truth Sadat's visit, for all the historical importance attached to it, was a near disaster. It was clear that there was little personal chemistry between himself and Begin, and he believed that by coming to Israel he had already made enough concessions and wasn't about to make any more in the near future. Just as the failure of the Arafat–Barak Camp David summit led to violence some 23 years later, there was a real and pressing concern among many Israeli and US officials that the failure of Sadat's visit to Jerusalem actually made war more rather than less likely.

With the hindsight of history and with the outcome of the negotiations between Israel and Egypt known and understood, we can place a slightly different spin on Sadat's visit. Both senior ministers in the Begin government – Moshe Dayan, who had left the Labour Party to become Begin's first Minister of Foreign Affairs, and Ezer Weizman, architect of Begin's electoral triumph and Minister of Defence – managed to establish cordial relations with their opposite numbers from the Egyptian delegation, as well as with President Sadat. Weizman, who often took his metaphors from habits of courtship, compared his meetings with Sadat to meeting a new woman – sizing each other up and planning the next moves.[35] These relationships, however, proved vital when it came to the negotiations at Camp David.

Beware, however, those leaders that still call for dramatic gestures by leaders to resolve conflicts. Unless you can pre-determine a successful outcome to the proposed gesture – which in the real world of international politics you simply cannot – then steer clear of such methods of peace-making, which can exacerbate the conflict just as easily as help resolve it. To go from no contact for nearly 30 years to one dramatic visit was fool-hardiness of the worst sort. A simple ministerial meeting would have proved a sufficient upgrading of contacts, and more politically productive. Such a round of talks would not have led to the increased expectations or fears of the respective popula-tions that heads of state meetings naturally create, and which are extremely difficult to control, particularly in democracies such as Israel with a free press.

The Camp David summit involving Israel and Egypt under the auspices of the United States was set up like a football match. Pundits speculated on who the winners and losers would be. There was little grasp of the win-win outcome that is today a basic component for successful conflict resolution. There was general agreement that it was a big gamble for President Carter, whose domestic agenda had become bogged down in the quagmire of Washington politics. In Israel there was growing frustration that Sadat's visit to Jerusalem had not produced any quick solution to the Arab–Israeli conflict. Israel's chattering political classes started to whisper that Begin was being too intransigent, and that he might not be capable of reaching an agreement with Sadat that meant evacuating a large part of the Sinai. To make matters worse, Begin's health was causing increased concern to a party which had no chosen or natural successor. Sadat was also in deep trouble. Arab leaders condemned his visit to Jerusalem. In truth, Sadat had given Arab leaders such as President Asad of Syria the opportunity to challenge Egypt's position as leader of the Arab world. Once more, the Arab–Israeli conflict acted as a sub-plot in the power struggle in the Arab world.

So all three leaders were in weak positions and needed a deal to protect their own rule. There is no denying that this was true, but this reason in itself was not enough to bring the parties together. In short, it was very apparent even to a young man that both Begin and Sadat were able, if pushed, to make difficult concessions and survive politically. Indeed, as I have just argued above, it was in neither's interest to maintain the *status quo*. This created a real dynamic impetus to the negotiations that is a vital ingredient to solving conflicts. In short, the risks of signing an agreement were less than the risks of not signing an agreement. President Carter was aware of this, as well as the fact that only high-level diplomacy would bring results. The higher the drama, the greater the chance of success, as both Begin and Sadat had to be directly identified with the process in order to gain the maximum political benefit from its outcome.

As political theatre goes, the Camp David summit produced some of the very best. In the relaxed atmosphere of President Carter's country retreat, the delegations and American officials dressed in casual clothes. Not so Menachem Begin who, as one American official is often quoted as saying, dressed as if he was going to a funeral in a dark suit and tie. Though Sadat embraced the casual relaxed regime, some members of his delegation felt uncomfortable about the dress code, complaining of having to be seen in pyjamas, conducting negotiations in sports shirts and feeling that Camp David was a large prison camp.[36] There were daily press briefings by the Americans, who tried to control the flow of information to the outside world. This was no easy task, as both parties leaked information to their respective press whenever they had a bone of contention. Much of the leaking reflected deep internal divisions within the two delegations, and was done to damage a rival member from within the leaker's own delegation.

It was soon apparent that any improvement in the personal chemistry between Begin and Sadat had not materialised. In fact, relations were so bad that President Carter did not even try to bring them formally together after a disastrous meeting on the opening day of the summit, though they did meet from time to time on the paths that linked the various cottages that make up the living quarters at Camp David.[37] Much later, in October 1995, Richard Holbrooke, the US Special Mediator to the Balkans, while preparing for a summit of Balkan leaders that was eventually to lead to the Dayton Accords, attempted to learn from the lack of chemistry between Begin and Sadat. Holbrooke called Jimmy Carter, who recounted all his attempts to get the two men to talk at Camp David. On one occasion, on a trip to the Gettysburg battlefield that was meant to illustrate the human waste of sacrifice, Carter sat between the two men in the back of the Presidential limo for hours while they continued to ignore each other.[38]

Both Begin and Sadat, on different occasions, threatened to leave Camp David. On one occasion, Carter had to put himself between Sadat and the door to prevent the Egyptian, whose bags were already on the porch, from walking out. The attention given in the media to the personal chemistry was interesting but very misleading. Behind it was the misplaced belief that only friends can make peace. In other words, Begin and Sadat had to develop a friendship before they could grapple with issues. The eventual success of the Camp David summit should have gone a long way to exposing this myth, but it didn't. Currently, many people uneducated in the art of making peace still fail to understand this point. As Yitzhak Rabin said about making peace with Yasser Arafat, 'you do not make peace with friends but with your enemies'. It is clear that the Rabin–King Hussein chemistry did contribute to the Israeli–Jordanian agreement, but this has proved to be the exception to the rule rather than the rule itself.

Camp David worked not because Begin and Sadat fell in love and went for long walks in the woods during which they discussed the troubles of the world, but rather because the historical conditions were ripe for such an agreement to be signed. That said, both leaders were important figurehead ingredients for success, and it is the image of Begin and Sadat smiling at the signing ceremony on the White House lawn in 1977 that sticks in the memory. One can speculate that rarely in the history of the Nobel Peace Prize had it been awarded jointly for a shared action to two people who had remained so distant from each other. In truth, President Carter, who did not win the Nobel Peace Prize until 2002, had managed to create a win-win situation. Peace for both sides was consequently perceived as a positive step by both countries, who could point to tangible political, military and economic gains as a result of signing the agreement. Twenty-three years later, Bill Clinton failed to understand the basic concepts of the strength and ability of leaders to sign agreements and the need to create win-win situations. Clinton would make the mistake not once but twice, and as a result condemn the Middle East to years of renewed and intensified fighting.

Even at the time, experts sensed that the peace between Israel and Egypt would not be a warm one, but rather a stable and cold one. Questions soon arose as to how to define peace, and what kind of peace participants in conflicts and mediators should aim for. This is an important question, because it creates the framework for the negotiations that will have to take place if it is to be realised. Suspicions that Israel and Egypt had not fallen in love were soon proved well founded. Admittedly, Egged, the Israeli national bus carrier, did a good initial trade in taking Israelis into Egypt, but this flow of tourists was not reciprocated by Egyptians rushing to visit Tel Aviv or the holy sites in Jerusalem.[39] Nor, despite much effort from Sadat, did professional exchanges take place in such fields as engineering and medicine.[40]

Egyptian reluctance was based, in part, on the fact that the section of the Accords that dealt with the Palestinians was never implemented. In truth, however, the cultural divide that had existed since Israel's creation was clearly not going to be broken overnight. Egyptians remained suspicious of an Israel that they still regarded as a pariah state, and the peace treaty was sold to the Egyptian population by its leadership as a pragmatic rather than ideological change in position. The simple but important fact that the signing of the peace treaty between Egypt and Israel did not bring to an end the ongoing Arab–Israeli conflict was often overlooked in the wave of optimism in Israel that characterised the period following the signing of the Camp David Accords.

In Israel, the general sense of pessimism that followed the initial euphoria was based on the reaction of the Arab world to the new situation in the Middle East. Arab leaders rushed to condemn President Sadat as a traitor, and accused him of abandoning the Palestinians. The British media was full of stories about how Egypt's isolation would cripple its economy and lead to a possible inter-Arab war. Neither prediction appeared well founded: Egypt became second only to Israel in receiving economic aid from the United States, and despite all the bluster from Arab leaders they were unwilling to commit their armed forces to quell what they viewed as Sadat's treason. Such stories of imminent economic collapse and warfare, however, tended to obscure the need for an important debate over the nature of peace. In simple terms, what does this word mean – a word which is often overused, and in too general a way, by commentators and participants alike.

To this we must also add the phrase 'peace process', which has its origins in the early 1970s when the State Department in the United States started using it to describe the process of seemingly endless diplomacy in the Middle East that aimed at ending the Arab–Israeli conflict. More often than not, the phrase was used to describe a stalemate. The term, however, did serve as a political crutch for all to lean upon, often giving the impression that leaders knew where they were going, and that they had a blueprint. Almost laughably, people used this expression with no real understanding of its meaning or context. In truth, a peace process needs two partners, both of whom want peace at the end of the road, with some idea of how to get to this mythical state, and some reference to a time-frame. This could not be further from the truth in terms of characterising the recent history of the Arab–Israeli conflict.

At the start of the 1980s, debates about the nature of peace were not widespread on either side of the Arab–Israeli conflict. Israel wanted, and demanded, full normalisation with the symbolic exchange of ambassadors. The Arabs, with the notable exception of Egypt, were committed to the destruction of the Jewish state, and as a result opposed any degree of normalisation with it. In Lebanon, the PLO continued launching terrorist attacks on northern Israel in the hope of provoking serious Israeli retaliatory raids that would widen and internationalise the conflict. For its part, Israel remained unclear whether the lands it had captured during the Six Day War improved its security. Those who supported this argument were quick to point out the importance of the lands during the Yom Kippur War. At least an Israel taken by surprise had had the opportunity to regroup. If Israel had not had the Sinai or the Golan Heights, then the Arabs would have been on the road to Haifa in the north and Tel Aviv in the centre of the country.

In short, the lands captured in 1967 ensured that battles would be fought away from the major centres of the Israeli population. Central to the argument of those who believed that the lands did not enhance Israeli security was the simple point that the retention of the lands led to the Yom Kippur War. Later critics would focus on the value of land buffers in the age of missile technology. This was brought into sharp focus during the Persian Gulf War of 1991 when it became clear that Israel's control of the West Bank did not help prevent the SCUD missile attacks by Iraq on Israeli centres of population. Other Israeli security experts disagreed. True, the land did not prevent missile attacks, but it removed the possibility of a surprise Iraqi land offensive through a Jordanian- or Palestinian-controlled West Bank into Israel. Arguments surrounding the relative security value of these lands became more important to the debate as the land for peace formula envisaged by probably the most important UN Resolution, 242, became the preferred option for resolving the Arab–Israeli conflict after its adoption on 22 November 1967.[41]

Returning once more to the Arab historiography of this period, it is clear that Arab accounts focus on and stress the importance of the Jewish biblical claim of 'Greater Israel' – a Jewish state on both sides of the River Jordan. To a certain extent, this concentration is understandable, given the political rhetoric of Menachem Begin who openly talked of Judea and Samaria as being an integral part of the Jewish state – a God-given right to the land. Arab historiography charges that post-1967, Israel became more militaristic, expansionist and messianic in outlook, with the biblical justification of Israeli legitimacy being widely employed by Begin and the radical elements of the Israeli settlers' movement.

On a superficial level, this argument holds up. It is true that Begin wanted to control the Occupied Territories for ever. His comment during the Camp David negotiations that he would sooner cut off his right hand than yield a single inch of these lands is often quoted as an example of the strength of his feelings on the issue. Israel, however, is a secular democracy, and while Begin may very well have believed in his religious rhetoric, the question of security has always been at the centre of the debate in Israel on the future status of the West Bank among the mainstream Israeli political élite and its military top brass. It is possible to compare Greater Israel to the Palestinian right of return for refugees. Both remain central ideological goals of the Likud and the PLO, but there is also a sense that such aims – though desirable – are highly impractical in the real world.

It seems inconceivable that a man of Begin's intelligence, when left alone with his thoughts, could have failed to realise that there was no chance that any American administration – Democrat or Republican – would allow Israel to annex the West Bank and bring the one million Palestinians living there under full Israeli sovereignty. Just as Begin used religion as a political and cultural weapon, so he used religious legitimacy as a unifying and rallying call for his followers. It should be remembered that Begin did not come from a strong religious background, nor in later life was he a strictly orthodox Jew. Over the years, however, he developed the reputation for being a humble and religious Jew, in contrast to fiercely secular Labour Party leaders.

Politically for Begin, this proved to be very important in helping him attract the Orientals, who identified more with his personal characteristics than the more secular and socially liberal Labour Party leaders. In short, while Begin the man would stress the biblical right to Judea and Samaria, Begin the politician could not face returning the lands to Jordan or the Palestinians because he knew at this time that any such moves would endanger Israeli security. So despite his religious rhetoric, Begin was in fact a security hawk. Here already we see the birth of an important distinction between those who wished to keep the West Bank for security reasons and those who argued for Israeli control on the grounds of religious legitimacy. Therefore, the tags employed by many historians about the characteristics of the new Israel were somewhat misleading, as events during the 1980s confirmed.

Maps

1 *The Sykes–Picot Agreement for the partition of the Middle East, 1916*

Based on a map in Howard Sachar, *A History of Israel: From the Rise of Zionism to Our Time*, New York: Knopf, 1996.

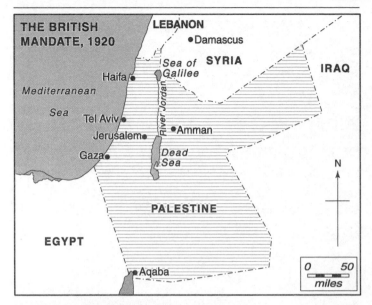

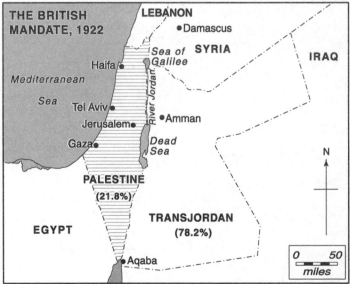

2 *The initial partition of Palestine, 1922*

Based on maps by Martin Gilbert, printed with permission from *The Routledge Atlas of the Arab–Israeli Conflict.*

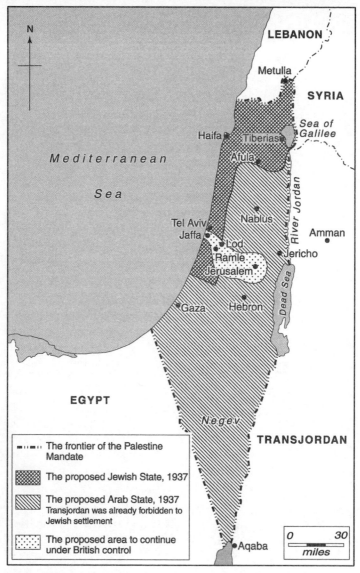

3   *The Peel Commission recommendation for the partition of Palestine, 1937*

Based on maps by Martin Gilbert, printed with permission from *The Routledge Atlas of the Arab–Israeli Conflict*.

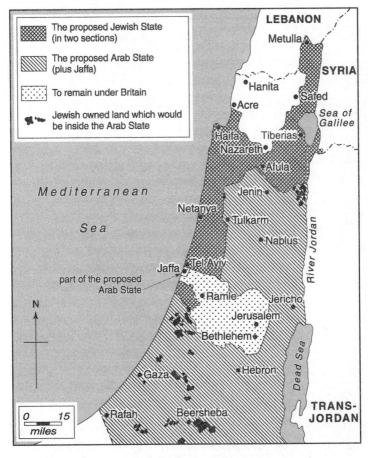

Legend

- The proposed Jewish State (in two sections)
- The proposed Arab State (plus Jaffa)
- To remain under Britain
- Jewish owned land which would be inside the Arab State

4 *The Woodhead recommendation for the partition of Palestine, 1938*

Based on maps by Martin Gilbert, printed with permission from *The Routledge Atlas of the Arab–Israeli Conflict.*

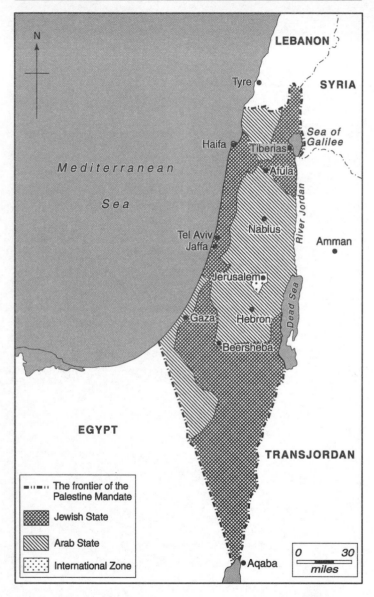

5 *The United Nations partition plan for Palestine, 1947*

Based on maps by Martin Gilbert, printed with permission from *The Routledge Atlas of the Arab–Israeli Conflict*.

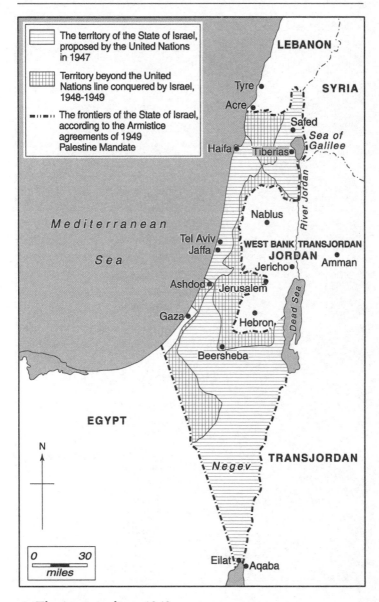

The territory of the State of Israel, proposed by the United Nations in 1947

Territory beyond the United Nations line conquered by Israel, 1948-1949

The frontiers of the State of Israel, according to the Armistice agreements of 1949 Palestine Mandate

LEBANON

SYRIA

Tyre

Acre

Safed

Sea of Galilee

Haifa

Tiberias

Mediterranean

Nablus

River Jordan

Sea

Tel Aviv

Jaffa

WEST BANK | TRANSJORDAN

JORDAN

Jericho

Amman

Ashdod

Jerusalem

Dead Sea

Gaza

Hebron

Beersheba

EGYPT

N

Negev

TRANSJORDAN

0   30

miles

Eilat | Aqaba

6   *The Armistice lines, 1949*

Based on maps by Martin Gilbert, printed with permission from *The Routledge Atlas of the Arab–Israeli Conflict.*

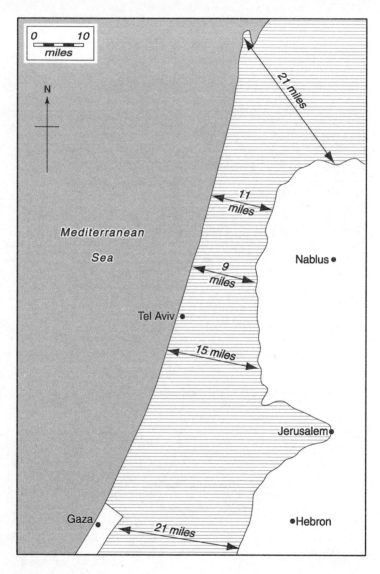

7 *Israel's strategic width, 1949*

Based on maps by Martin Gilbert, printed with permission from *The Routledge Atlas of the Arab–Israeli Conflict*.

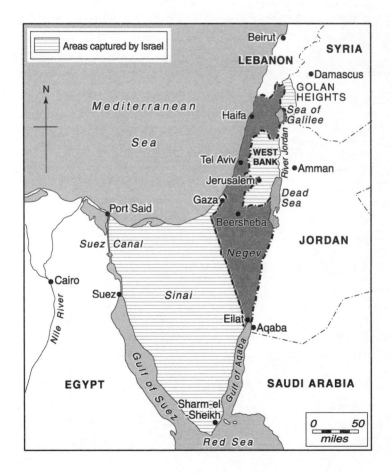

8   Israel's borders after the Six Day War, 1967

Based on maps by Martin Gilbert, printed with permission from *The Routledge Atlas of the Arab–Israeli Conflict*.

Legend:
- Israel 1949–1967
- Occupied

N

LEBANON •Beirut

SYRIA

•Damascus

Mediterranean

Haifa *Sea of Galilee*

Sea Nazareth

Nablus

Tel Aviv Jericho •Amman

Jerusalem

Gaza Hebron *Dead Sea*

Port Said Beersheba

ISRAEL **JORDAN**

Suez Canal *Negev*

Suez *Sinai*

Eilat •Aqaba

Gulf of Suez *Gulf of Aqaba* **SAUDI ARABIA**

EGYPT

Sharm-el-Sheikh

0   50
miles

Red Sea

9   Israel's borders, 1993

Based on maps by Martin Gilbert, printed with permission from *The Routledge Atlas of the Arab–Israeli Conflict*.

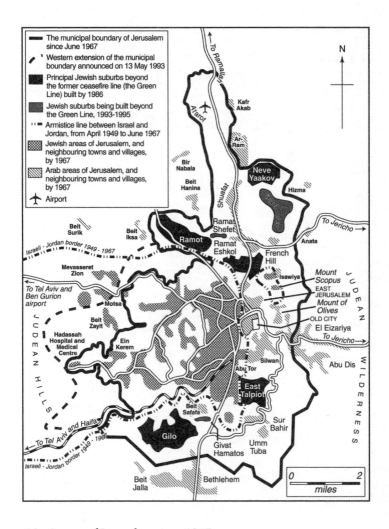

10 A map of Jerusalem since 1967

Based on maps by Martin Gilbert, printed with permission from *The Routledge Atlas of the Arab–Israeli Conflict.*

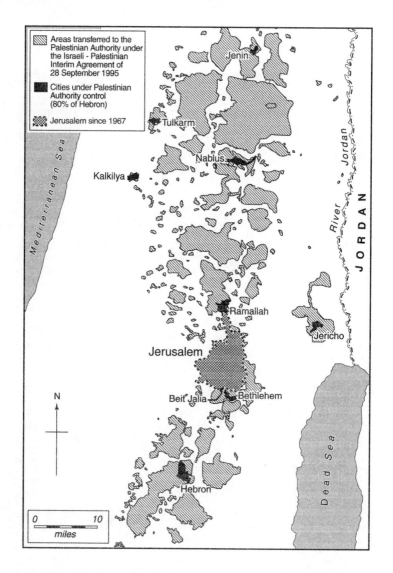

Areas transferred to the
Palestinian Authority under
the Israeli - Palestinian
Interim Agreement of
28 September 1995

Cities under Palestinian
Authority control
(80% of Hebron)

Jerusalem since 1967

Mediterranean Sea

Jenin

Tulkarm

Nablus

Kalkilya

River Jordan

JORDAN

Ramallah

Jerusalem

Jericho

Beit Jalia   Bethlehem

N

Hebron

0   10
miles

Dead Sea

11 The Oslo Redeployment map

Based on maps by Martin Gilbert, printed with permission from *The Routledge Atlas of the
Arab–Israeli Conflict.*

CHAPTER FIVE

Follow Thy Leader: A Crisis of Confidence

There was a joke that did the rounds in the Knesset restaurant during the early 1990s which went like this. Question: what do you get when you add Yitzhak Rabin and Shimon Peres together? Answer: a Prime Minister. In truth, Israelis have long developed a love-hate relationship with their leaders, but following the demise of Menachem Begin the humour tended to get blacker – reflecting the growing crisis of trust and confidence in the country's political and military leadership. Though the roots of the leadership crisis can be traced back to the 1950s, there were a number of contributing factors in the 1980s that led to an intensification of the crisis of confidence.

Here it should be remembered that Israeli leaders – unlike their Arab counterparts – operate in a democracy in which there is an open and free press. Stories of wrong-doing and political intrigue in Israel are difficult to suppress in the same way that, for example, royal court gossip in Jordan or Saudi Arabia is kept from the public view by a highly controlled and censored media. Such are the levels of scrutiny in Israel nowadays that many potential leaders and parliamentarians do not even bother to throw their hat into the ring, preferring instead the calmer waters of business, academia or law. One is reminded of the torrid time that elements of the Israeli press gave Benjamin Netanyahu and his wife Sara during his period of office. The reporting of the story concerning the alleged mistreatment of the Netanyahu nanny marked a real low point in Israeli journalism. Sadly, and partly as a result of this over-intrusiveness, there has been a marked decline in the calibre of the 120-member Knesset, the Cabinet and even at the very top itself.

It should not be forgotten that despite all the diplomatic, media and academic interest that Israel attracts, it is even today a small state with a population of only 6.5 million, out of which some 5.5 million are Jewish – and therefore eligible to occupy senior positions in the Jewish state. This means that is has a very limited pool upon which to draw for its leadership. Unlike their American counterparts, Israeli leaders generally do not disappear from view following an electoral defeat or resignation brought on by scandal. Shimon Peres has contrived to lose five national elections (1977, 1981, 1984, 1988 and 1996), and yet at the age of 80 he still continues to occupy leadership positions. Peres's mentor David Ben-Gurion resigned from office in order to retire and live on a Kibbutz. He was soon, however, back at the helm preparing Israel for the Suez War. Yitzhak Rabin became Prime Minister for a second time some fifteen years after resigning from the position due to the scandal that involved his wife failing to close foreign bank accounts. More recently, Benjamin Netan-yahu tried to reverse this trend by announcing that he was quitting public life following his election defeat by Ehud Barak in 1999. Four years later, however, and we find Netanyahu once more holding senior office in the government and looking odds-on to become Prime Minister once more when Ariel Sharon steps down. Even Barak, who retired from public office after suffering a humiliating electoral defeat at the hands of Sharon in 2001, looks set fair to return to active politics in the near future.

Before looking at the growing crisis of leadership in Israel during the 1980s, it is worth outlining the conceptual framework that political and military leadership is assessed within. In simple terms, how much does leadership really count in shaping the history of Israel and the Arab–Israeli conflict? Conversely, how much are developments shaped as the result of the successes or failures of logical processes? A basic example of this could be: how much is the hostility of Arab states towards Israel shaped by the failure of modernisation in the Arab world? Similarly, how much do specific events that leadership has no control over impact on shaping history? For example, how could leaders legislate for the actions of Baruch Goldstein in carrying out the Hebron massacre in 1994?

In the case of Israel, the relationship between leadership, process and events in shaping the nation's destiny altered throughout the decade to the extent that the central political decision of the 1990s – to negotiate with Arafat and the PLO – was not instigated by the action of leadership in the form of Peres and Rabin. The changes reflected the growing crisis between leadership, secondary élites and the wider population.

The roots of the leadership crisis in Israel can be traced back to the 1950s, and specifically the Lavon Affair of 1954. The Lavon Affair itself began with the arrest of an Israeli spy ring in Cairo and their subsequent trial and conviction. At first, the Israeli government denied to the Israeli public that this was a spy-ring, and claimed that the accused were put on trial because they were Jewish. There were instances of anti-Egyptian rallies in Israel, as it was presumed that the accused were innocent and that their trial was effectively a show trial. It soon became apparent, however, that it was not only a spy ring, but also a very active one. Members of the ring had been captured red-handed planting crude bombs in Cairo. The Egyptian police caught up with the group when an attempt to bomb a Cairo cinema went wrong. A device went off prematurely, setting fire to the trousers of the bomber. As a result, two members of the cell received the death sentence and six others long prison terms. The apparent aim of the mission had been to sabotage relations between Egypt and the West at a time when Nasser was negotiating over a British withdrawal from the Suez Canal.

The central political charge around which the whole sad affair revolved was that Pinhas Lavon, the Minister of Defence, had not informed or got authorisation from the government to carry out the operation. Ben-Gurion's bitter rival and successor as PM, Moshe Sharett, thought that the operation was a plot by the hard-liners in Israel to wreck the diplomatic contacts that had been taking place between Egypt and Israel in Paris.[1] Furious, he implied that Ben-Gurion and his supporters were behind the operation, which did indeed succeed in ending the contacts with Egypt. From a domestic perspective, the affair had important ramifications for civil–military relations, with attempts made to clarify the need for clear political approval for covert operations. Lavon strenuously denied having ever given the order for the operation, but the head of Israeli intelligence insisted that he had received oral instructions from Lavon to carry it out.

A special committee appointed by the PM, Moshe Sharett, was unable to verify the claims of the head of intelligence, but as a result of the affair and other issues Lavon decided to resign in February 1955. His replacement was David Ben-Gurion, who had previously retired from active politics to live at Sde Boker, a Kibbutz in the south of the country. It was not long before Ben-Gurion once more assumed the premiership in addition to the Ministry of Defence. In 1961, another special committee consisting of seven ministers was set up to investigate the affair, and it concluded that Lavon had not given the order for the operation to take place, nor had he even known of it. The findings of the committee were endorsed by the government, but not by Ben-Gurion. Consequently, Ben-Gurion resigned and called new elections. He argued that, with the inter-party affiliations, the group of seven ministers were not independent enough to judge the case. After the elections Ben-Gurion returned once more as both PM and Minister of Defence, but only after Lavon had been dismissed from his post as Secretary-General of the Histadrut.

Within two years, Ben-Gurion retired again and returned to Kibbutz Sde Boker. This time Levi Eshkol, a man renowned for his skills in bringing groups and factions together, replaced Ben-Gurion as PM. Eshkol's skills were soon put to the test when, the following year, Ben-Gurion demanded that he appoint a new and independent commission of inquiry to discover whether the 1961 commission had acted correctly. Eshkol refused Ben-Gurion's demand. By this stage, Ben-Gurion had become obsessed by the issue and a new struggle developed within Mapai. Eventually, matters came to a head in 1965, at Mapai's conference which ended with 60 per cent supporting Eshkol and 40 per cent Ben-

Gurion. The majority verdict was not accepted by Ben-Gurion who, along with some of his close followers, left the party he had helped found in 1930 to form a new party, Rafi. At the time, Ben-Gurion's challenge to Mapai was seen as serious, but in the subsequent elections Rafi performed badly and in 1968 the majority of members rejoined forces with Mapai and another Labour party, Achdut Ha'avodah, to form the Israeli Labour Party.

Clearly, somebody was lying to the Israeli public, either elements of the military leadership or the political leadership. Ben-Gurion's pursuit of what he saw as justice in the case – the vindication from the charge that the military had not operated without proper military authority – had implications for the degree of trust in politicians. Ben-Gurion was by this time a sad, lonely, isolated figure who was regarded as something of a spent force in Israeli politics. The cliché expression that all political careers end in failure must be applied to the man on whom hangs much of the Israeli myth and symbolism. Sadly, there are parallels between the demise of Ben-Gurion and Israel's other father figure from the founding generation, Menachem Begin.

The issues at the heart of the leadership crisis resulting from the Lebanon war are different from those of the Lavon Affair, but the overall question remains the same: that of trust and account-ability of both the political and military leaderships. Israel's first offensive war was largely a consequence of the multi-faceted mixture of the Lebanese civil war and the resulting struggle for control of the state, and the presence of Syria and the PLO in the country.[2] There is no doubt that Israel's war in Lebanon, which lasted initially from June 1982 until 1985 (although Israel occupied a self-declared security zone up until 2000), was a military success. Equally, there can be little doubt that the war was a spectacular political failure. The three main Israeli actors – Begin, Sharon and Chief of Staff of the IDF, Raful Eitan – all contributed to the problems. Israeli leaders suffered from the delusion that they understood the conditions of the theatre of conflict.[3] Ignoring for a moment the over-ambitious nature of the political goals of the war —

1 Eliminating the PLO as an independent political force
2 Inserting a pro-Israel Christian Maronite government in Beirut
3 Reducing the Syrian threat to Israel
4 Improving co-operation with the US while reducing the role of the Soviet Union in the Middle East

— the central question of the post-war fallout rested on the issue of who knew what, and when, in the Israeli Cabinet, and was the action authorised?[4] In truth, what materialised was a complex round of claim and counter-claim. What is clear is that the normal processes of checks and accountability were not fully functional during the war. The Israeli population, which was initially supportive of the war and the removal of the PLO from southern Lebanon, became increasingly sceptical about the war as the IDF entered an Arab capital for the first time, and openly hostile following the massacres of Palestinians at the Sabra and Shatilla refugee camps in September 1982. Some 400,000 Israelis – around 10 per cent of the total population – gathered in Tel Aviv's main square (renamed as Rabin Square in 1995) to demonstrate for a full judicial inquiry into the massacres.[5]

The massacres at Sabra and Shatilla were one of the modern Middle East's darkest hours. The resulting Kahan Committee Report stated that, while the massacre had not been carried out by Israeli forces, as Israel had control of the camps at the time, it bore indirect responsibility for not having prevented the killings.[6] The massacres were in essence a product of domestic Lebanese politics, with the Christian Phalangist forces entering the camps to seek revenge for the assassination of their leader, Basher Gemayel. At the time the Palestinians were blamed for his killing, though it now seems more likely that Syrian intelligence was behind the massive car bomb that killed him and many of his supporters. Could Israel have done more to prevent the massacre? Absolutely. Allowing the Phalangist gunmen into the camps – for whatever reason – was simply foolhardy, and an illustration of Israel's lack of understanding of Lebanese politics.

Several senior IDF officers were removed in the ensuing investigation, and the Israeli architect of the war, Ariel Sharon, was forced to resign as Minister of Defence and his political career was severely hampered during the 1980s. Still today, much of the ill will in the Arab world towards Sharon is based on the Arab historiography on Sabra and Shatilla, which paints Sharon, and not the Phalangist gunmen, as the murderer. In a wider sense, much of the ill will towards Israel from Europeans stems from the events in the camps. It seems that a whole generation was brought up on Robert Fisk's book, *Pity the Nation* – a highly descriptive, shockingly stark, but politically loaded account.[7]

Within Israel the events triggered widespread demonstrations, and on a deeper level a sense of mistrust not only of the government, but the military as well. The actions of Ben-Gurion – as irrational as they may have become in the 1960s – were to a large extent governed by his attempt to ensure that the IDF that he had helped shape was exonerated of any wrong-doing in the Lavon Affair. There can be little doubt that Israeli civil–military relations were compromised during the Lebanon war, with the result that it was sometimes unclear who was in control of the conflict. The powerful Ministry of Defence in Tel Aviv appeared to control the flow of information to the political sector. Sharon, in defending his position, stated that he at all times briefed the Cabinet and the Knesset Foreign Affairs and Security Committee. In truth, the war revealed the complex nature of the relationship between Israel's elected leadership and the military top brass. Also it revealed the difficulties of Israel's politician generals, which in part led to the crisis in leadership.

If the small population of Israel dictates the relatively small group of national leaders available, the Arab–Israeli conflict represents an additional conditioning feature of the leadership. Both the centrality of the conflict in Israeli politics and its length, spanning as it does the entire history of the state, mean that experience gained in the top tier of the IDF can be translated very quickly into the political sphere. Israeli history is full of examples of generals who have been parachuted into senior political leadership positions soon after their retirement from the IDF.

These range from Dayan, Rabin, Ezer Weizman, Sharon and Barak to Shaul Mofaz, who became Minister of Defence in 2002, only months after retiring as Chief of Staff of the IDF.

Why are so many generals parachuted into leadership positions over career politicians? And what difficulties has this caused?

Essentially in the pre-Lebanon war era, Israelis viewed leaders of the IDF as being above the political fray. This trust, of course, was not always well placed – there was a great deal of politicking going on in the IDF, and political back-stabbing, but the vast majority of this took place far from the gaze of the public eye. As the leadership generation of the founding fathers started to retire or die, the battle for succession became a central issue. It was clear that there was not an abundance of talent among the political élite, many of whom had reached their lofty positions thanks to patronage networks rather than on merit. This provided the opportunity for the generals to enter politics and, with their expert knowledge of the Arab–Israeli conflict and the respect of the public, assume a high-ranking position.

Though this trend started mainly with the Israeli Labour Party, once the Likud appeared to become the natural party of government from 1977 onwards, the trend was mirrored in that party. Indeed, since the political turnover of 1977 and the frequent reversals of power during the 1990s, the hand of the generals has been strengthened, in that some play the Likud off against the Labour Party in the hope of winning a better political deal. Usually, generals request political support from the party leader to ensure a high place on the party list for the Knesset elections and the promise of a leading portfolio in any government that the party forms after the election. In a telling indictment of this policy, only three career politicians – Shimon Peres (Labour), Moshe Arens (Labour) and Menachem Begin (temporarily) – have held the portfolio of Minister of Defence since 1967. The other eight holders of the office during this period were all ex-generals or ex-lieutenant-generals (Chiefs of Staff). In the same period, three of Israel's Prime Ministers – Barak, Rabin and Sharon – were ex-generals.

Expert knowledge of military matters, however, is one thing; ability to manage either a non-defence-related ministry or the country as a whole are altogether very different things. In short, the vast majority of ex-generals have – to varying degrees – struggled to become effective Cabinet Ministers in areas such as education, or even minor portfolios such as Minister for Tourism. Of the three who made it to become Prime Minister, none has shown much understanding of economics and all have given their respective Ministers of Finance a great deal of freedom – in some cases, such as Menachem Begin, too much rope. Similarly, all have lacked vision of the other major issue in Israel – that of secular versus religious rights. In terms of being classified as good negotiators and able to play the political game, perhaps only Sharon has excelled in this area. Rabin was mediocre, and Barak little better. Even some of the generals who have been appointed to the position of Minister of Defence have found it extremely difficult to make the transition from soldier to politician. Rabin, while serving as Minister of Defence in the 1980s, often had a difficult relationship with the General Staff of the IDF, particularly when it came to setting policy for Israel's response to the Palestinian Intifada. Difficulties were perhaps at their greatest when a Minister of Defence found himself dealing with a Chief of Staff who had originally been passed over in favour of him. It was largely for this reason that relations between Ehud Barak and his successor Amnon Lipton-Shahak were complicated.

Another charge placed at the door of the generals – and specifically to Barak and Mofaz – is that both allowed their decisions as Chief of Staff to be influenced by the knowledge that one day they would enter the political sphere. In effect, Barak and Mofaz were acting as politicians while still in uniform. This charge was particularly relevant to these two individuals, given the remarkably short period of time between them retiring as Chief of Staff and assuming high political office. In the case of Mofaz, it was clear that while he was in uniform he was being actively courted as a king-maker in internal Likud politics and the battle of Sharon and Netanyahu for the party leadership. But perhaps the worst exponent of this trait was Moshe Dayan, whose involvement in party politics in the mid-1950s, while he was Chief of Staff, went as far as attempting to replace the party leadership – a blatant violation of the rules governing civil–military relations.[8]

To a certain extent, the breaking of the Israeli public's absolute trust in the IDF as a result of the Lebanon war did damage the credibility of generals trying to get into politics, but if the war damaged the credibility and integrity of the military leadership, it caused twice as much damage to the political leadership. Begin resigned largely on his own terms on 15 September 1983, citing an inability to continue in the job – code for a complex state of affairs that included ill health, coming to terms with the Israeli loss of life during the Lebanon war, and the recent death of his wife.[9] In resigning, Begin avoided much of the criticism that was directed towards the political élite. Begin withdrew from public life, not giving interviews or commenting on debates, and died in 1992. His son Benni (Ze'ev) Begin followed his father into politics and was involved in a running dispute with Sharon over the charge that Sharon had misled his father during the war in Lebanon. Whether or not Begin was duped by Sharon before and during the war, it was, as Conor Cruise O'Brien summed up: 'as sad an end as might well be conceived to a long political career, which had been entirely devoted to the selfless service of Israel.'[10]

The demise of Begin heralded a new era of leadership in Israel, despite the fact that his successor, Yitzhak Shamir, was of the same generation as Begin. Shamir was no orator, and indeed, even though he had served as Knesset Speaker and subsequently as Minister of Foreign Affairs under Begin, he was seen as a stop-gap appointment, much in the same way as Sadat was viewed in Egypt when he succeeded Nasser in 1970. Shamir, however, was to prove extremely durable and became Israel's second longest serving Prime Minister. Paradoxically, Shamir's position during his time in office rarely appeared secure, with numerous challenges to his leadership made by various groupings within the

Likud. Nationally, Shamir was never held in high esteem by the Israeli electorate – even by his own supporters. He was, however, an extremely intelligent and charismatic man, and for Israel a far better leader than Begin.

Shamir's rival during the 1980s was Shimon Peres who, like Shamir, was not particularly admired by the majority of the Israeli electorate. Peres had taken over the leadership of the Labour Party following the resignation of Yitzhak Rabin in 1977, just prior to the election that saw Likud win power for the first time. For all the rational explanations that can be applied to Israeli history, the strange case of Shimon Peres falls into the irrational category. Peres is simply not trusted by the bulk of Israelis, and least of all among the Jews of Oriental origin. There is no one event or decision that can be used to account for the distrust – no financial, sex or other scandal. In the plain and simple terms favoured by Israelis, Peres is seen as too aloof, arrogant and clever. In most democracies these characteristics would not hinder a political career. Not so in Israel. The 'Israeli street', as it is called (market traders, taxi drivers and other amateur pundits always willing to offer their opinions to fellow Israelis and unsuspecting tourists) do not even like Peres's Hebrew – too wordy and clear, they argue. Their preference is for the strong, guttural Hebrew of Rabin – who was once described as an American general who spoke some Hebrew. The ability to speak the language of the Israeli street is a very important aspect of national leadership in Israel, and Peres – like the veteran diplomat, writer and broadcaster, Abba Eban – simply didn't have it. In later years, the Israeli street and others viewed Peres as being too anxious to agree a deal with the Arabs, and looking for his place in the history books.

For much of his career, Peres adopted a much harder line in relations with the Arabs. Though he never served in uniform – another major point that was held against him – he was the man most responsible for building up the IDF in terms of the purchase of weapons and Israel's nuclear programme. During the early 1970s he had enjoyed close links with the settlers' movement Gush Emunim, and during the first Rabin government he was seen as less conciliatory towards the Arabs than the Prime Minister. During the 1980s his position shifted, and he soon acquired the tag of the leading dove in the national leadership. Just as, to a large degree, Shamir's hands were tied by internal party challenges to his leadership in the Likud, the same was true for Peres and the Labour Party. Peres's nemesis, Yitzhak Rabin, soon returned from a brief period of political exile following his resignation in 1977, and challenged Peres unsuccessfully on several occasions before eventually regaining the leadership of the party at the start of 1992.

So, just at a time when the crisis in national leadership in Israel was developing, the two main parties – Likud and Labour – had at their respective helms leaders who for varying reasons were considered to have serious flaws. In retrospect, opinion polling at the time – and Israelis are probably the most polled people in the world – reveals the extent of the problem, with Rabin for Labour and Sharon or Levy for Likud in more cases than not outscoring their respective leaders in the popularity stakes. It was largely as a result of these internal challenges and near parity between the two parties that followed the 1984 Knesset elections that both leaders bowed to the inevitable and formed the National Unity Government (NUG). A failure by either Shamir or Peres to secure at least a share of power would have cost them their job as party leader.

Give this fact, it was perhaps unsurprising that, during the difficult negotiations, more problems were encountered over the allocation of Cabinet portfolios to the parties and the question of who would be PM than in devising an agreed programme for the government. Eventually a formula was reached whereby there would be an equal division of portfolios between Labour and Likud blocs, and a rotation of the position of PM. As leader of the largest party, Peres served for the first two years, with Shamir as Minister of Foreign Affairs, and in 1986 they switched jobs. So strong was the fear in both leaders that they would be dumped by their respective parties, that the formal agreement for the rotation named Peres and Shamir just in case their respective parties did harbour any plans to replace them.

In terms of the performance of the NUG, the first two years (1984–6) proved to be highly successful, in that the government managed to address the two major issues: a withdrawal from Lebanon, and the economy. Peres brought a new style of leadership that was based on the use of technocrats rather than party functionaries in government. He appeared to revel in at last being number one, and even his harshest critics concede that he was one of Israel's most dynamic and successful leaders. In the short term, Peres would appear to have reversed the leadership crisis. Despite his near heroic efforts in rescuing the Israeli economy from the brink of disaster and his clear dynamic leadership in other areas, Peres would never have the opportunity again of enjoying an electoral mandate to govern. Once more, events and processes would combine to derail Peres's ambitions and further deepen Israel's leadership crisis. Peres once more would suffer at the hands of the religious parties, who by this stage were firmly established in the Likud coalition bloc, making it extremely difficult for any Labour Party to form a government, and by the outbreak of the Palestinian Intifada – an event that in the short run shifted Israeli public opinion towards the Likud and parties of the radical right. Also, some credit needs to be given to Shamir for the success of the Peres premiership, though it was in his interest to ensure that the Labour Party was not provided with an excuse to quit the government and so deny him his opportunity of becoming PM in 1986 under the terms of the rotation agreement. Indeed, the major issue during the first two years of the NUG became this very question: would Peres and Labour renege on the agreement and leave the NUG after two years and not hand over to Shamir?

The NUG between 1986 and 1988 failed to function as effectively as during its pre-rotation period, and this led directly to the crisis of leadership at the end of the decade. There were a number of reasons for this, which in the main centred on differences over the conduct of the peace process. In the domestic arena there were factors that added to the paralysis of the government. Firstly, the parties were looking forward to the elections that were scheduled for 1988 and positioning themselves for the coming campaign, which everyone agreed would be close.

The question of blame came to play an important role, with both the major parties accusing each other of being responsible for the growing difficulties in the peace process. Secondly, key figures in the government no longer saw the need for its continuation, especially Peres who became increasingly frustrated over Shamir's leadership, which was of a very different nature to his own dynamic style. The end result of all the differences was that it appeared highly probable that the government would collapse before 1988, and this fact heightened what effectively became a two-year election campaign. Within Israeli society there was a palpable sense of frustration at the state of the government, and both of the major parties were held to blame, a point that was confirmed by the relatively poor showing of both the Likud and Labour in the 1988 elections.

Almost unnoticed during the years of National Unity Government, significant changes were taking place in the relationship between the leadership of the major parties – but especially the Labour Party – and their Members of the Knesset (MKs). Indeed, the changes within the Labour Party were, in part, to help provide the impetus for the growing pressure on the leadership both to start talking to the PLO and to accept the concept of a two-state solution to the Israeli–Palestinian conflict. In other words, this was the real political starting point of the road that was to lead to the Oslo Accords and subsequent agreements with the PLO.

In the Labour Party, the decision to join forces with the Likud led to only one MK leaving the party, Yossi Sarid (later to become leader of Meretz). Within three months of the formation of the NUG, however, there were clear signs of the emergence of a strong doveish element within the parliamentary party, with its new Secretary General, Uzi Baram, as its unofficial head. In the long term, the growing independence of the parliamentary party from the leadership became highly significant. With a government comprising around 85 out of the 120 seats in the Knesset, it was natural that much of the opposition should come from within the Labour Party itself. Mapam was the largest opposition party, and had only six seats in the Knesset. The long road to the Oslo Accords has its origins in this growing independence of

MKs, and the way in which the 'young guard' of the party used it to develop and put forward alternative strategies and visions to those of the leadership.

In a development that helped cement this new-found independence, the Labour Party introduced American-style primary elections to select and order its election list. Though the process was, at this stage, restricted to members of the Central Committee, it was a clear sign that the process of internal democratisation of the party was under way. This in effect made it harder for the party leadership to prevent any dissenters by evoking the threat of placing the relevant sinner in an unrealistic place on the party list for the Knesset. The importance of this change cannot be over-estimated, as it altered the political culture of Israel. Whether or not the changes improved Israeli democracy is another question. There was widespread attempted political fixing, and primary leadership elections could produce a leader such as Amram Mitzna, who was highly popular with the party faithful but clearly not a potential Prime Minister.

In the wider sense, the consequences of the formation of the NUG for the Israeli left became clear almost immediately with Mapam's decision to leave the Alignment and return to opposition. This split represented a major realignment in the Israeli left, with the Labour Party leadership drifting further to the right in pursuit of power while Mapam started to offer an alternative, more radical path. By 1988, the extent of these differences was apparent, with Mapam becoming the first Zionist party to accept the notion of direct negotiations with the PLO and, under certain conditions, to accept the establishment of a Palestinian state.

The period following Mapam's withdrawal from the Alignment also saw the start of attempts to forge a new party of the left uniting Mapam, RATZ (the Citizens' Rights Movement Party) and parts of the peace movement, which eventually resulted in the formation of Meretz in 1992. Yossi Sarid, a senior figure in Meretz, quipped after the secret negotiations between the Israeli government and the PLO became public that he felt like a paratrooper in a war lying on a barbed wire fence so his colleagues could run over the top of him. He went on to say that he was lying on his back so he could see who was running over him to talk to Arafat. This comment says a lot about the role of parties to the left of the Labour Party on the political spectrum in paving the way for the Oslo Accords. Sarid and others were both privately and publicly reconciled to the concept of the two-state solution long before the more pragmatic centrist leadership of the Labour Party. In this respect, Meretz helped fill the void caused by the growing crisis of leadership from the mainstream parties in Israel who, in coming together to agree a joint platform, had in effect postponed the difficult decisions that needed to be taken about peace.

What role did the ongoing crisis in Israeli leadership play in the Palestinian Intifada? And how did this Intifada impact on Israel?

The popular uprising known by its Arabic name 'Intifada' started on 9 December 1987, after four Palestinian workers from the Gaza Strip were killed by an Israeli agricultural vehicle. In the highly charged atmosphere of the time, rumours soon started to spread that it was not an accident, and during the funerals violent demonstrations broke out in the Jebalya refugee camp and other parts of the Gaza Strip. This incident proved to be only the catalyst, and the popular uprising in the West Bank and Gaza Strip that followed took both the Israeli government and the PLO leadership by surprise. The deeper socio-economic and political reasons for the Intifada are complex, ranging from a marked decrease in economic prospects to political issues such as the effects of rising Israeli settlement in the West Bank and Gaza Strip.[11] The Intifada was to last for nearly six years, and it came to have a profound impact upon the peace process and the eventual decision of the Israeli government to open a dialogue with the PLO.

The Intifada started against a general background of increasing Palestinian frustration in the Territories over the failure of the peace process, and amidst signs that the PLO was adopting a new and more pragmatic approach to dealing with Israel. Yasser

Arafat declared that the PLO accepted the two-state solution to what he termed the Palestine question. In addition, he also appeared to embrace the diplomatic path to achieving the goal of a Palestinian state. Though the US administration of Ronald Reagan had some concerns over Arafat's phrasing in the statements he made to confirm this new position, they eventually accepted that this marked a positive development in the peace process.

During the initial weeks of the Intifada, there were widespread demonstrations and strikes throughout the West Bank and Gaza Strip. Such events had taken place before, but this time there was no sign that they would subside, and indeed the demonstrations grew progressively more violent. At first it appeared that no one in particular was organising them, a clear sign that this was a genuine uprising and not a PLO-orchestrated manoeuvre. Indeed, it was some time before the PLO mobilised its members and took over the running of the Intifada from its headquarters in Tunis. The Israeli Minister of Defence, Yitzhak Rabin, was on a visit to the US at the time of the outbreak of the Intifada; he failed to understand the implications of the outbreak and did not cut short his visit. When he did return, he found the IDF struggling to deal effectively with the situation. In the early months of the unrest the IDF, untrained in dealing with young Palestinians throwing stones and firebombs at them, responded with force. As a result, during the first two months of the Intifada, at least 51 Palestinians were killed.

From day one, the crisis was given extensive coverage in the international media, and the images shown, particularly in the USA, caused concern even among some of Israel's strongest supporters. The fact that the international media tended to paint a one-sided picture of events and grew increasingly hostile towards Israel further damaged the Israeli position. Israel's two senior leaders, Shamir and Rabin (in Israel, Minister of Defence is number two, with Foreign Affairs number three), were not particularly effective spokesmen at countering the increasingly effective PR machine of the PLO. Over time, the IDF learnt new methods of dealing with the stone throwers, and to some degree the violence levelled off. Although the unrest never disappeared, Israel managed to contain it without the Intifada developing into a wider regional conflict.

By the end of the first year of the Intifada, the number of Palestinians killed had passed the 300 mark, and the number of wounded had reached 20,000. During the second year, the Intifada took a more sinister turn, with widespread intimidation aimed at preventing any Palestinians from co-operating with the Israeli authorities, and the brutal murder of around 150 Palestinians for allegedly collaborating with Israel. On top of this, some 300 more Palestinians died in clashes with the IDF. Despite the high numbers of Palestinians being killed by their own people, the international media continued to focus on the confrontations between the IDF and Palestinians. Many of the former type of killings took place at night and a long way from the assembled galleries of cameras. Still, the lack of coverage of these killings reinforced the belief of many Israelis that all the media were interested in was the sport of Israel-bashing.

It was against the background of a worsening of the Palestinian uprising and the election of President Bush Sr in the United States in November 1988 that the four-point Rabin–Shamir Peace Plan was put forward on 14 May 1989. Both events had had a profound impact on Rabin and Shamir. Rabin had gradually come to realise that force alone could not end the Intifada, and that there was a need for a negotiated solution from within the framework of the NUG. Shamir was also extremely concerned about Israel's deteriorating image abroad, and especially in the United States, where the 24-hour news media was bringing disturbing images from the West Bank and Gaza Strip to homes around the nation. After eight years of warm relations with the Reagan administration, there was concern over whether Bush would prove to be such a strong supporter of Israel. Shamir's staff had monitored Bush's statements during his time as Vice-President and during the Presidential campaign, and forecast (correctly) more problems dealing with him than with Reagan. Consequently, Shamir saw the need to act in order both to improve Israel's image abroad and to win over the new US administration.

The Rabin–Shamir Peace Plan called for elections in the West Bank and Gaza Strip leading to a degree of autonomy for Palestinians. The plan cleared its first obstacle, the Israeli Cabinet, only after attacks from two Labour Party ministers who felt the plan did not go far enough, and from three ministers from the Likud who felt that the consequences of the plan would be detrimental to Israeli interests. Stalemate once more. The three Likud ministers, Ariel Sharon, David Levy and Yitzhak Moda'i – known collectively as the 'shackle ministers' – rejected the plan because they felt that it would lead to a Palestinian state in the Territories. At the time there were increasing calls from some elements of the Labour Party to open a dialogue with the PLO, and indeed one minister, Ezer Weizman, actually attempted to start such a dialogue despite the fact that under Israeli law contacts with the PLO were illegal. Meanwhile, the 'shackle ministers' attempted to insert four new clauses into the plan: no participation of East Jerusalem Arabs in elections; an end to the Intifada; no dialogue with the PLO; and no Palestinian state and the continuation of the Israeli settlement programme in the West Bank and Gaza. The central aim of their strategy was to keep Jerusalem away from the negotiating table and to prevent the slide to a PLO-led Palestinian state.

Eventually, Shamir was forced to back down and include the new clauses in the plan, a fact that made it totally unacceptable to the Labour Party. Shamir's decision marked the beginning of the end of the NUG and relations between himself and Rabin deteriorated from here onwards. As a result, the NUG came to be dominated by Peres and Sharon, who for ideological and personal reasons wanted to see its demise. The emergence of two externally sponsored peace initiatives further destabilised the Israeli government.

The peace initiatives put forward by President Mubarak of Egypt on 4 September 1989 and by US Secretary of State James Baker on 14 October 1989 brought matters to a head, and the US-sponsored plan led to the eventual collapse of the government in Israel in March 1990. The Likud was concerned that the US administration was trying to move the NUG too far from its agreed positions. Shamir, who had supported the Rabin–Shamir Plan, was against the two external initiatives and accepted the view of the 'shackle ministers' that no Palestinian representatives from East Jerusalem be allowed to take part in the Palestinian electoral process. Yitzhak Rabin attempted to find a compromise formula that allowed for Palestinians from East Jerusalem to take part in the process but not vote. However, Shamir rejected the compromise, a decision that led Rabin to conclude that there was little point in remaining in the government. In a last-ditch attempt to solve the crisis, the Likud Minister of Foreign Affairs, Moshe Arens, came to a private agreement with Secretary of State Baker. They concluded that Israel would consider the Palestinian participants on a name-to-name basis and accept that the list would include people who were not officially resident in Jerusalem but who merely had a second address there. However, when Arens took the plan to Shamir he rejected it out of hand, and this proved to be the final nail in the coffin of the NUG.

More importantly, the moment when Shamir said no to Arens marked one of the key turning points of Israeli history.[12] For the next decade, the consequences of it would be felt from Oslo to Washington. In the short term it soured relations between Israel and the US, and led to the formation of a narrow-based ruling coalition in Israel that for the first time included parties from the far right. In the long term this was the moment when the leadership of the Labour Party started on their road to Oslo and direct negotiations with the PLO. Other pieces of the jigsaw remained to fall into place, but from this point onwards it was clear that either Peres or Rabin would have to talk directly with the PLO, as there were no other options for partners. The Likud, on the other hand, moved towards a more hard-line position, with Shamir now seemingly in tune with the wishes of the 'shackle ministers' and their radical right-wing allies. Despite this, a strange twist of history was to present Shamir with the opportunity of becoming the first Israeli PM to hold direct negotiations with the Arab governments of Jordan and Syria, the PLO being indirectly represented in the delegation of the former.

During 1990, it was clear that the popular enthusiasm that had driven the first two years of the Intifada was in decline. There were still large-scale demonstrations and outbursts of sporadic violence, but not on the scale seen in the first two years of the uprising. This was partly due to new tactics that the IDF started to employ, which called for the avoidance of what they termed confrontation points. There were, however, increasing tensions among the Palestinians in the Territories between the supporters of the PLO and those who supported Islamic fundamentalist groups such as Hamas. These tensions, which resulted in many deaths of Palestinians under the charge of collaboration with Israel, were in essence turf wars mixed together with a degree of nationalist politics. As the PLO appeared to shift towards a negotiated settlement with Israel, these divisions turned to violence, Hamas rejecting any notions of compromise with Israel. Another factor in the decline of the intensity of the Intifada was the 'war weariness' of the international press, who were now looking for new stories to cover. CNN, along with liberal papers such as *The Guardian* and *New York Times*, ran out Israel-bashing television reports and column inches.

What role did the religious parties play in the downfall of the NUG?

The era of the National Unity Government was finally brought to an end by Peres's 'unholy (dirty, smelly) exercise', a phrase coined by Rabin. Peres's master-plan was to end the NUG and then replace it with a narrow-based Labour-led government which included one or more of the religious parties, without holding fresh elections. The dirty exercise became one of the most unsavoury episodes in the history of the Knesset, and its ramifications were to be felt for much of the 1990s.

The most likely coalition partner for Peres was Shas, the ultra-orthodox movement which had shown signs of moving closer to the Labour Party's position on the peace process. The spiritual leader of Shas, Rabbi Yosef, had commented while on a visit to Cairo that the saving of human life was more important than the issue of land. In addition, during his stay at the Ministry of

Finance (1988–90), Peres attempted to soften up Rabbi Deri, the parliamentary leader of Shas, with increased funding for the development towns where Shas's support was strongest, and for Shas-related educational projects. Yet despite all the ground-work, the establishment of a grand coalition between the Labour Party and Shas proved impossible to achieve. True, Shas did help Labour bring down the NUG, but when it came to supporting the second part of Peres's exercise they withdrew their backing. In short, Shas could join Labour only if the latter held a winning majority – otherwise Shas supporters drawn from the ultra-orthodox/Oriental/low-income groups would not have tolerated the move.

Unfortunately for Peres, just as he was about to present his winning coalition to a packed Knesset, with his wife in the visitors' gallery, it became clear that two members of the religious party Agudat Israel would not support the coalition. This reversal happened despite the fact that they had signed a deal live on Israeli television that they would do so. Clearly, Peres had not calculated for the intervention of non-parliamentary Rabbis and spiritual leaders, many of whom were not even based in Israel. Both Shas and another party, Degel Hatorah, were prevented from helping any Labour-led coalition by the intervention of their supreme mentor, Rabbi Schach (even Rabbi Yosef, the spiritual leader of Shas, deferred to him). In effect, a few senior Rabbis were determining the political colour of the next govern-ment in Israel.

Israeli democracy had reached one of its lowest points. However, things went from bad to worse. The extent of Peres's desperation led to unprecedented offers, such as potential Cabinet portfolios and financial incentives being made to Agudat and to various so-called rebels whom he approached. Such offers led to a heated debate about the very nature of the Israeli electoral and political system, as well as widespread public condemnation and protest. In the end, President Herzog passed the baton to Shamir, who was able to form a narrow-based Likud-led government. This happened only after another attempt at NUG collapsed due to internal opposition from within both the Likud and the Labour Party. Unfortunately for Shamir, in order to form an administration he had been forced to match Peres's offer, but when – as he put it – the religious parties came 'to cash their cheques', he simply said that he could not do it. For Shamir, trying to keep an increasingly hostile coalition together, the next two years proved to be very difficult.

Even prior to the dirty exercise, there had been a growing sense of unease from Israel's mainly secular élite that the religious parties were gaining too much influence, and that their actions were turning Israel into a strongly religious country. Headlines at the time included 'Israel's Ayatollahs' and 'Is Israel the next Iran?'. These types of headlines were wild exaggerations, but nonetheless there was a sense in Israel that the best way to clip the wings of the smaller political parties – code for religious parties – was through a process of electoral reform that would prevent the situation of the minority holding effective control over the majority. The question of religious parties and the wide issues of secular versus religious rights and Israeli law versus Jewish law have always been complex in a state that, after all, defines itself as a Jewish state. The fact that many of the parties do not even recognise the state does not appear to stop them demanding generous government handouts for their schools and social activities. One of the major failings of the period of the various NUGs was that a rare opportunity was missed for the secular parties to frame a written constitution free from the fear that the religious parties would be able to topple the coalition. Leaders from both the Likud and Labour, however, had one eye on future coalition negotiations with Israel's religious parties (who were strongly opposed to the imposition of a written constitution), and chose not to pursue constitutional reform.[13]

Israel's leadership crisis was characterised by a state of inertia that in many ways mirrored the period between the Six Day and Yom Kippur Wars. Back then, the deep divisions and lack of meaningful debate were encompassed within the ruling Labour Party. This time, the divisions lay both within and across the two major parties, which were bound together in a marriage of convenience to preserve the position of key leaders. In retrospect, looking at the elections held during the period, the lack of choice being offered to Israelis by the major parties was conducive to maintaining position rather than advancing any radical peace proposal.

In some respects, the period of the 1980s in Israel can be characterised as one of coming to terms with what needed to be done to try to solve the Arab–Israeli conflict, and to deal with the pressing issue of economic liberalisation and the growing gap between rich and poor, without actually being able to take the resulting required action to help resolve the issues. The phrase 'Israeli democracy under stress' is often used to describe this period. A more apt title would simply read 'The wasted years'. Luckily for Israel, its leadership was to a degree saved from having to make decisions by the lack of a real partner for peace. Yasser Arafat's statement in 1988 calling for a two-state solution and renunciation of violence was greeted with a great deal of scepticism in Israel. While Arafat talked peace, the Palestinian Intifada continued, with PLO-sponsored violence being used against both Israeli soldiers and other Palestinians. Any hope the Israeli leadership had clung to of talking to local Palestinian residents of the West Bank and Gaza Strip all but evaporated. From here on, the question was when – and if – the Israeli government would be willing to talk with Arafat.

The failure of Israeli leadership was further seen in the growing international consensus that a solution to the Arab–Israeli conflict would have to be imposed by the outside world. This view was prevalent among many of President Bush's advisers, in Europe and in the Soviet Union under Gorbachev, and was manifest in such international institutions as the Socialist International (at this time still a powerful body of which both the Israeli Labour Party and Mapam were members, and in which the PLO enjoyed observer status). These pressures were brought to bear on Israel during the 1990s, which saw major developments both in the Arab–Israeli conflict and within Israeli society.

CHAPTER SIX

Waiting for Godot: False Dawns and Shattered Dreams

To many people in Israel, the 1990s will be remembered as the decade of false dawns and sad realisations about the nature of the hatred that is directed towards Israel from the Palestinians, Arab states, and other parts of the world. If one were writing an entry for an encyclopaedia, the account would focus on the drama of the Rabin–Arafat handshake, which the then British Foreign Secretary Douglas Hurd described as the Middle East equivalent of the fall of the Berlin Wall, and the peace agreements that followed that handshake. In the years to come, someone who read such an entry might easily conclude that the 1990s were characterised by a growing sense of building towards peace and reconciliation between Arab and Jew that all went horribly wrong at the end of the decade. Others would no doubt view the 1990s as a period of coming to terms with the past and a maturing of the Israeli state – illustrated by the increase in the number of non-fiction and fiction books written by Israelis that adopt a critical approach to Israel.

The reality is of course very different. In political terms, the period could equally be characterised as the decade of concessions, starting with Yitzhak Shamir's decision to attend the Madrid Peace Conference in 1991 – when he knew that the PLO would be in Madrid as part of the Jordanian delegation – and moving on to the recognition of the PLO and the general acceptance of the disastrous land for peace formula that Israel either made or was coerced into making – concessions that when taken together came close to amounting to a collective form of national suicide. Predictably, these concessions did not satisfy the aspirations of the Arabs, but rather fuelled them to new heights. The Israeli return on these concessions was diminished even further by the fact that once the outside world had persuaded Israel to accept the notion that compromise was the only way forward, it did not give it due reward or offer it the kind of reassurances that it needed to help convince an increasingly sceptical Israeli public that such moves were in the best long-term interest of the Jewish state. But perhaps the greatest mistake was made by Yitzhak Rabin, who pioneered the policy of continuing to make concessions even while his designated peace partner was doing little to stop violent attacks on Israelis, the 'concessions under fire' formula. The message behind this decision was not lost on the Palestinian leadership, who throughout the decade continued to use tactical violence in order to apply pressure on Israel and win additional concessions to the ones already placed on the table by Israel.

People who say that an election victory in itself doesn't change a country are absolutely right. But just as the victory of Menachem Begin and the Likud in the 1977 elections was a defining moment in Israeli history, so the same can be said of Yitzhak Rabin's and the Labour Party's triumph in the 1992 elections. Israeli television hailed the result as an upheaval or earthquake, while the international media described it as a victory for peace – or the 'peace camp', as some label the left-of-centre parties in Israel. In truth, it was a narrow win caused, to a large extent, by the reduction of votes for the Likud and the fragmentation of the nationalist camp vote. Indeed, the nationalist camp actually won more votes than the so-called peace camp. So what?, you might ask. It is important, however, to remember that the election did not produce the mandate for the radical changes that were to follow. More significantly, the election confirmed important changes that were taking place within Israeli society.

The arrival of immigrants from the Soviet Union at the end of the 1980s and the start of the 1990s naturally transformed Israeli society and culture once more, just as the arrival of the Orientals had done previously. Prior to this influx, the ethnic Jewish balance of the state had been shifting away from Ashkenazi Jews towards the Orientals and their descendants. The arrival of the ex-Soviets – the vast majority of whom were of Ashkenazi origin – readjusted this ethnic balance. In truth, the Soviet Aliyah to a certain extent led to a redefining of the divisions within Israeli society, the labels of 'new immigrant' versus 'veteran immigrant' replacing the old ethnic divisions. The challenge of absorbing 750,000 immigrants in a period of less than a decade was considerable for Israel. Not only this, but the aspirations of this Aliyah were higher and more immediate than those of most previous Aliyahs. As a result of this, and the almost inevitable period of alienation that new immigrants in Israel experience, there was soon widespread dissatisfaction among this group – despite the fact that the economic indicators pointed to this Aliyah as being the most successful of all immigrant groups. Politically speaking, this group were initially seen as natural Likud supporters, and Likud leaders had hoped that the arrival of this Aliyah would help cement their position as the dominant force in Israeli politics. In the minds of the Likud leaders, the arrival of the Soviet Aliyah had other implications for Israel. They hoped that the new immigrants would settle in the West Bank, and consequently reshape the demographic balance of the area in favour of Jews. Such a change would have strengthened Israeli claims to incorporate these lands into Israel proper. Leaders such as Yitzhak Shamir hoped that by stalling the peace process they could buy time to help create these additional realities on the ground. The Likud was to be disappointed by the Soviet Jews on both counts. In 1992, the vast majority of the new immigrants – angry at their absorption process led by a Likud government – supported the Labour Party, and the vast majority did not settle in the West Bank but chose Israel proper.

The introduction of a new electoral system in Israel for the 1996 elections, in which voters cast two ballots – one for Prime Minister and the other for the Knesset – had a profound impact on Israeli political culture during this crucial period of the state. The new system was – not to mince words – a disaster, giving more power to the smaller parties and weakening the hand of the

Prime Minister. While the outside world, and in particular President Clinton, called for additional concessions, consecutive Prime Ministers from the Israeli left and right – regarded as the best of the young turks – struggled with the seemingly impossible task of balancing the pressures of the outside world with keeping their rainbow coalitions of eight or more parties intact. In Israel, each sector of society demands an increased share of a decreasing central government economic pie. At the top of the list were the Immigrant Party, a new party founded by the veteran refusenik Natan Sharansky who was pushing for increased funding and political influence for the Soviet immigrants, and the ultra-orthodox Jews led by Shas, who were pushing strongly for additional funding for their social and education programmes.

In 1994 the Labour Party lost control of the Histadrut for the first time since its creation in 1920. In reality, the Histadrut was by this stage little more than a relic of a bygone age, with its oversized Russian-style headquarters in Tel Aviv living on past glories and uses. The Histadrut had been the central agency in the battle to build the economic structures for a Zionist state. To many, the decline of the Histadrut marked the death of the socialist dream for Israel. At the height of its power the Histadrut had played a role in the life of most Israelis, and even today its health fund is the most heavily subscribed in Israel. Along with the Kibbutzim (which came under its umbrella), it was perhaps the most potent symbol of the Labour Zionist economic miracle. From a wider perspective, the 1990s saw profound changes in the structure and performance of Israel's economy. A decade that started with the arrival of the wave of immigrants from the former Soviet Union, an economic recession and the blocking of the loan guarantees by the Bush administration, ended with the Israeli economy in seemingly better shape than at any time during its 55-year history.

Israel's so-called hi-tech miracle, however, obscured a much more complex picture of the economy, one in which the dual conditioning factors of Zionism and the Arab–Israeli conflict still play a central role. In statistical terms, between 1990 and 1996 there was a rapid 6 per cent annual average increase in GDP and a very strong 7–8 per cent expansion of business sector product. By the end of 1996, per capita income in Israel had reached a level similar to that in developed countries such as Great Britain and Ireland, and higher than that in Greece, New Zealand, Portugal and Spain. Exports of goods increased by 7–8 per cent on annual average during this time, although there was an increasing balance of payments deficit that rose to nearly 5 per cent of GDP at the end of 1996. However, these statistics paint only a part of a much more complex picture of the development of the Israeli economy.

How did the Israeli economy change over the years to create this situation?

The Israeli economy has changed substantially since the formation of the state, with the economic well-being of the majority of the population increasing significantly, to the extent that by the end of the 20th century the standard of living in Israel was on a par with that of the United Kingdom and other Western European countries. These changes are all the more remarkable given the fact that Israel has never had any real natural resources, and has faced the difficult burdens of dealing with massive waves of immigration and constant Arab hostility which, in the economic sphere, has manifested itself as a boycott of Israeli goods. The successes of the Israeli economy, however, cannot hide other less impressive facts such as the failure to develop an egalitarian society (as the founding fathers had intended). The gap between rich and poor has continued to widen throughout its history, and the number of Israelis living below the poverty line at the end of the 20th century was greater than in the US and Western European countries. The non-Jewish population of Israel has not developed at the same economic pace as the rest, leaving it far behind. Among the Jewish population, the major inequalities are largely based on ethnic origin.

Central to the quest of the Zionist movement for a Jewish homeland was the awareness of the importance of developing a strong economic sector. A country had to be not only sustainable in terms of its ability to defend itself, but also economically viable – and as far as possible self-sufficient. This was particularly true in a country such as Israel (and in the pre-state period) which relied upon the arrival of immigrants to maintain its population development. A drop in immigration due to an economic down-turn, or an increase in emigration from Israel, was a security issue; it endangered the development of the state through unfavourably altering the demographic balance between Arab and Jew. On top of this, the role of the Arab–Israeli conflict has been important in determining the development of the Israeli economy. For example, Israel has traditionally had to invest large sums in defence, and more recently in developing a military industrial complex in order to maintain its qualitative edge in weaponry over the Arab states. There has been little or no trade with Israel's neighbours, who have imposed boycotts on such economic activities, some of which remain in place at the start of the 21st century. These two factors meant that there was a very direct relationship between the economy and the nation's security, and this fact has been at the centre of the development of the Israeli economy since 1948.

The structure and development of the economy was largely determined by the founding fathers of the state from the Second and Third Aliyahs. The development of a strong public sector economy was seen as vital in securing the future of the state, and this remained largely unchanged until the mid-1980s and the onset of economic liberalisation (deregulation and privatisation).[1] The fact that many of the newly arriving immigrants to Israel (and Palestine) brought little capital with them meant that strong dependence ties formed, as the immigrants relied on the state for their basic economic needs. Even those immigrants that did bring capital were still dependent upon the state in the short term in terms of absorption and education.

As previously discussed, realising the extent of the dependency ties is vital to understanding the development of the Israeli economy. The individual was dependent on the state for their everyday needs, while the state itself became increasingly dependent on foreign aid to meet the economic needs of Israel. In terms of ideology, the mainstream leadership of the Labour movement was social democratic in nature, rather than socialist as some claimed. This was clearly shown by the reluctance to redistribute economic resources to the newly arriving immigrants and away from the established population. In simple terms, this meant that the economic position of the first immigrants was stronger than that of those who arrived later. This fact has continued throughout the history of Israel, with each new Aliyah entering the economic ladder at the bottom, and over time working its way up to a higher position.

The historical characteristics of the Israeli economy can be summarised as follows: highly centralised, with a high degree of government influence and interference. Despite attempts at encouraging enterprise and the development of new business élites, the economy has always been dominated by a small number of actors, many of whom have close connections to the political élite. Many of the economic high flyers can be seen socialising with the political big guns at the 4 July party held by the US Ambassador at his residence in Herzliya, the high point of the Israeli social party season. Repayment of debt has been a major burden on an economy that has been heavily dependent on gift capital (loans and grants) from foreign countries, especially the United States. The cost of the defence effort is the single largest expenditure, and influences the rest of the budget. At times of high tension in the Arab–Israeli conflict there is a marked increase in defence spending at the expense of other sectors of the economy, such as in the periods prior to the Suez War (1956) and the Six Day War (1967). Another important characteristic has been the subsidising of basic consumer goods and transport by both the Labour Party and the Likud. The relationship between the economy and politics is more direct than in many other developed economies. Politicians from all parties have taken political and organisational benefits from manipulating the economy in terms of increasing distribution of state funds to their constituents, or simply by the process of pre-election spending increases, known locally as 'electionomics'.[2]

In terms of political economy, the impact of the economy in

determining the outcome of national elections was not really seen until 1977 with the rise of the Likud. Before the 1967 Six Day War, economic and social issues had played an important role in determining the composition of the various Labour-led coalitions, but without threatening the dominance of Mapai in the short term. After 1967, the future of the territories captured by Israel during the war came to dominate the political agenda, with economic and social issues pushed more and more into the background. By the late 1990s, with the emergence of a broader and stronger national consensus on the future of the Territories and the peace process in general, socio-economic issues started to play a much greater role in determining the political colour of Israel's governments. This was compounded by the introduction of direct elections for Prime Minister which, as we have seen, allowed Israelis to cast two votes: one for PM and the other for the Knesset. Israelis appeared to use their ballot for the Knesset to cast a vote on economic issues. For instance, a voter from a lower-income group could cast one ballot for a right-wing candidate for PM to reflect his own hawkish views on the peace process, while casting another vote for a different group such as Shas, who are perceived as representing the interests of the ultra-orthodox and lower-income earners in Israel.

The Israeli economy has not developed as Shimon Peres's vision of the new Middle East originally intended. This vision foresaw Israel providing the technological expertise helping to harness the financial resources of the Gulf States and the labour of Arab and North African countries to develop a Middle Eastern version of the Common Market.[3] There are a number of reasons why, even during the period of accelerated peace-making in the early to mid-1990s under the Rabin and Peres governments, such visions did not reflect the political and economic realities of the region. There was Arab suspicion that Israel's efforts to integrate itself into the Middle East and develop regional financial infra-structures similar to the EU model marked an attempt at a form of economic colonisation.

These suspicions were partly based on the size of the Israeli economy, whose GDP is greater than that of all its Arab neighbours put together. The majority of trade does not presently take place between countries in the region (Israel–Arab or between Arab countries), but rather between individual countries and external powers, for example the US. In short, Israel's economy is not yet fully normalised, but has taken significant steps in that direction over the last decade. On the downside, as the economy becomes more immersed in the global markets so it will be more vulnerable to international downturns. For example, if the US sneezes, Israel will catch a cold. In the long term, as the levels of US aid to Israel are reduced, its economic dependence on the US will shift to a more indirect inter-dependence on the health of the American economy.

How did the questions of secular versus religious rights shape Israel during the 1990s?

If Israeli leaders were being constantly pressurised into making concessions in order to attempt to reach peace with Israel's neighbours, and on economic matters to keep governing coalitions in place, the same can certainly be said in the area of secular versus religious rights. During the 1990s, the changes in Israel's election system helped dramatically increase the number of members of the Knesset from orthodox or ultra-orthodox parties. Ironically, the framers of the changes had devised the new system to reduce the level of representation for the smaller parties, which included the religious ones. Admittedly, it would be superficial to argue that the growth in representation for religious parties was based solely on electoral politics. Demographically, the orthodox and ultra-orthodox were growing at a much faster rate than secular Israelis. The average number of children within an ultra-orthodox family was twice that of a secular family. In a country where the demographic balance between Arab and Jew is so central to the continued existence of the state, large families are encouraged by government agencies.

In recent years, the birth rate among Israeli Arabs (living within the Green Line – i.e. in Israel proper) and the West Bank and Gaza Arabs has been rising much more rapidly than the

Jewish birth rate. As a result, it is highly likely that by 2020 there will be an Arab majority in the lands from the East Bank of the River Jordan to the sea. So, yes, Israel's religious Jews – whether or not they accept the legitimacy of the Jewish state – are extremely important to Israel's future security. Politically, Shas, the largest of the ultra-orthodox movements, started to attract votes on ethnic and socio-economic grounds as well as religious ones. With its linkage to the Orientals, Shas became the natural home for many traditional Likud supporters of Oriental background who had become disillusioned with the party's attempts to provide economic solutions for the constituency.

The increase in Knesset representations raised important questions about the very nature of Israeli democracy. Should Shas, for example, be able to effectively hold the casting vote in ratifying peace agreements signed by Israeli leaders? To some Israelis, particularly on the left, this was almost too much to bear. Yet perhaps the most historic and controversial decision in Israeli history was taken in September 1993 with Shas Members of the Knesset (MKs) holding the decisive votes. To outsiders it would appear strange that MKs who did not even accept the full legitimacy of the government in which they served would ratify a peace accord. In Israel, however, it has become the norm, as parties such as Shas have become the political king-makers. The fact that the ultra-orthodox do not serve in the armed forces further upsets many Israelis. It should be remembered that the linkage between army service and citizenship is very strong. For example, the other grouping that does not serve in the army, the Israeli Arabs, are considered not to be full citizens of the state of Israel, while the ultra-orthodox are considered full citizens. The question of army service for the ultra-orthodox has become a political hot potato, with leaders such as Ehud Barak calling for them to serve. In essence, while there has been some movement towards a limited number of ultra-orthodox Jews serving in the army, Israeli leaders have yet to take a strong stand on the issue for fear of antagonising religious leaders and their political representatives. All of this poses difficult questions for the long-term development of Israeli democracy – questions on which many in Israel appear resigned to postponing debate until after the resolution of the Arab–Israeli conflict.

In the meantime, Israel needs to be careful to check the growing political power of the ultra-orthodox – the new mayor of Jerusalem is an ultra-orthodox Jew – and make sure that any future debates and votes on peace agreements between Israel and the Palestinians and Israel and Syria are not held hostage to the whims of Shas and other ultra-orthodox parties. In short, the future of the state of Israel must not become a bargaining chip or concession that Prime Ministers offer to appease such parties. Thankfully, at present, there is growing evidence that the political influence of the ultra-orthodox at the heart of government may prove to be on the decline. It must be remembered that while Israel is a Jewish state – or a state for the Jews – it was founded along secular lines by secular members of the Zionist movement, and has taken its place among the democratic nations. Israel must not allow itself to be hijacked into becoming a Jewish version of Iran.

The general viewpoint of the Arab world is that Israel has already taken that path – that it is, in effect, a strongly observant religious state that does not tolerate non-Jews. The perception is heightened by the linkage between religion and the land – particularly the West Bank – which is highlighted in the Arab media, and the role of settlement in the Israeli political agenda. Arab papers talk of the lack of civil marriages in Israel – all marriages, to be legal, must be performed by a Rabbi. Likewise, the Arab media also highlights what it sees as the decadence of Western democratic values such as divorce, abortion, prostitution and pornography in Israel. To many Arabs, Israel is a mixture of the worst of both worlds. Perhaps the clichéd Arab picture of an Israeli is of an observant Jew wearing a kippa who indulges in all the nationalist vices of Israel, as well as all the sexual ones too.

Both perceptions are of course somewhat misguided, but it is clear that Israel underwent important cultural change during the 1990s, partially as a result of the peace-making activities of the political leadership, and in part due to the wider trends of globalisation from which Israel was not immune. Perhaps the central development was that of the Israeli yuppie. Okay, so this was perhaps the defining characteristic of the 1980s in the UK and USA, with films such as *Wall Street* and books such as *The Bonfire of the Vanities* chronicling the thirst for money and power. On a deeper level, the term 'yuppie' implied a preference for the individual over notions of collective good. In Thatcherite Britain and Reagan's America these values dominated the decade, the downside of the yuppie get-rich culture not being felt until the end of the 80s. In Israel the yuppie culture arrived in earnest in the 1990s, and if anything its impact was much greater than in the UK or USA. Israel was a country that was founded and built by the principles of self-sacrifice and the collective good. The notion of sacrifice was never more apparent than in the battlefield, which had been part of the national ethos since the 1948 War of Independence.[4]

While it is questionable just how socialist Israel's founding fathers were – they were forced to put nationalist goals above socialist ones – nevertheless with the ever-present threat of war and destruction of the state, personal advancement (while still an important feature of Israeli society) was not the dominant feature it became in the 1990s. The rise of the yuppies was indicative of a trend in Israel of the individual coming before the state, which manifested itself in areas such as the growing number of middle-class families attempting to get their sons exempted from army duty (currently three years followed by around 60 days each year until middle age). Though Israel's protracted war with Hezbollah may have had something to do with this, it remains perfectly clear that many Israelis appeared unwilling to put themselves in the line of danger. Many of the recruits who served in combat units were new Soviet immigrants who viewed army service in the IDF as less stressful than undertaking their national service in the armies of the former Soviet Union.

To many veterans, young Israelis were simply becoming too soft. The presence of cable television and channels such as MTV appeared to have hypnotised many Israelis, who aspired to the kind of lifestyle enjoyed by young Americans. Record numbers bought Levi jeans, drank Coke and visited fast-food halls. Even McDonald's arrived in 1994, opening up in Tel Aviv and Jerusalem. The Tel Aviv Stock Exchange, with new liberalisation and further deregulation, became an investment game for Israelis eager to see quick returns on their money. The national lottery craze took off, with some people buying excessive numbers of tickets (here Israel was no different to the UK or USA). All these developments were not lost on the Arabs, many scholars forecasting that Israel was sowing the seeds of its own decadent destruction.

The clear message that such cultural developments sent out to an Arab world was that if they (the Arabs) made life as difficult as possible, the Israelis were not ready for the fight. To put it another way, war weariness had set in in Israel. The first successful exploiters of this situation were Hezbollah, who used PR gimmicks such as filming attacks on Israeli soldiers in Lebanon and distributing them to news agencies in the full expectation that Israel's liberal television channels would show them in prime time. The effect of such videos was both an increase in draft dodging – or at the very least the avoidance of combat unit duty – and a marked increase in the debate in Israeli society over whether Israel should remain within its self-declared security zone in Lebanon.

Eventually, under intense pressure from key segments of middle-class Israeli society, Ehud Barak withdrew the army from Lebanon in a lightning manoeuvre that, while no doubt saving the lives of retreating Israeli soldiers, created an image of the IDF withdrawing with their tails between their legs. This image was not lost in the Arab capitals, which noted that Israeli leaders, if pressurised by the use of violence, would make additional concessions in order to placate an Israeli public increasingly yearning for an end to the conflict. Put in political terms, elements of the Arab leadership sensed the start of the endgame with Israel, wanted to obtain maximum concessions from it, and were seemingly prepared to use any tactic in order to secure them.

Crucially, Yasser Arafat was one such Arab leader who thought he understood the new Israeli frailty. As he walked away from the Camp David summit – at which Barak had offered concessions that went far beyond anything that Israel had put on the table up to that point – his mind was already made up to use violence – or residence, as he terms it – to extract further concessions from Israel. Central to Arafat's strategy was his belief that Israeli society would not tolerate being blown up on buses and would force its leaders to return to the negotiating table and offer additional concessions. Many Palestinian leaders were quite open about the fact that they were employing the same model used by Hezbollah in its war with Israel. Palestinians talked about the decay of Israeli society and about the increase in homosexuality in places such as Tel Aviv. In truth Israel, and in particular Tel Aviv, has in recent years always had a thriving vocal gay scene, much of which takes place in the middle-class bars and parks near the beach. The fact that an Israeli trans-sexual, Dana International, won the Eurovision Song Contest contributed to this impression of decadence and an increasingly hedonistic society. Arafat's advisors were filling his head with stories of the well known Shenkin area of Tel Aviv, where Israel's café society had stopped talking about politics and started talking fashion and other normal topics. To this extent, the return to a state of war between Israel and the Palestinians came as a great shock to those Israelis who had either wholeheartedly presumed or hoped that wars were a thing of the past. For Arafat, the great shock was that Israelis did not buckle, but rather, as we shall see later, were in the short term reinvigorated with a new sense of resistance.

The change to a more individualised society may have been the most important change within Israeli society, but the most curious must surely have been the reaction to the murder of Yitzhak Rabin in November 1995. Rabin's assassination by Yigal Amir, a Jewish zealot, left Israeli society and the political élite in a state of shock. Prior to the killing, the Rabin administration had been struggling, and the Oslo peace process was in deep trouble. On 20 October 1994, a Hamas bomber had blown himself up on the number 5 bus just as it came out of the under-pass at Dizengoff Street. The resulting carnage was shown live on television for hours on end, while Israeli protestors gathered at the scene shouting death to the Arabs. There had been other suicide attacks before this one in the northern towns of Afula and Hadera, but this was something else. Suddenly, Israeli cities had become war zones. In the past, the war stopped at the front line, in the desert in the south or on the Golan Heights or the West Bank. Attacks had taken place in Jerusalem, which was considered to be the front line by Israelis, but nothing on this scale had taken place in Tel Aviv. As more attacks followed, with no discernible pattern except to kill as many Israeli citizens as possible, so Rabin's government looked more shaky. The withdrawal of Shas – over a long-running dispute with the fiercely secular Meretz coalition partner – left Rabin dangerously exposed to votes of no confidence in the Knesset. In short, this was a government living on borrowed time. As in America, Israeli leaders are addicted to polling, and Rabin's internal figures had him at best running neck and neck with Netanyahu in the contest for direct elections for Prime Minister. Israeli society, as previously mentioned, was deeply split over the concessions that Rabin was offering, and was even more divided about the kind of compromises that appeared necessary in the coming months and years.

Rabin's death changed all this in the short term. Suddenly there was a new consensus among Israelis to continue making concessions in the hope – rather than certainty – that they would bring peace. Rabin's immediate successors – Peres, Netanyahu and Barak – all made concessions, although only Peres enjoyed overwhelming support for the concessions he offered between November 1995 and February 1996. The murderous cycle of suicide bombings carried out by Hamas and Islamic Jihad in February and March 1996 put an end to this consensus.[5] The only difference between before and after the Rabin killing was the tone. The debate about the extent of the concessions that were required within the land for peace formula was muted, partly out of respect for what had happened to Rabin, and also as a result of the blurring of the differences between the candidates for Prime Minister.

What appears on the surface difficult to explain, however, is that in the elections held only six months after the assassination of Rabin, only 22 per cent of voters cited his killing as having influenced 'to a great extent' how they cast their vote, with some 19 per cent stating that it had 'to a certain extent' affected their vote.[6] In truth, as soon as the suicide bombings started in February 1996, Israelis moved on from the trauma of the assassination and started to deal with the trauma of the bombings. This is of course extremely unhealthy, but in a country where one collective trauma has rapidly followed another, it is the norm. There is a tendency among Israelis to internalise traumatic events and deal with them only on a superficial level. This, for many, helps keep them sane and able to focus on another strong Israeli trait – getting on with it. So, in the long term, the death of Rabin did not impact on the implementation of the Oslo Accords as much as many had originally predicted.

A direct consequence of Rabin's death was that Palestinian elections were held on time in the areas governed by the Palestinian Authority in January 1996. Prior to this, Shimon Peres and the government had used Rabin's death to give impetus to the withdrawal of IDF forces from several Palestinian towns and villages, placing them under either joint control or sole Palestinian control. The Peres government viewed Rabin as a victim in the search for peace and they saw it as their duty to continue, and indeed speed up the process in order to commemorate their fallen leader.[7] The resulting elections produced the expected victory for Arafat and his political faction, Fatah. The international media were quick to dub the election a popular Palestinian endorsement of the Oslo Accords. Israeli politicians added that their partner for peace had been given a degree of legitimacy by the people in order to move the process to the next stage – final status talks that were to start, briefly, in 1996. Many Israelis hoped that Arafat would use his mandate to launch a more pro-active policy against Hamas and Islamic Jihad. He did not. Instead, Palestinian jails continued to operate a 'revolving door policy', with the Palestinian justice system resembling Captain Renault's system in the movie *Casablanca*, characterised by the shout of 'round up the usual suspects'.

Following the failure at Camp David in 2000, Arafat threw in his lot with the suicide bombers – a decision that on the surface appeared an irrational one politically. On closer examination it was rational, given the continuing context of the United States granting concessions to the Palestinian Authority, many of whose members by this stage were privately endorsing attacks on Israeli civilians. As more and more evidence came to light linking Arafat and his close aides with attacks on Israelis, there were calls to isolate him, expel or even kill him. While the Bush administration moved to find an alternative, European countries continued to deal with him. Many used phrases such as 'cycles of violence' – thus giving credibility to the argument that Israeli responses to violence were no better than the original attacks.

At the centre of much of Europe's beef with Israel was the policy of targeted assassinations, or 'extra-judicial killings'. This policy was not new in Israel: the perpetrators of the killing of the Israeli athletes at the Munich Olympic games in 1972 had been tracked down and assassinated by Israeli agents. Likewise, ex-Nazi scientists working on Arab nuclear programmes had met a similar fate. What was different this time was the increased use of this weapon by Israel, and the fact that it was being carried out under the full glare of the international media, who had returned to the West Bank and Gaza following the start of the war in 2000, equipped with motorcycle crash helmets, flak jackets and *Arab–Israeli Conflict Made Simple* guidebooks at their side. On top of this was the frequently pointed out fact that Israeli security forces routinely torture Palestinian detainees. Torture still takes place, despite the fact that the Israeli Supreme Court ruled to disallow any form of physical pressure on detainees – even those that are considered to be 'ticking bombs' (have information that could prevent an imminent attack, thus saving life).[8] Such forms of non-lethal torture were used by the British in Northern Ireland and by many police forces in other Western-style democracies during the interrogation of suspected terrorists. In Northern Ireland, IRA prisoners were routinely tortured by Special Branch officers – particularly at the notorious Castlereagh Interrogation Centre.[9] Torture methods included beatings, sleep deprivation and cold hosing down. European courts were extremely critical of such actions, and ruled that all interrogations had to be recorded or monitored. Among even moderate elements of the nationalist community in Northern Ireland, the torture issue was the cause of much hostility towards the security services. Similarly, British security forces employed at varying times in Northern Ireland a shoot-to-kill policy that included the infamous 'death on the rock' episode when the SAS shot an active IRA unit in Gibraltar. In truth, Israeli and British security forces learnt much from each other's *modus operandi*.

In a general sense, just as Israel arrests Palestinians it suspects of being members of organisations such as Hamas and the PFLP (Popular Front for the Liberation of Palestine) and – in the old days – the PLO, the British did exactly the same in the mid-1970s in Northern Ireland through the policy of internment, which saw hundreds of suspected IRA members arrested and imprisoned without trial. Indeed, to suggest, as many do, that Israel is uniquely hard on what it terms terrorists is really rather misleading. On the contrary, it may come as a surprise to hear that Israel – which is famed for its tough stance against terrorists – has a history of freeing hundreds of prisoners from its jails in prisoner exchange deals, often just to get the bodies of dead Israelis back.

On a human level it is easy to understand such decisions, given the Israeli doctrine of getting all their boys back home. Israel is a small country of only 6.5 million inhabitants. Despite all its problems, it is a small, closely-knit society in which everyone knows someone who has been hurt or killed in action. This, together with traditional Jewish values of wanting to give everyone a decent burial, have meant that over the years Israel has gone to great lengths to get its prisoners of war and its dead returned to the country.

This casualty issue has always been Israel's Achilles heel. Arab leaders have always known this, and have acted accordingly. Hezbollah, however, have in recent years taken this to new lows. As we saw earlier, during Israel's occupation of southern Lebanon the organisation filmed its attacks against Israeli soldiers, often showing in graphic detail the bloody aftermath of its actions. Tapes were quickly distributed to Arabic news organisations and shown on cable channels in Israel. The aim of groups like Hezbollah is two-fold: to create fear and doubt among Israelis and to help translate this into public pressure on the government to release their prisoners (and Palestinians) from Israeli jails.

While it is easy to understand the action of the Israeli government on humanitarian grounds, it is more problematic to understand how they pushed aside the political and security considerations of the deal. In Northern Ireland under the terms of the Good Friday Agreement, nearly all paramilitary prisoners have been released from jail, on licence that their respective organisations stick to the terms of the agreed ceasefire. The attitude of the vast majority of these prisoners is that the war is over, and they have not returned to violence.

Sadly, it appears that the war is not over for the Hezbollah and Palestinian prisoners that Israel unleashes back into the free world. The brutal reality is that, of those released, a sizeable majority will carry out additional attacks against Israelis. Following a recent wave of prisoners released by Israel – as a goodwill gesture to the then Palestinian Prime Minister, Abu Mazen – some six have been involved in serious crimes since their release, including several in organising suicide bomb attacks against Israeli cities. One wonders what the attitude of the families of the future bereaved will be when they learn that the attack was carried out by someone whom Israel released from prison.

Despite all the violence and killing, the political framework of the deal between Israel and the Palestinians has remained in place.

Back in 1996, Yasser Arafat's deputy, Abu Mazen, and the main Israeli architect of the Oslo peace process, Yossi Beilin and his academic friends, held a series of secret meetings in Stockholm and Tel Aviv to produce a blueprint that was to form the framework for a final agreement between Israel and the Palestinian Authority.[10] The resulting Beilin–Abu Mazen Plan (or Stockholm Document) was not published at the time, and never officially endorsed by either Arafat or the then Israeli PM, Shimon Peres.[11] The reason that its importance still resonates today is that it is the main indication of what the Palestinians will settle for to end the conflict, and what the Israelis are willing to offer. The Beilin–Abu Mazen document also formed the basis of the talks between Ehud Barak and Yasser Arafat at Camp David in 2000, and more importantly the current negotiations between the Israeli and Palestinian Prime Ministers. The agreed content of the plan will shock many, particularly its section on the status of Jerusalem, which has appeared an intractable issue up to now.

The centrepiece of the plan was the linkage of the status of Jerusalem to an Israeli acceptance of a Palestinian state in the West Bank and the Gaza Strip. The key articles are listed below:

1   A Palestinian state to be created in Judea and Samaria (West Bank) and the Gaza Strip.
2   The capital of this state would be called Al-Quds, namely those parts of Jerusalem that are located outside the municipal borders of Israeli Jerusalem, but which are considered by the Palestinians to be part of the city.
3   The PA would recognise Israeli sovereignty over West (Jewish) Jerusalem, while sovereignty over East (Arab) Jerusalem would remain open for discussion.
4   The Palestinians would respect the principle of the open city of Jerusalem.
5   The Temple Mount would come under Palestinian control and a Palestinian flag would be raised on the site.
6   The Old City would be without official sovereignty, but Israel would maintain control over it.

The ambiguity over the amount of the West Bank to be included in the Palestinian state was later cleared up, with between 88 and 95 per cent to be handed over. Though not discussed in the plan, its consequences would lead to control of key water sources in the West Bank – which Israel is highly dependent on – being handed over to Palestinian control.

It is the issue of Jerusalem, however, that is the most interesting.

The idea that the Palestinians would accept Al-Quds as the capital of their state was not borne out at the Camp David talks in 2000, where the negotiations collapsed over the failure to reach agreement on this issue. In 2003, when the Palestinian delegation was led by Abu Mazen, it is clear that there had been significant movement on this issue by the Palestinians – a return to the Beilin–Mazen formula – but whether this is a long-term commitment remains to be seen. A Palestinian flag flying over the Temple Mount sends shivers down the spine of most Israelis, and many non-Palestinian Arabs. This appears, however, to be the price that Israel will have to pay to reach any accord over the status of Jerusalem.

Commentators such as Daniel Pipes are absolutely right in suggesting that Israel is winning its current war with radical Palestinian terror groups. Like all previous Arab–Israeli wars, however, it looks like Israel will not be able to turn a clear-cut military victory into political gain. There is a widespread misconception that because the current Prime Minister Ariel Sharon is considered to be a hawk, he will be able to drive a harder bargain with the Palestinians than his predecessor, Ehud Barak. This is complete nonsense. The truth is that Sharon will strike a deal that resembles the Beilin–Abu Mazen Plan. The only difference between the current PM and his predecessors lies in his ability to sell the deal to a sceptical Israeli population.

Few are more acutely aware of this point than Sharon himself. His astonishing comments when he referred to the Israeli 'occupation of the West Bank' were not a slip – or a sudden change of ideological perspective. Rather they were part of preparing Israelis for the shocks that will come in future years. They also marked a brave admission that the *status quo* is untenable for Israel, and that the Jewish state must move to protect its most sacred lands such as Jerusalem. The terms of the deal based on the Beilin–Abu Mazen Plan are already in place. The 'road map' peace plan presented by the Americans in May 2003 must create the conditions that allow each side to sell the deal to their respective constituencies. Both Arafat and Peres failed to endorse the original plan back in 1996 because they believed that they could not successfully achieve this and survive politically. It is here that the US-sponsored road map for peace is intended to step in.

Will the road map end the violence? And does it have any chance of long-term success?

The answer to the first is no. Even before the statement of rejection by Hamas, secular militant Palestinian groups – some close to Yasser Arafat – concluded that they would continue with the violence as well as the political dialogue. From their perspective, this is easy to understand. Why change a winning formula? The United States, Russia and Europe have, in effect, rewarded the Palestinians for two years of murderous violence, much of it directed against innocent Israeli civilians. In Ireland we refer to this as the 'bomb and ballot box' strategy, in Israel as the 'suicide bomb and political concession' strategy. In a perfect world, there would be no room for any of these killers at the negotiating table.

Ignoring the moral issue of dealing with killers, the road map has little practical chance of being implemented. Just like a dumb schoolboy who makes the same mistakes time and time again, so the US State Department (the main framers of the plan) continue to fail to learn the lessons from the disastrous Oslo peace process. Even the most strident supporters of Oslo now accept that interim stage agreements are a bad idea – given that there are rejectionist forces such as Hamas at large who thrive on derailing timetabled agreements, particularly ones in which progress from one stage to another depends on 'performance' (a ludicrous US phrase) at the previous stage.

To call a new international conference, as the road map proposes, is foolhardy when we are still trying to get over the last one, held in Madrid in 1991. In Madrid the parties almost came to physical blows when the Syrians accused the then Israeli PM, Yitzhak Shamir, of being a terrorist. Imagine the scene this time around, assuming, as appears highly likely, that Ariel Sharon leads the Israeli delegation into the conference room: Palestinians waving their Sabra and Shatilla banners, shouting 'killer' and 'fascist'. With all this showboating going on, there will be little chance of real progress.

So what is the alternative to the 'shiny suit' school of State Department diplomacy?

We are already seeing the alternative at work (or rather we are not). Sharon has had a working relationship with key members of the PA leadership, excluding Arafat, for some time. Indeed, their contacts can be traced back to the pre-Oslo period when it was illegal for Israelis to meet with PLO officials.[12] Today, both sides are keen to talk in private, and to agree solutions to the key issues before presenting them to the outside world. Both, for domestic reasons, prefer secret diplomacy. The key to progress, however, remains any Palestinian leader's ability to rein in Hamas and its international network of bombers and financiers. Though both parties have signed up to the road map, the real diplomatic action will be taking place in private meetings at Ariel Sharon's official residence in Jerusalem, where key Palestinian leaders are regular visitors.

Perhaps the greatest contribution of the road map will be to help provide a smokescreen, and a safety net, to direct talks between the Israelis and Palestinians based on the Beilin–Abu Mazen framework. In the meantime, Israel must be given all the necessary international support to destroy the increasingly international infrastructure of Hamas and other radical Palestinian groups. Israel, however, must find ways of getting out of the culture of making concessions in the hope of securing peace. The formula 'land for possible peace' simply doesn't add up. In recent times, Israeli society has shown itself to be much more resilient than appeared possible during much of the 1990s. By taking the battle into the heart of Israel, the Palestinians may have made a historic tactical mistake.

Finally, an issue that came to greater prominence during the 1990s was the question of the role of women in Israel, and the relatively few women who are in the Knesset or who occupy other political leadership roles. This imbalance is indicative of deeper issues and problems that surround the position of women in Israeli society. Here, two images come to the mind of the outsider. The first is of Golda Meir, Israel's fourth Prime Minister and one of the first female leaders of a Western-style democracy, and the other is of the Israeli army – the people's army – in which women serve compulsory national service alongside their male colleagues. Neither image, however, reflects the real picture. Golda Meir was the exception to the rule.

In Israel, women remain greatly under-represented within the élite.[13] So unique was Meir in terms of gender that she was considered almost asexual. While in private she had a string of lovers and enjoyed the nickname of 'the mattress', in public she acted as a traditional Zionist leader. Since Meir's resignation in 1974, no Israeli female has held high office or been involved in areas of the security establishment. During the 1990s, vocal MKs such as Yael Dayan spoke of the need to increase the representation of women in the Knesset. Debates have taken place about the merits and pitfalls of quotas – in which women have specially reserved positions in a party's list of candidates for seats in the Knesset.

In the arena of extra-parliamentary politics women have proved more successful, with groups such as the Four Mothers being very influential in helping pave the way for a withdrawal of the IDF from southern Lebanon. But apart from this and other notable exceptions to the rule, women in Israel remain far more politically alienated than in almost any democratic country. Why is this? Once more, it is a case of the survival of the state coming first, with other causes such as women's issues a poor second. The key argument put forward once more by the male-dominated élite is that 'once we have peace, then we can address these issues'. The trouble is that Israeli women have been waiting for peace for 55 years, and it is commonplace now for even the older generation of women who lived in the so-called egalitarian Kibbutzim to argue that they were given the worst jobs to do.

The IDF, as the central social conditioning agent and shaper of attitudes, has a very poor record in terms of women. Most young girls doing army service are given administrative jobs, and few occupy the kind of position that could help their long-term career prospects in the civilian sector. Recently, a young air cadet won the right to train to become a fighter pilot, but again she is a high-profile exception to the rule. In recent years, there have been a number of cases of sexual wrong-doings coming to light involving Israeli commanders at the highest level.

Female immigrants arriving from the former Soviet Union during the 1990s found Israel to be backward in terms of women's rights. Israeli women have much more in common with their Palestinian counterparts, who are given the same message from their male-dominated élite – nationalism and the battle for the state comes first, and all else will follow. In the meantime, Palestinian women are murdered in 'honour' killings, and raped and beaten in one of the most repressive regimes for women in the world. So much for the Palestinian Authority offering new hope for the women of the Middle East. In Israel, despite the growing awareness and reassessment of the role of women in winning and developing the Jewish state, reflected in the output of a new generation of female writers, there is much work to be done if Israel is to fall into line with other democratic nations in this respect. In truth, with Jewish culture promoting the values of women staying at home cooking and having children, it may never come into line. At the very least, in the short term women need legal protection from the increasing number of violent attacks at home. At a political level, more funds are needed to launch the careers of female candidates. It takes around $150,000 minimum to fund a successful primary election campaign to win a place on the Knesset list.

Perhaps the best name for Israel during the 1990s is 'Israel waiting for Godot'. So much in terms of the development of Israeli society has been suppressed by the conflict with the Arabs. During a brief window when it appeared possible that the Oslo Accords – which appeared at first to provide Israel with a negotiating partner – could really succeed in ending the conflict, we got a taster of the things to come in the future. To those Israelis who say that we cannot wait for peace before making substantial changes to social and political frameworks, it is worth pointing out that though Israeli society is far from perfect, in an era when the political élite is offering substantial concessions to the Arabs, social cohesion at home is vitally important. Any breakdown in this, as the Rabin assassination confirmed, can lead to disaster.

CHAPTER SEVEN

Learning the Lessons and Crystal Ball Gazing

Currently, there are signs that Israelis are not sure which lessons need to be learnt from the collapse of negotiations with the Palestinians. Perhaps, with Hegel's belief about a lack of learning from history, it is important to debate rather than jump to conclusions at this stage about what needs to be learnt. The underlying subtext to the lesson-learning debate is the desperate search to fill the political void caused by the demise of the Oslo peace process. The philosophical parameters of the debate over how best to bring peace to Israel remain partially obscured by political rhetoric. The debate centres on the definition of 'strong' and, in terms of the Israeli–Palestinian conflict, the fundamental difference between a military victory and a political one.

On the one hand, the Israeli left emphasise that past military victories – and present-day military might over the Arabs – have not resulted in peace, and that political victory (recognition of the right to exist) will come only through negotiation and concession. The left also stress the centrality of the economy to Israel's security, citing the need for a peace-time economy in order to attract new immigrants and to prevent emigration of other Israelis. With Arab birth rates still much higher than Jewish ones, this issue has taken on new resonance. In short, the left highlight the importance of the linkage between security and the economy, arguing that the Zionist priority is that of immigration, not maintaining control over lands captured in 1967. In short, there is no viable alternative to negotiations and compromise with Yasser Arafat and the PLO.

On the other hand, the Israeli right argue that the actions of the left raise the political aspirations of the Arabs and reduce the strength of Israel's military deterrents. They cite the withdrawal of Israeli forces from Lebanon in 2000, and the proposals that Ehud Barak put on the table at Camp David, as compelling evidence to suggest that the Israeli left has failed to learn basic lessons from history and experience. The basic lesson, they argue, that needs to be absorbed is that Arafat, and the vast majority of Arabs, do not want to make peace with Israel, and will do so only when they have realised that they cannot destroy it by military force or through economic isolation. For the right, any negotiations must take place under optimum conditions for Israel. These conditions include a weak and divided Arab world in which Arab political aspirations have been previously clipped. In terms of Zionist priorities, they place the retention of land over the absorption of immigrants. They perceive the acquisition of additional lands as enhancing Israeli security, not as a burden on it.

Transposing the often hijacked and abused term 'third way' into Israeli politics, we are essentially talking about identifying the natural successors to David Ben-Gurion and Moshe Dayan. While both were part of the Labour movement, they were the pioneers of the Israeli 'third way' not in terms of party politics, but rather in developing a workable, pragmatic framework for dealing with Israel's relations with the Arabs that drew inspiration from both sides of the Israeli philosophical debate. To a certain degree, the current Prime Minister, Ariel Sharon, and the Minister of Foreign Affairs, Benjamin Netanyahu, can be classed as the natural successors to Ben-Gurion and Dayan. Both have shown resolve during respective premierships in checking Arab aspirations and maintaining Israeli military deterrents, while making also, at certain junctures, tactical concessions in order to try to reach a political settlement with the Arabs.

Writing in 1859, John Stuart Mill, the great libertarian philosopher, argued that 'a party of order or stability, and a party of progress or reform, are both necessary elements of a healthy state of political life'. If Israel is to exceed Hegel's expectations of government, its leaders need to develop – and articulate – a third way that contains elements of both parties outlined by Mill.

So, what lessons need to be learnt?

The stark reality is that peace-making efforts have actually led to an increase in terrorism in Israel. Personal security has become a major issue within Israeli cities that hitherto were considered safe. When President Clinton, Ehud Barak and Yasser Arafat made their way home from Camp David in 2000, conventional wisdom appeared to point to the summit having confirmed the deeply held belief that the Israeli–Palestinian conflict was intractable and would last for at least another generation. This does not have to be the case, providing that both sides learn the lessons of what went wrong. As a result, it is timely to examine the deeper issues at stake here.

Why have peace agreements – signed in seeming good faith – failed to end conflicts? What are the root issues that have largely determined the causes of these conflicts? And how has the international community got its peace-making attempts wrong?

In the search for peace, it is generally presumed that the signing of peace agreements is the best method of securing an end to a conflict. This is wrong. Recent history has taught us that peace agreements primarily serve the purpose of securing the legacies of political leaders rather than actually bringing an end to the violence and bloodshed. Indeed, peace agreements can actually lead to a worsening of a conflict. Note, for example, the Middle East where, since the signing of the Oslo Accords in 1993, the number of Israelis and Palestinians who have died in the conflict has increased dramatically. As a result, there is a clear need to identify alternative strategies of peace-making that do not rely on such crude devices of conflict resolution.

Before applying the remedy, it is important to identify the root causes of these conflicts. What forces lead a man to plant an explosive device intended to kill and maim? What leads men to send suicide bombers into centres of towns to cause carnage? The traditional view is that there are two forces at play here:

nationalism and religion. This is true, but there is a lack of under-standing as to what is meant by these vague terms. Religion, and in particular religious fundamentalism, is often cited as a major factor in conflicts in the Middle East, Ireland and the Balkans. However, nationalism remains the most important determining factor in these conflicts. Contrary to the accepted wisdom of policy-makers, nationalism is not simply a struggle for statehood. In this increasingly complex globalised world, nationalism takes a very different form. Nowadays the winning of statehood is viewed as only a provisional stage of a national struggle, and not the endgame that politicians appear to believe it to be. In the Middle East, Hamas and Islamic Jihad seek legitimacy to create an Islamic fundamentalist state. In this respect, their war against Israel is directed as much against secular Palestinians as it is against Israelis. As for the PLO, after nearly a decade of control they still have not secured a degree of legitimacy among the Palestinian population for a secular Palestinian state. Indeed, within the Arab world the question of legitimacy of rule has been the major issue in the development of states since the creation of the Arab state system. In order to govern with any degree of legitimacy, the ruler must enjoy the support of either the majority of the population or, as in many Arab cases, a powerful minority (usually the economic and military élite).

Related to the issue of legitimacy are questions of economic nationalism or, put simply, the need to develop a strong economy if a national struggle is to survive. Currently, this is particularly relevant within the areas controlled by the Palestinian Authority, where it has clearly not materialised. The Palestinian business élite, the majority of which is based outside of Palestinian areas (in the Diaspora), has not been motivated by nationalist reasons to invest in a future Palestinian state. The brutal economic realities are that this group prefer to invest in the world markets based on economic – not nationalist – motives. Consequently, the perilous position of the Palestinian economy makes the threat of a declaration of a state appear like an empty vessel. In this case, the creation of a state would merely increase the alienation of society from its leadership and lead to a crisis of legitimacy of rule. This in turn would fuel the Israeli–Palestinian conflict, with the Palestinians increasing their ambitions to grab hold of an Israel that appears like a land of milk and honey in contrast to their own economic position. Hence the notion that even secular, more moderate Palestinians will never accept a two-state solution to the conflict.

The most important consequence of the emergence of what we can loosely term 'new nationalism' and the question of legitimacy is its effect on peace-making. It would appear that traditional approaches to peace-making are out of date. What is required is in effect an attempt by mediators to reduce the aspirations of national struggles and not – as currently happens – increase their desire for creating new states. Mediators such as the USA need to reinforce the message that such states are largely unsustainable and are likely to lead to civil strife or anarchy, which is liable to spill out into neighbouring countries. In short, such states constitute a danger to themselves and to others.

Current peace-making is very much based on the dictate of Woodrow Wilson, who said that there should be a state for each individual ethnic group or religion; or, as Elie Kedourie points out, Wilson wanted self-determination as the basis for the new and better world order.[1] This policy, although framed during the First World War, became more entrenched following the Second World War, and even more visible following the demise of the Soviet Union in 1991, with the new Central Asian Republics and the fragmentation of the Balkans. However, this policy has not reduced the number of nationalist-based conflicts in the world. In truth, it has had the opposite effect. The international community needs to move to stop the creation of further new states that are likely to become destabilising influences.

Peace agreements that lead to the creation of such states will prove to be unworkable in the medium to long term. Nationalism will remain a strong negative force upon mankind, with new groups of fanatics ready to take over when those who carried out the attacks are buried or put behind bars. Deal with the problem at source, and do not merely fuel the flames of the problem by creating more unsustainable states.

Are there any specific lessons we can learn from the failure of the Oslo Accords?

There are currently two schools of thought about the failure of the Israeli–Palestinian Oslo Accords. First, that the Palestinians and Arafat didn't want peace and duped the Israelis. There is growing evidence to suggest that this was the case. The second is that the technical failings of the Oslo Accords were so great that they never provided any real chance for peace to take root. My argument concentrates on the latter, and suggests that the Accords were so flawed that Arafat's own personal motives and actions were of secondary importance in determining the outcome of the ten-year process.

History

Few will forget the moment on the White House lawn in September 1993, when a reluctant Yitzhak Rabin, encouraged by then US President Bill Clinton, offered his outstretched hand to a beaming Yasser Arafat. The ceremony marked the culmination of eighteen months of secret diplomacy between the Rabin government and the Palestine Liberation Organisation in the signing of a formal peace agreement, meant to end nearly a century of conflict. What became apparent from the White House ceremony was that the image of the handshake had taken on almost as great an importance as the details of the agreements, if not more. The famous handshake was not, however, a spontaneous act. President Clinton's advisers had spent the previous Saturday planning just how to ensure that it took place. George Stephanopoulos described the planning: 'Then the President would turn to his left, shake Arafat's hand; take a half step back with his arms slightly lifted from his sides and hope that Arafat and Rabin reached across his belt for the picture of the decade.'[2] Even the expression that Clinton would have on his face was rehearsed, with a preference for a closed mouth smile.[3]

The agreement, officially entitled The Declaration of Principles, was followed by a second agreement signed in Cairo in 1994. Both agreements dealt with the transfer of parts of the West Bank and Gaza Strip to Palestinian control, but postponed discussion of the core issues of the conflict, such as the future of Jerusalem and the fate of the Palestinian refugees, until the 'final status' talks, scheduled to start three years later. The agreements contained a series of interim stages that aimed at achieving peace through a gradual, carefully timetabled process. Collectively, the agreements are better known as the Oslo Accords, after the city where the initial negotiations had taken place.

From the outset, however, the Oslo process started to go wrong. In analysing why, it is important to avoid playing the blame game, or even identifying the winners and losers. With hindsight, it is clear that the process was technically flawed from the very beginning, and those who cling to what remains of the process – the Mitchell Report or Tenet Agreement – are, to say the least, misguided. Oslo may have failed to end the conflict and may have helped escalate it to the level of violence we are witnessing today, but there are important lessons, both positive and negative, to be drawn from it.

I have identified seven key aspects of peace-making, Oslo style, that we need to learn from.

1. Secret diplomacy

As one of Israel's greatest diplomats, Abba Eban, writing in 1983, pointed out: 'There has hardly been a success for international conciliation in our time without the option of secrecy having been used at a crucial stage of the negotiating process. Many breakthroughs in conciliation would have been impossible if the negotiators had not found at least temporary shelter from public scrutiny.'[4] Some twenty years later, during the Oslo negotiations, both parties considered the use of a secret channel to be essential in securing an initial peace agreement that included statements of mutual recognition. Secrecy allowed direct negotiations to take place despite an Israeli law forbidding direct contacts with the PLO. Moreover, both sides agreed to complete deniability, making it easier to put forward ideas and discuss positions and potential trade-offs.

The secret channel obviated the need for public posturing and playing to domestic audiences that had marred previous public negotiations such as the Madrid Peace Conference in 1991. The secret nature of the talks helped to deepen relationships between the participants, enabling them to come up with creative solutions for previously intractable issues. One of the major problems, however, was that when details of the clandestine meetings slowly and inevitably started to emerge, the parties had to secure an agreement quickly before their cover was totally blown. Finally, as even Edward Said acknowledges, part of the Rabin–Arafat handshake's moment of beauty was the realisation that the Israelis and Palestinians had achieved this agreement themselves, and without the help of the United States.[5]

2. Interim staged agreements

It was the Palestinian side that insisted on the interim stages in the Accords. The idea was to give the Palestinian Authority time to increase the territory it controlled and to develop the Palestinian economy before final status talks. The Palestinians wanted to go into these final status negotiations in a stronger position than when the talks began in Oslo in 1993. They were not government-to-government talks, but rather government-to-revolutionary-movement negotiations. Consequently, the PLO wanted time to develop the foundations for the Palestinian state which it saw emerging at the end of the process.

In theory, the idea of interim stages held several advantages for both sides. It allowed for the postponement of difficult compromises until the latter part of the process, and it provided time for both sides to develop support for the deal at home. In practice, however, the interim stages provided the groups that opposed the Accords (rejectionists) ample opportunity to derail the process through suicide bomb attacks against Israeli cities carried out by such Islamic radical groups as Hamas and Islamic Jihad. Thus the interim stages actually weakened the prospects for peace. The terrorist attacks damaged the level of support for the Oslo Accords in Israeli society and brought about a strong economic and security response from the Israelis, such as closure of the borders between Israel and the West Bank and Gaza Strip, which damaged the already weak Palestinian economy. The final failure of the notion of interim stages was that the Palestinians saw them exclusively as a way for the Palestinian Authority to strengthen its position. But Israel made similar efforts as well, apparent in its renewed expansion of key settlements in the West Bank. There is a strong case, in fact, for arguing that Israel benefited much more from the interim agreements than the Palestinians, who did not gain the amount of territory in the West Bank they originally believed they would prior to final status talks.

3. Opponents of peace

In retrospect, more careful consideration should have been given to methods for dealing with the rejectionist groups that resorted to violent attacks. A major charge against the Oslo Accords by the Israeli right was that successive Israeli governments had to leave the job of preventing such attacks to Palestinian Authority forces, an approach that clearly did not work. All Israeli governments since 1993 have accused Yasser Arafat of not doing enough to dismantle the infrastructure of such groups, and Israeli military action in recent years – especially the surrounding of Arafat's compound in Ramallah – is a direct consequence of this failure. Though there are no easy solutions to dealing with such groups as Hamas and Islamic Jihad, Arafat needed to make a more concerted attempt to solve this problem, and to back it with increased co-operation with Israeli security forces (particularly in intelligence gathering). In the prevailing climate of mistrust, however, such co-operation was neither easy to develop nor to maintain.

4. Mutual trust and confidence

The late Yitzhak Rabin said that you cannot choose your partners for peace, and that on the White House lawn in 1993 he would rather have shaken the hand of anyone else than Yasser Arafat. He argued that you make peace with enemies, not friends. However, once partners for peace-making have been identified and accepted, then there is a need for a sea change in political thinking to help create an atmosphere of mutual trust between the two parties. The Oslo Accords highlighted the importance of mutual trust and confidence by including much 'constructive ambiguity' in its wording. This was initially designed to allow both sides slightly different interpretations of certain points. Under the government of Yitzhak Rabin, there was enough trust to make the process work. This trust, however, was based on the somewhat false assumption (particularly on Arafat's part) that the Palestinian Authority would obtain the majority of its goals in the final status talks. Under Benjamin Netanyahu and Ariel Sharon, Israel's positions have not radically altered, but the element of trust between the two sides has collapsed.

5. Problems of mediation

As the primary external party in the Middle East peace process, the United States was meant to play three interrelated roles: that of mediator, messenger and guarantor of agreements. The role of the United States in the current crisis in Israel has highlighted three important lessons for future negotiations. First, the need for mediation is a sign of weakness and should not lead to the external party's over-involvement if there is little prospect of success. Next, there has been an over-reliance on shuttle diplomacy involving US special envoys or Secretaries of State, which tends to mask the distance between the parties. The US support of Israel disqualifies it in the eyes of some (mainly Arab and Third World) countries from its role as mediator. But at the moment, no other country qualifies, and any other willing parties, such as the European Union, are viewed by Israel as biased toward the Arab side. Even US President George Bush's call for Israel to pull out of Palestinian areas in the West Bank has not altered the Arab perception that Israel is, in effect, the United States of Israel. Neither the Israelis nor the Palestinians maintained commitments that were made in the Hebron Agreement (1997) and Wye Memorandum (1998), commitments that the United States was meant to guarantee. Consequently, the US was drawn ever deeper into the endless accusations and counter-accusations from each side. As Margaret Thatcher concedes, despite all these problems, the US remains the only viable mediator for the conflict.[6]

6. Peace-making in democracies versus dictatorships

The election of Benjamin Netanyahu in Israel in 1996 was expected to put the Oslo Accords at risk because, as leader of the opposition, Netanyahu had rejected the Accords. During the 1996 election campaign, however, he changed tack, and after assuming office he moved to implement the accords, albeit at a slower pace. The Oslo Accords had survived a change of government in the only Western-style democracy in the region.

Would this continuity have happened had Yasser Arafat been replaced? Probably not, and herein lies the crux of the problem of signing peace deals with non-democratic parties. Palestinian critics of the Oslo Accords argued that they were a private agreement between the Israeli Labour Party (supported by big business) and the right-wing part of the Fatah movement (also with large business interests). Clearly, the failure to expand the basis of support for the agreement on the Israeli side almost led to its downfall. Thus, the biggest lesson we can learn in this area is the need for both parties to build as wide a base of support as possible for the agreement.

7. Building a new society and region

Clearly, a central, if negative, lesson of the Oslo Accords has been the need to translate political advancements in the peace process into visible economic improvements in the lives of the majority of the populations. This failure to provide any peace dividend gave the rejectionist groups an opportunity to further their radical agendas – particularly in areas controlled by the Palestinian Authority, where the radical Islamic groups are funded by the

Gulf States – and attract local support by investing these resources into infrastructure such as Hamas hospitals, charitable works and services.[7] The provision of social services became one of the biggest sources of influence that the organisation had on many Palestinians. It was vital for Israel and the Palestinian Authority to create conditions likely to attract investment. For Israel, this meant not using closures of the West Bank as a political weapon. For the Palestinian Authority, this included developing a modern system of government and successfully addressing the problem of corruption.

Once the war is over, both sides will have to find a new peace-making framework within which to work. Initially, this will involve questions of disengagement, but one day the parties' attention will return to peace-making. This time around, policy-makers should take note of the real lessons of Oslo, and devise much more sophisticated methods of peace-making.

Summarised, they are:

1 Secret diplomacy offers the best opportunity for the most rapid advancement of a post-Oslo peace process, providing the will and means exist on both sides.

2 A new peace deal that includes interim stages needs to be more clearly defined. At the very least, provisions need to be made for dealing with rejectionists who would use the period of the interim stages once again to destabilise the situation on the ground.

3 A degree of personal trust must be developed and maintained. This can be partial, as in the case of Rabin and Arafat, but it should take the form of confidence-building measures such as reinstating security co-operation. Such trust is even more significant when agreements (such as the Oslo Accords) contain a high degree of 'constructive ambiguity', which should be kept to an absolute minimum. Both sides need to make it clear to their respective constituencies exactly what concessions are being made in signing an agreement – no more deception or smokescreens.

4 The role of the external parties in the peace process needs to be

more clearly defined. In short, they should act either as mediators or messengers, but not as guarantors of agreements.

5 An economic peace dividend must underpin any political deal. This is increasingly important because the Palestinian economy is close to collapse and the Israeli economy has moved into recession. Where leaders have had to make significant political compromises, there needs to be the carrot of economic improvement.

By incorporating these five points, any agreements will stand a greater chance of success. The bottom line remains, however: both parties must be motivated to reach an agreement, and the Israeli and Palestinian leaderships must be politically strong enough to implement a prospective deal. Today, both factors are absent. When conditions are ripe, however, there will be fewer excuses for getting it wrong the next time.

Thought also needs to be given to the deeper problems that lie behind this failure. Ignoring the nuts and bolts of the Accords, the key philosophical aim of Oslo was to integrate Israel into the Middle East. Underpinning this hope was the perception that the Arab world was shifting towards political and economic liberalisation, and that the Palestine Liberation Organisation would be at the forefront of the development of democracy and improved human rights (including rights for women) in the Middle East. Palestinians, like Israelis some 40 years earlier, were deemed to be a special case. Surely these people, many of whom had lived in refugee camps for nearly half a century, would demand more than rule by a despot or family dynasty?

The development of Palestinian civil society was, in turn, central to the success of the peace process. Peace between Israel and the Palestinians would be impossible without the development of strong democratic institutions. Leadership was also viewed as a pre-requisite. In the heady days of 1993, it was presumed that the Palestinian leadership, most of whom lived in exile, would come flooding back to the West Bank to develop the political and economic infrastructure for a future state. The reality was different. Those who returned were the political and security élite – one cannot survive without the other. In effect, Yasser Arafat, his political cronies and the various military elements of Fatah set about constructing an elected dictatorship that has come to dominate Palestinian life. The economic élite remained in the Diaspora, reluctant to invest in what many saw as a corrupt regime, while others did try but got burned and withdrew their initial investments. Ironically, it was this group that was keenest to see the peace process succeed. Economic leaders had long since stopped viewing Israel as an obstacle to a strong regional economy. Rather, they viewed it as the gateway to economic success through the development of joint projects that used the region's two greatest commodities: Israeli high-tech knowledge and cheap Arab labour.

Without the needed investment from its own élite, together with the non-arrival of most of the promised aid from Arab countries, Palestinians living in areas under PA control saw their economic position worsen, not improve. In the absence of any economic improvement and with increased potential for civil strife, Arafat and the PA turned their backs on any real democratic reforms (if they had ever embraced them in the first place). Monies were increasingly diverted into developing the two rival security forces which Arafat deemed necessary to maintain power. Opposition was not tolerated. Journalists who attempted to expose the corruption in the PA were barred or thrown in jail.

The PA came to resemble other Arab dictatorships that shape their myths and their place in history through control over the print media and television. Arafat turned to Israel-bashing during times of internal crisis. Since the signing of Oslo – at a time when the leadership of the PA should have been preparing Palestinians for peace – we have witnessed the most overt use of the media for propaganda purposes (anti-Israel) in the Arab world for some time. Even children's cartoons were not exempt from this: one famously depicted Israelis as pigs. Stories that Israel was routinely poisoning the Palestinian water supply were given coverage in news bulletins.

As a result, Palestinians today are no more prepared for peace than before the peace process started. Israel is blamed for the economic ills – the PA leadership is careful to talk up the effects of Israeli closures of the West Bank and Gaza Strip that routinely follow a terrorist attack in Israel. This blame game deflects from the real source of the ills of the Palestinian people – the PA. The Palestinians should put their own house in order before talking peace. In addressing the economic ills, the PA must launch a massive programme of public works to help, for example, alleviate the chronic shortage of housing in the West Bank and Gaza Strip. Research indicates that over 450,000 new housing units are needed to meet demand.[8]

To be fair, democracy in Israel is also under great stress, but at least there is a relatively free and lively press and people hold governments accountable for their actions. The message to the Palestinians should be clear: embrace democracy and human rights, spend less on ensuring the continuation of Yasser Arafat's regime, and develop a genuinely free press that is prepared to debate the issues surrounding peace in a mature and open way. Failure to address these problems will mean that any future peace process or agreement will be a road to nowhere, just as, with the benefit of hindsight, Oslo was from the outset.

Sadly, despite the best intentions of 'the peace-makers', it is the schoolyard bully who continues to dominate in the world of international conflict. The difference between a schoolyard bully and a tough gentleman is that the latter may drive a hard bargain, may even refuse to come to an agreement; but when he does, he gives his word and keeps it. With the schoolyard bully, you must require him to deliver before you do. If you are persuaded to deliver before he does, then chances are he will make you deliver time and time again on other issues before he keeps his side of the original deal – that is, if he ever does.[9] Morally, we must, as the former Mayor of New York, Rudolph Giuliani points out, stop treating the schoolyard bully on the same level as the tough gentleman, as 'roughly morally equivalent'. Sometimes there is a need to negotiate with people who 'are maybe evil, but we shouldn't treat him [Arafat] the same way we treat Rabin, Peres or Barak or Sharon or Netanyahu ... [who] all roughly share our sets of values'.[10] Sadly, Colin Powell appears to differ from Giuliani's position, lumping Arafat and Sharon together, as Bob Woodward points out, as 'two bad guys'.[11]

These bullies strike at the soft underbelly of Western democracy, against targets where attempts at co-existence between two sets of people have resulted in a degree of normalisation that is wholly unacceptable to the mind-set and ideology of the bully. If Israel and other Western-style democracies are to emerge victorious in this conflict, then they must find ways of dealing with these people who specialise in perpetrating the cruellest acts in the name of nationalism or religion.

Cut to the Hebrew University in Jerusalem, an institution famed for its efforts in bringing Arabs and Jews together. The shock of the attack in 2002 on its Frank Sinatra Cafeteria was compounded by the revelation that the bomber was an Israeli Arab employee of the university. Indeed, the following day the very same person was asked to help clean up the blood-covered room and decorate the cafeteria so it could re-open. It transpires that his accomplices came from East Jerusalem, where the university is located. They planted the bomb knowing that it could kill Arabs as well as Jews. The university was chosen because of its openness and the fact that it represented one of the few places in Israel where Israelis and Arabs can easily meet.

The sad conclusion from this example (and countless others) is that the schoolyard bully can always wreck the work of others trying to co-exist. From this we can also deduce that while such people are at liberty there is no hope for meaningful peace in any of the world's major conflicts. Many argue that the best way to get rid of the bully is to form coalitions to oust him. This achieves little other than replacing one bully with another who, given time, will become just as sadistic as his predecessor. What is required is a concerted attack on all bullies (real and potential) using all the military and judicial tools available in the West.

In philosophical terms, the underpinnings of the Western world lean too much towards the libertarianism of John Stuart Mill and the consensualism of Jean-Jacques Rousseau. What is needed is a return to a more Hobbesian approach of the 'absolute sovereign'. More specifically, we need to acknowledge the key problem that Thomas Hobbes underlines: that man is naturally in a state of war, and ceases attacks only when he fears the penalty for getting caught. In practical terms, if we are to protect Western-style democracy, then we must have the courage to actively defend ourselves. This starts at home, with a stronger emphasis on law and order. Here, there are two current problematic trends. The first lies in policing, where too often police and paramilitary forces are not able to take a hard enough line with known bullies. The second concerns the liberal tendency of some judiciaries in terms of applying and interpreting the law. All too often, a smart defence lawyer can work the many loopholes that exist in legal systems to get their client off the hook.

In Israel, robust police and army operations have resulted in many successes against terror networks, both in terms of preventing attacks and in bringing those such as the Hebrew University bombers to justice. The liberal-dominated judiciary, however, has prided itself on overturning government and security force initiatives on security. Israel's Supreme Court is probably the most liberal of any in Western democracies, and clearly needs reforming if Israel is to win its war on terror. Israel needs more coherent and aggressive strategies for dealing with schoolyard bullies. To be sure, this will involve changing our current liberal-based strategies, and will lead to some short-term infringements on civil liberties. The latter, however, is a price worth paying if it prevents barbaric attacks such as those that have taken place in Jerusalem and elsewhere. Perhaps our leaders need to start reading more Hobbes and less Mill and Rousseau. If they did, they might learn that we have not yet inflicted heavy enough defeats on the schoolyard bullies to be a position to solve international conflicts through written political agreements.

Ironically, for years, Israel has been derided by liberal elements of the international community as paranoid about its security. All it had to do to solve its terrorist problem was to make increasingly generous concessions to the Arabs. How wrong this was. Important lessons need to be drawn from the Israeli experience if international terrorism is to be contained. You cannot reduce levels of international terrorism without concerted action – in terms of military intervention, intelligence gathering and political co-operation. In short, a large part of military budgets needs to be devoted to the fight against terror in all nation states. This battle is likely to define the first part of the 21st century, and may take decades rather than years to resolve. Pre-emptive strikes against terrorists and their supporters are vital in preventing attacks.[12] Here, the key question remains: will the American population be able to stomach more aggressive defensive actions being undertaken on their own soil?

The multi-national links of terrorist organisations mean that it is misleading to talk of only one country being singled out as responsible for harbouring terrorists. We live in a global era, and terrorist groups are drawn from many different tribes and states. Intelligence gathering in Israel concentrates more on the individual than on the organisation. US intelligence agencies have over-concentrated on tracking organisations that often change name. Identify likely targets and protect them. In Israel these are perceived as air travel, public transport and major shopping malls. Anyone who has been through security at Ben-Gurion airport in Tel Aviv can vouch for the fact that it would be very difficult for terrorists to get onto a plane. Israel also places an armed guard on each El-Al flight as an added precaution. All Israeli planes (El-Al and charter companies) are fitted with state-of-the-art defence systems, including anti-missile devices. The presence of such technology prevented an Israeli charter plane from being shot down in Kenya in 2002, when terrorists fired heat-seeking missiles at it.

It is vital not to enter into negotiations with terrorist groups or their supporters. Any form of dialogue will be viewed as a sign of weakness by the terrorists.

The bottom line, however, is that it is *impossible* to eradicate all forms of terrorism, particularly that directed against Israel. There will also be deranged radicals willing and able to mount attacks against soft targets. We need to start talking in realistic terms of containing terrorism and cutting off its supply lines. This is where countries that sponsor state terrorism still need to be brought to book. There are major difficulties, however, in achieving this goal. Many of these countries have weapons of mass destruction. Libya's unilateral decision in December 2003 to get rid of its WMDs is an illustration of the results that such international pressure can bring. A recent assessment of Iran claimed that it would have nuclear bombs within five years. Israel adopted a two-pronged approach to dealing with these states: attempting to make the world aware of the links between these states and terrorists, and using military action to destroy the nuclear menace. In 1981, Israeli jets bombed Iraq's nuclear installation near Baghdad. Experts claimed that Saddam Hussein was only months away from becoming a nuclear power. In the long run, Israel may need to take similar action against Iran.

Unfortunately, it is clear that some weapons of mass destruction may have already fallen into the wrong hands. New missile technology means that terrorists in the near future could fire missiles from the relative safety of Iran at targets across Israel. As a result, the next terrorist attack will in all likelihood be different in nature to the September 11 attacks in New York and Washington DC – perhaps a missile fired at an urban population centre or, as many leading Israeli security officials predict, a missile armed with a chemical or biological warhead. In short, Israel needs to put in place mechanisms that first contain the levels of violence. This is more important than a simple one-off military strike on a single state or on training camps – most of which will be empty anyway.

Israel has not succeeded in defeating terrorism. It is able, however, to prevent a lot of the attacks that are mounted. Other countries need to learn quickly that there will be a price to be paid for implementing such preventative measures. Those that argue, for example, that the United States should not abandon its open society are wrong. It must. The nature of the conflict means that US citizens will have to get used to a more intrusive security presence on the street and a more aggressive military campaign abroad. This is a price worth paying if it prevents attacks and saves innocent human life.

Accepting that a political solution to the Israeli–
Palestinian conflict is a long way off, what practical
steps can be taken to help de-escalate the conflict?

There are clear and compelling arguments for physical separation of Israelis and Palestinians as the best means of reducing the violence in the West Bank and Gaza Strip. Any measure short of this is doomed to failure, and may actually inflame a deteriorating situation. A potential plan for achieving separation, in the form of the construction of a security fence between Israel and the PA areas, has taken shape as a last resort to avoid all-out war, and was endorsed by the Israeli Prime Minister in 2003. Below is a basic outline of the complex plan.

Understandings

Agreement is reached over a series of unilateral withdrawals and annexations based on the basic principle that Palestinians – wherever possible – should live in areas under Palestinian Authority control, and that Israelis should live under Israeli sovereignty.

Borders

A slight redrawing of the Green Line – the line between Israel proper and the West Bank – would take place. Israel would seek to expand its coastal plain eastwards and to widen both sides of the Jerusalem corridor, the narrow area that connects Jerusalem with the coastal plain.[13] Israel is at its most vulnerable in these areas, and previous Israeli governments of all political persuasions have called for this modification. Some Palestinian villages that lie within Israel proper would be handed over to the Palestinian Authority. This handover of land that is not in the West Bank would help the process of separation and would be compensation for Israel's annexation of the lands.

There is a philosophical problem here, however, as well as an issue with defining Israeli identity. Writing back in 1986, the Israeli writer and fully paid-up member of the Israeli left,

A.B. Yehoshua, in a magazine interview addressed a well known Israeli Arab poet, Anton Shammas: 'I say to Anton – if you want your full identity, if you want to live in a country that has an independent Palestinian personality, that possesses an original Palestinian culture, rise up, take your belongings, and move 100 metres to the east, to the independent Palestinian state that will lie beside Israel.'[14]

In response, Shammas stated that if and when such a state is created, he did not wish to leave his country and kindred and his father's house for the new lands of a Palestinian state. From this, Shammas aspired to create a single Israeli nationality that would be common to all those living in Israel, both Arab and Jewish.[15] For Yehoshua, however, Israeli identity was inseparable from Jewish identity. In recent years, it has become clear that it is not only the question of the dual identity of Israeli Arabs that drives their desire to remain in Israel, but also economics. The economic position of Israeli Arabs is not very strong, but it remains much better than that of their Palestinian brothers across the Green Line. Consequently, it might prove difficult to convince the Israeli Arabs that a moving of the Green Line is in their best interests.

Settlements

Israel has some 144 settlements in the West Bank and 22 in Gaza. Of the 170,000 residents of these settlements, more than half live in the nine largest settlements. As 90,000 settlers live in the area of greater Jerusalem and in settlements near the Green Line, it would require only relatively minor changes to the Green Line for the majority of settlers to live within Israeli sovereign territory. The settlements in Gaza should be abandoned by Israel, as should other outlying and isolated settlements in the West Bank.

Water

Over 60 per cent of Israel's water originates directly from the West Bank or from aquifers that are connected to the West Bank. Israel does not trust the PA in this area, and will have to supervise the sources or turn to the international community to act as monitors – though many Israelis fear this would set a dangerous precedent. Alternatively, Israel will have to be encouraged, both politically and financially, to develop desalination technology, which in recent years has come down in cost and now produces much more water. It is conceivable that with the correct investment, Israel might not need the aquifers in the West Bank after all.

Physical barriers

Once there is agreement, the physical building of fences and walls – complete with guard towers – can take place along most of the border. Palestinian workers would be prevented from entering Israel. Israelis, in turn, would be barred from PA-controlled areas.

Outstanding issues

This plan makes no attempt to reach agreement on issues related to the peace process, such as the future of Jerusalem and the right of return for Palestinian refugees. The plan resembles an armistice agreement more than a peace plan.

Separation of peoples leaves some deeper questions that obviously need to be addressed.

Critics argue that in Israel it would lead to an almost apartheid-style state in which the rights of the Arabs who remained under Israeli control would be in grave danger. With the United Nations once more debating the 'Does Zionism equal racism?' question, liberals in Israel argue that this is not the time to give the Arabs and the UN ammunition by addressing such emotive subjects. Unfortunately, however, time is running out. The Israelis and Palestinians are at war in all but name, and action needs to be taken now. Separation would, in all proba-bility, lead to the creation of a Palestinian state, with all the problems that would bring. At present, however, this is not the major issue. There is a *de facto* state already in existence, and separation may force Palestinian leader Yasser Arafat's hand. Today, he is telling his people they are involved in a war of liberation for a Palestinian state. Separation may just expose this myth.

On the ground, it will be difficult to enforce separation. There will be terror attacks as groups try to destabilise the situation. The violence, however, will be more limited and localised than we are witnessing at present. One of the major successes of the Israeli army in recent years has been to avoid causing serious Palestinian casualties by withdrawing from potential flashpoints. If the forces were further separated, this would increase the chances of reducing the violence to more acceptable levels. In Israel, separation would vindicate those who argue that Israel will have to rely on an 'iron wall' to protect itself, over those such as Shimon Peres who advocate integration and co-operation. Former Prime Minister Ehud Barak's recent comments on the subject in *Newsweek* were very telling. Barak does not believe that Arafat will ever agree to peace, and consequently separation is inevitable. Policy-makers need to abandon the dead end of the current peace process before it is too late and accept that, given Arafat's reluctance to end the conflict with Israel, separation is the only real way of preventing a major war.

What are the demographic implications of any separation plans?

By the year 2020, Jews will constitute a minority in the geographical area between the River Jordan and the Mediterranean sea. This startling fact has sent shock waves through the Israeli political establishment and is already having a profound effect in reshaping the political map of Israel. According to a recent report, Jews will constitute around 40 per cent of the population in this area, while Arabs and 'others' will make up around 60 per cent. The report, published by an academic at Haifa University in Israel, proposes a map of separation between Arab and Jew as the best way of ensuring the future of the Jewish state. Today, the old political lines in Israel – between those that favour exchanging land for peace and those that believe in Greater Israel (a Jewish state on both banks of the River Jordan) – are being redrawn. As no deal appears likely with Yasser Arafat in the foreseeable future, many leading Israelis have called for Israel to unilaterally address the demographic time bomb. This is code for a separation plan – the current hot potato, as politicians argue over how effective it would be at increasing Israeli security. In private, however, security is code for demography – the two are highly related. Israeli leaders are concerned that the higher birth rate among the Arab population is the biggest threat to Israeli security.

Two well known right-wing proponents of 'Greater Israel', President Katsav and the Mayor of Jerusalem, Ehud Olmert, both came out in favour of unilateral separation from the Palestinians. On the surface, their reasons for supporting the plan were populist – the plan enjoys strong support among an increasingly anxious Israeli population. Most Israelis believe that by separating themselves from the major Palestinian population centres and building physical barriers such as fences, they will be allowed to go about their daily business without the fear of being killed or maimed. On a deeper level, however, we are witnessing the realisation among the Israeli right that the dream of 'Greater Israel' is over. The cost in terms of the threat to the Jewish nature of the state of Israel is too high a price to pay. Today, the choice is simple: Zionism or Greater Israel. You can no longer have both. Many leading members of the right in Israel had clung to the idea that even after Israel's troop withdrawal from the West Bank, Israel would one day return and exercise full sovereignty over these lands. These dreams are unrealisable unless we witness an exodus of Palestinians from these areas on a par with that of the 1948 war. Another leading Likudnik, Dan Meridor, has endorsed the separation plan, despite his well known personal commitment to 'Greater Israel'. Meridor argues that Israel has to deal with the dual problems of security and demography now – and that this will entail the evacuation of some of the Israeli settlements in the West Bank and Gaza Strip.

The left in Israel is experiencing other tensions. It is struggling to come to terms with the fact that Yasser Arafat duped them. In his first political speech since leaving office, former PM Ehud

Barak stressed that he now knows that Arafat was never a partner for peace, and never will be. If Barak has learnt his lesson, many on the left have not. Leading architect of the Oslo Accords Yossi Beilin still clings to the hope that there will be a peace deal reached between Israel and the Palestinian Authority along the lines of the 2000 Camp David summit. Beilin and the left are taking a big gamble. If no agreement is reached in the next twenty years – as appears a distinct possibility – then, as we have seen, Jews will be a minority in the lands from the River Jordan to the Mediterranean. Beilin counters this argument by stating that, if Israel does instigate a unilateral separation from the Palestinians, then it would be closing the door on ever reaching a peace agreement with them. For many Israelis, this particular risk appears well worth taking.

New groupings are being formed in Israeli politics that transcend party colours. We have already seen the formation of a group that supports separation and that draws leading names from across the political spectrum. Even Ariel Sharon called for a copy of the report and the accompanying separation map that details how Israel can defuse the demographic time bomb. Many argued that the price that Israel paid for making peace would transform its political and party systems. What was unforeseen was that the price for not reaching peace is likely to be just as significant. The transformation needs to come quickly, as Israel needs to regroup and make its choice between separation or the long-term gamble that Arafat or his successors will make peace with Israel. For the Palestinians there is no hurry, but for Israel it is a race against time. Israeli leaders need to act decisively and, despite all the logistical and political problems involved, opt to unilaterally separate the Jewish state from the Palestinians.

What about a re-division of Jerusalem?

Today, as in most of its long history, Jerusalem is at the centre of a war between two peoples who wish to control it and its holy places. For Israelis, the majority of whom are secular in nature, Jerusalem represents the crowning glory of the Zionist dream to build a state for the Jews. For the Palestinians, Jerusalem also represents the centrepiece of their nationalist aspirations. In the nationalist literature of both sides, a state without Jerusalem as its eternal capital is described as a body without a heart. Delving deeper, the issue of the future status of Jerusalem is not exclusively about nationalism or even religion, but rather the myths, rituals and symbols that dominate Middle Eastern history and shape contemporary opinions and events. Perhaps the most significant of these are the symbols. In this world of winners or losers in conflicts, whoever controls the city at the top of the mountain is seen as the victor, while the defeated party has to make do with Jericho or Ramallah. In short, Jerusalem is a symbol of strength and a link with past conquests, a living reminder of everything that went before and the perils of losing control over the city.

Somebody once asked me why so many attacks and counter-attacks have taken place in Jerusalem, or within its wider municipal boundaries. The answer is simple: attackers tend to go for the heart. The symbolism involved in launching a successful attack on Jerusalem has, in history, made or broken military campaigns. In Israel's War of Independence in 1948, the Arabs devoted much of their resources to ensuring that the siege of the city was not broken. Without Jerusalem, they argued (correctly), there would be no meaningful Jewish state. West Jerusalem held out against all the odds and thus became one of the most important Jewish symbols of that war. In the contemporary world, Jerusalem is the front line of the Arab–Israeli conflict – in this case, the Israeli–Palestinian war of attrition. It is important when analysing recent events to place them in the deeper context outlined above, if one is to fully understand their significance.

Israel's seizing of the unofficial Foreign Ministry of the Palestinian Authority in Jerusalem's Orient House in 2002 was undertaken on one level to remind the Palestinians that Israel still controls the entire city. The current Israeli government regards the previous government's decision to hand over land on the outskirts of the city to full Palestinian control as a terrible mistake. On a deeper level, it was intended to send a clear signal that the current government will not accept, at this stage, an official PLO presence in the city. Israeli actions in taking over Orient House were undertaken not for strategic or political reasons, but rather for these deeper symbolic reasons. The Palestinian leadership fully understand the deeper message behind the Israeli actions. For them, a state without a heart is not worth having. As previously mentioned, the Palestinians view Israeli housing projects as political settlements with the aim of encircling the city and cutting off Arab East Jerusalem from other nearby Palestinian population centres such as Ramallah. Despite Israeli efforts in Jerusalem, it is losing the demographic battle for control of the city. Birth rates among the Arab residents of East Jerusalem, while lower than among the Palestinian Arabs of the West Bank, remain considerably higher than among the Jewish population of West Jerusalem (including the ultra-orthodox Jews). On top of this, in recent years there has been something of a backlash from secular Jews living in the city about the increasing dominance of the culture of the ultra-orthodox. Many secular Jewish residents of Jerusalem are choosing to move outside the city. This has, as a result, further weakened Israel's long-term prospects of Jerusalem becoming a Jewish city.

The culture of language and the meaning of war

There are three seemingly quite separate wars being fought in the Middle East at present. For the sake of simplicity, let's say that one is being conducted in Hebrew, another in Arabic and a third one in English. Each is clearly illustrated in the media coverage of the conflict in Israel, the Arab world and the West. The basis and subtext of each war is different, but few people appear able to read between the lines and deduce the true nature of the conflict. The differences are apparent in the terminology used by the protagonists. For Israel, this war is a continuation of 'ebb and flow', the term it uses to describe the Palestinian violence which started in October 2000. The Palestinians prefer the more loaded term Intifada (uprising). Israel terms its actions as defensive, the Palestinians' as offensive. Israel defines its operations as reprisal raids, the Palestinians' as reoccupation. Israel defines the conflict as being about Palestinian nationalism, while the Palestinians talk in terms of a state (this is meant to reassure Israelis that they still subscribe to a two-state solution). Israel makes the demand for reciprocity, the Palestinians for more concessions.

These linguistic differences are important when examining the deeper rationales for the war.

The Hebrew version of the war is not about Israel attempting to defeat the Palestinians. Rather, it chronicles a defensive response to the widely held belief among the Israeli political and military élite that Yasser Arafat is attempting to impose a solution on Israel by unleashing tactical violence to win political concessions. In this respect, Arafat has done what no Arab leader since the late President Nasser of Egypt managed some 35 years ago – namely, unified Israelis. On a recent visit to Israel, I was struck by the return of a feeling of national awareness and solidarity. Arafat, in attempting to push Palestinian nationalism, may have woken a sleeping giant. Yes, there are disagreements, but these are over tactics, and not war aims.

In Arabic, the war is viewed as one of national liberation of the Palestinian state from Jewish occupation. Surprisingly, given the fact that Arafat and the vast majority of the PA are secular in nature, there has been a strong religious streak to the justification for the war. This may well be because, in terms of justification, there is very little less that a Palestinian leader who was offered such a state by an Israeli Prime Minister at Camp David in 2000 can do. In recent speeches in Arabic, Arafat has increasingly used religious and historical references to Islamic lands, sending martyrs to Jerusalem, and talking of Palestine in terms of all the lands to the west of the River Jordan.

The Arabic press does not mention the Camp David summit of 2000, or the fact that some 80 per cent of Israelis still accept the creation of the Palestinian state. Ehud Barak, the then Israeli PM who offered these concessions, is portrayed as a hard-liner, and the veteran dove Shimon Peres as a puppet of Ariel Sharon. Interestingly, the press in some Arab states argues that Arafat was duped by Israel into signing the Oslo Accords in 1993, and that Israel has done little to enhance Palestinian security – a novel departure from Western conventional wisdom. In closed, non-democratic societies, however, the power of such messages remains very strong. Most Arabs I talk to (and these tend to be academics) really believe that Israel is to blame for most Arab hardships.

The English version of the war is the crudest, with complex issues analysed in black and white. At the centre is the good guy–bad guy division, questions of right and wrong, and subjective interpretations of the concept of justice. Israel is often portrayed as the bad guy, and its actions in the West Bank are viewed as wrong. Many Western journalists attempt to give balance to what they see as the two central issues of the conflict – Israeli security needs and Palestinian nationalism – but, like their political leaders, they fail to comprehend the deeper issues involved. At times, their reporting is too underpinned by Western rational thought. They call for both sides to agree to address both security and nationalist issues, or in other words for an Israeli withdrawal in return for a promise by Yasser Arafat to end Palestinian violence. If only it were that simple.

The truth is that this very Middle Eastern war is about gaining strategic advantage prior to agreeing political terms. Israel is saying to the Palestinians, 'remember you cannot destroy us, and that you must lower your expectations in the political negotiations to come'. In layman's terms, Arafat and his paramilitaries cannot lay siege to Israeli cities and settlements and force it into political concessions. For the Palestinians, the war represents the completion of the strategy started in October 2000 of using violence to obliterate the memory of Camp David and win back Arab and international sympathy for Arafat and the Palestinian cause. The international community seems to miss these simple points. It needs to wake up to the true nature of the conflict if it is to help disengage the two sides and start some form of political dialogue in the future.

Perhaps if Arafat, Barak and Clinton had all spoken the same language at their meetings in the hut at Camp David, then they would have at least understood the futility of continuing with the negotiations. This could, to some degree, have prevented raising the expectations of their respective constituencies that there was a chance for a final agreement to emerge from the talks. Instead, Arafat spoke as someone who saw the need for national struggle, Barak spoke as victor, and Clinton spoke the international language of ignorance. At a recent academic conference in Tel Aviv University that analysed the events of Camp David, a rather defensive-looking Barak sat through nearly the entire proceedings. His input at the end says much about this language of the victor. To summarise, in basic terms he argued that he would not have done anything differently. In earlier comments he argued that the talks were a useful laboratory experiment that showed Arafat once and for all to be an enemy of Israel. It is fair to say that much of what Barak says today is done with one eye on his future return to public life in Israel, but still it resonates as the language of the victor.

To many Arabs, Ariel Sharon is the cheerleader of the victors' club. In reality, this is far removed from the true picture. Sharon lacks the bravado and arrogance of a Barak-type figure. His is the language of the insecure. Israel, for all its progress over its 55-year history, remains extremely isolated and vulnerable in a dangerous neighbourhood that is growing increasingly hazardous as natural resources such as water become scarcer, and where long-term demographic trends favour the Arabs. Sharon knows that Israel needs to both strengthen its position in the region and achieve some type of settlement with the Arab states and the Palestinians. The trick for Israel, and his leadership, is to buy a little more time in the hope that future generations of Arabs will soften their stance to the presence of Israel among their brothers.

To those who view Sharon as a hate figure – and here there are many Jews as well as Arabs – a tale comes to mind from the Knesset. During the post-Oslo period, Sharon was the only leader of the right who recognised that the clock could not be turned back, and he spent much of the period walking around the lobbies of the Knesset carrying armfuls of maps, pausing to show them to anyone who would listen. The maps contained his vision of a political solution to the Palestinian problem and they embraced, albeit in code ('entity' was the substitute word used for 'state'), the concept of a Palestinian state. Years later, in the summer of 2003, Sharon made his daring comments to a packed Likud meeting about the Israeli 'occupation' of Arab lands. To say this in the lions' den of Israeli nationalism took courage and, most of all, vision. If Sharon can find a Palestinian partner who shares the language of the insecure, then there may be a chance for progress. At the time of going to press, it remains unclear whether the Palestinian Prime Minister Abu Ala is such a figure.

Throughout Israel's history, the clock has appeared to be resting at one minute to midnight. In retrospect, much of the decision-making that has taken place in Israel over the years has been governed by the need to secure the state's survival. This has placed a great deal of emphasis on the short term over more sophisticated long-term planning. As a result, Israel has made more than its fair share of mistakes, ranging from the Lebanon war to Rabin's decision to negotiate under fire. Israelis continue to grumble about health care and the cost of living, while facing increasing risks to their personal security. The gap between the rich and poor in the country continues to grow at an alarming rate. The middle class do all they can not to catch a bus, while those in poorer neighbourhoods have little choice but to play the Russian roulette game of taking a bus back and forth to their place of work. Though there are no figures on this, it is fairly certain that of those 750 Israelis who have died in the recent war, a disproportionate number could be classified as poor.

Israel needs peace to address its growing poverty gap and other issues. But most of all, Israel needs the conflict with the Arabs to end in order to secure its existence. The question remains: how much do Arab regimes need the conflict to end? If history has taught us one thing it is that the Arabs do not respond well to military defeat, and in the political arena the Arab–Israeli conflict remains a useful card to play in times of trouble for many Arab leaders.[16] Until this changes, there would appear to be little chance of a comprehensive peace in the region. Despite improvements in Israel's situation over the past decades, the clock today still rests at one minute to midnight.

Postscript

At the time of this book going to press, there were signs that at least some of the lessons of the Oslo Accords had been learnt by the original negotiators. The signing of the Geneva Accords on 1 December 2003 by an Israeli delegation that included many of the architects of the now defunct Oslo Accords (now sitting on the opposition benches in Israel) and a Palestinian delegation that included individuals close to Yasser Arafat, however, raises important questions about peace-making strategies. Ignoring the polemic arguments about whether or not these negotiations should have taken place at all, to the casual observer of the conflict the most salient question remains: why can't the respective Israeli and Palestinian governments adopt this agreement as the basis for a final status deal? Deeper questions surround the issue of how the Accords' sponsors aim to develop public support for the difficult concessions that the agreement calls for both sides to make. And how useful – or otherwise – are the Accords to both the Israeli Prime Minister Ariel Sharon and his Palestinian counterpart, Abu Ala?

Critics of the agreement have pointed to the fact that the negotiators from both sides acted independently of their respective governments, and consequently that the agreement does not reflect the political realities of the day. Much has been made in the local media about the so-called cynical motives of the participants who, it is charged, were looking to re-invigorate their political careers. Take, for example, Yossi Beilin, the main Israeli architect of the Oslo Accords, who is charged with blatantly using the publicity from the Geneva Accords to aid his campaign to become leader of the new Social-Democratic Party in Israel. Anyone, however, who has met Dr Beilin would not doubt his commitment to peace-making and the personal danger he has put himself in. The same can equally be said about the Palestinian delegation. The disturbing images of some members of the delegation being jostled and spat at by Palestinians as they left Gaza to attend the signing ceremony serve as a timely reminder of their political and physical bravery.

The high-profile signing ceremony in Switzerland, attended by Jimmy Carter, Mikhail Gorbachev and a who's who of international peace-making, was clearly designed to maximise the public pressure on Sharon and Arafat to endorse at least parts of the agreement. Here, neither Sharon nor Arafat want to comment on the substance of the Accords for fear of weakening their respective negotiating positions in future talks.

In private, Arafat would accept the Accords as the basis for ending the conflict with Israel. Unlike the Oslo Accords, which reflected the political and economic weakness of the PLO at the time – allowing Israel to effectively attempt to impose a solution to the conflict – the Geneva Accords take their precedent from the Camp David Agreement signed by Israel and Egypt. There, Israel offered more than the political realities of the day dictated they had to, in order to secure a deal with President Sadat. For Palestinians who have not been using the peace process as a cover for the piecemeal destruction of Israel, the Geneva Accords offer almost everything they demand, except the full right of return for refugees: a state including nearly all of the West Bank and Gaza Strip (the latter expanded in exchange for Israel keeping two large settlement blocks); half of Jerusalem (including the Dome of the Rock); and control over the water sources in the West Bank. In short, the guiding principle of the Israeli team was to create a just and therefore stable peace between the two sides. Better to be generous now rather than see an unstable peace collapse in ten or twenty years. Others, of course, would say that such thinking is like playing Russian roulette with Israel's future. The current Israeli Prime Minister, in private, sits somewhere between the two viewpoints here. Remember, it was his support for Mena-chem Begin during the Camp David negotiations that persuaded Begin to offer Egypt all of Sinai, and for Israel to agree to dismantle the Jewish settlements there.

Learning an important lesson from the Oslo Accords, both the Israeli and Palestinian delegations have already started to educate their respective populations about the merits of the agreements, and the extent of the concessions that each side has to make. There has already been a mail-drop to every Israeli household with leaflets detailing the plan and asking for support. Details of the Accords have been published in the Palestinian press (the small print of Oslo was never publicised in this way).

In public, both Israeli and Palestinian leaders make all the usual noises about the US-sponsored road map for peace being the only peace plan in town. In private, however, both are keen to use the impetus that the Accords have generated to push for an agreement. Both leaders also understand that when an official government-to-government agreement is eventually reached, it will resemble the Geneva Accords. It is for this reason that the agreement may prove to be historic. Only time will tell if this is the case, or whether the Accords merely represent another false dawn in bringing about an end to the conflict.

Notes

Introduction

1 *The West Wing*, 'The College Kids', 2 October 2002 (US airing).
2 Ian McIntyre, *The Proud Doers: Israel After Twenty Years*, London: BBC, 1968, p. 98.
3 Martin Gilbert's works on maps remain the best available source in English. See Martin Gilbert, *The Routledge Atlas of the Arab–Israeli Conflict*, London and New York: Routledge, 2003.
4 'Admit it: Israeli Cities Have Become War Zones', *National Post*, Toronto, 28 January 2002.
5 John Simpson, *News From No Man's Land: Reporting the World*, London: Macmillan, 2002, p. 228.
6 Bernard Lewis, *The Middle East: 2000 Years of History from the Rise of Christianity to the Present Day*, London: Phoenix, 1996, p. 368.

Chapter 1

1 David Halberstam, *War in a Time of Peace: Bush, Clinton and the Generals*, London: Bloomsbury, 2003, p. 484.
2 Hillary Rodham Clinton, *Living History: Memoirs*, London: Headline, 2003, pp. 517–18.
3 Elie Kedourie, *The Crossman Confessions and Other Essays*, London and New York: Mansell, 1984, p. 226.
4 Martin Gilbert, *Israel: A History*, London: Black Swan, 1999, p. 3.
5 On the Ottoman Empire, see: Lord Kinross, *The Ottoman Empire*, London: Folio Books, 2003.
6 Lord Kinross, *The Ottoman Empire*, pp. 477–80.
7 Mitchell Cohen, *Zion and State: Nation, Class and the Shaping of Modern Israel*, Oxford and New York: Blackwell, 1987, p. 71.
8 On the development of early Zionist thought and organisation, see: David Vital, *Zionism: the Formative Years*, Oxford and New York: Oxford University Press, 1982.
9 Adam Garfinkle, *Politics and Society in Modern Israel: Myths and Realities*, Armonk, NY: M.E. Sharpe, 1997, p. 86.

10 On the effects of the fall of the Ottoman Empire on the Middle East, see: David Fromkin, *A Peace to End All Peace: The Fall of the Ottoman Empire and the Creation of the Modern Middle East*, London: Phoenix Press, 2000.

11 Gabriel Sheffer, 'British Colonial Policy-Making Towards Palestine, 1929–1939', *Middle Eastern Studies*, Volume 14, Number 3, October 1978, p. 320.

12 See: Isaiah Friedman, *Palestine: a Twice Promised Land – The British, the Arabs and Zionism*, New Brunswick and London: Transaction Publishers, 2000, p. 219.

13 For a useful summary of the change of Feisal's position, see: Walter Laqueur, *A History of Zionism*, New York: Schocken Books, 1989, pp. 237–8.

14 Mark Tessler, *A History of the Israeli–Palestinian Conflict*, Bloomington and Indianapolis: Indiana University Press, 1994, p. 210.

15 Winston Churchill, speech to the House of Commons, 1 August 1946, in Winston S. Churchill (selected and edited), *Never Give In: the Best of Winston Churchill's Speeches*, London: Pimlico, 2003, p. 426.

16 For more on the complexities of the British decision, see: Miriam Joyce Haron, 'The British Decision to Give the Palestine Question to the United Nations', *Middle Eastern Studies*, Volume 17, Number 2, April 1981, pp. 242–8.

17 Naomi Shepherd, *Ploughing Sand: British Rule in Palestine, 1917–1948*, London: John Murray, 1999, p. 244.

Chapter 2

1 For a detailed summary of Truman's motives, and the importance of the Cold War setting in framing US policy towards Palestine, see: Bruce J. Evensen, 'Truman, Palestine and the Cold War', *Middle Eastern Studies*, Volume 28, Number 1, January 1992, pp. 120–56.

2 Elie Kedourie, *The Chatham House Version and Other Middle Eastern Studies*, London: Weidenfeld and Nicolson, 1970, p. 230.

3 Benny Morris, 'The Causes and Character of the Arab Exodus from Palestine: The Israeli Defence Forces Intelligence Branch Analysis of June 1948', *Middle Eastern Studies*, Volume 22, Number 1, January 1986, p. 18.

4 It is important to acknowledge that Arab historiography claims that there was an expulsion plan. This is a case of drawing different conclusions from the same documentary evidence. For a summary of this position, see: Nur Masalha, 'A Critique of Benny Morris', in Illan Pappe (edited), *The Israel–Palestine Question: Rewriting Histories*, London: Routledge, 1999, pp. 211–20.

5 Yaacov Bar-Siman-Tov, 'Ben-Gurion and Sharett: Conflict Management and Great Power Constraints in Israeli Foreign Policy', *Middle Eastern Studies*, Volume 23, Number 3, July 1988, pp. 330–1.

6 Michael B. Oren, 'Secret Egypt–Israel Peace Initiatives Prior to the Suez Campaign', *Middle Eastern Studies*, Volume 26, Number 3, July 1990, p. 366.

7 Madeline Albright, *Madam Secretary: a Memoir*, London: Macmillan, 2003, p. 484.

8 Minutes of meeting of PLO Central Committee, 9–10 September 2000, *Al-Hourriyah*, Number 821, 17 September 2000, p. 4.

9 Ghada Hashem Talhami, *Palestinian Refugees: Pawns to Political Actors*, New York: Nova Science Publishers, 2003, p. 171.

Chapter 3

1 Uri Bailer, *Between East and West: Israel's Foreign Policy Orientation, 1948–1956*, Cambridge: Cambridge University Press, 1990, pp. 15–16.

2 Enoch Powell, *Reflections: Selected Writings and Speeches of Enoch Powell*, London: Bellew Publishing, 1992, p. 257.

3 Robert D. Kaplan, *The Arabists: the Romance of an American Elite*, New York: Free Press, 1993, pp. 98–9.

4 For a military history of the war, see: Chaim Herzog, *The Arab–Israeli Wars: War and Peace in the Middle East from the War of Independence Through Lebanon*, New York: Vintage, 1984, pp. 109–42.

5 Keith Kyle, *Suez*, New York: St Martins Press, 1991, p. 549.

6 Henry Kissinger, *Diplomacy*, New York: Touchstone, 1994, p. 538.

7 On Israel's complex political and economic history with the EU and wider Europe, see: Howard M. Sachar, *Israel and Europe: An Appraisal in History*, New York: Knopf, 1999.

8 Margaret Thatcher, *Statecraft: Strategies for a Changing World*, London: HarperCollins, 2002, p. 246.

9 On Blair's private conversations with Arafat, see: Peter Stothard, *30 Days at the Heart of Blair's War*, London: HarperCollins, 2003, pp. 47–8.

10 Avner Cohen, *Israel and the Bomb*, New York: Columbia University Press, 1998, p. 137.

11 Samuel P. Huntington, *The Clash of Civilizations and the Remaking of World Order*, New York: Simon and Schuster, 1996, p. 184.

12 Majid Khadduri and Edmund Ghareeb, *War in the Gulf, 1990–1991: the Iraq–Kuwait Conflict and its Implications*, Oxford and New York: Oxford University Press, 1997, p. 171.

13 Philip Bobbitt, *The Shield of Achilles: War, Peace and the Course of History*, London: Penguin, 2002, p. 686.

14 Edward Said, *The Politics of Dispossession: the Struggle for Palestinian Self-Determination, 1969–1994*, London: Chatto and Windus, 1994, p. 90.

15 Yossi Beilin, *Touching Peace: From the Oslo Accord to a Final Agreement*, London: Weidenfeld and Nicolson, 1999, pp. 249–50.

16 Author's interview with Yitzhak Shamir, Tel Aviv, 17 August 1994.

17 Abraham Ben Zvi, *Decade of Transition: Eisenhower, Kennedy and the Origins of the American–Israeli Alliance*, Chichester, West Sussex: Columbia University Press, 1998, p. 6.

18 Bernard Lewis, *The Multiple Identities of the Middle East*, London: Weidenfeld and Nicolson, 1998, pp. 134–5.

19 Edward Said, *Orientalism: Western Conceptions of the Orient*, London: Penguin, 1995, pp. 318–19.

20 Martin Edelman, 'The New Israeli Constitution', *Middle Eastern Studies*, Volume 36, Number 2, April 2000, p. 12.

21 For background on Reagan and Bitburg, see: Edmund Morris, *Dutch: A Memoir of Ronald Reagan*, London: HarperCollins, 1999, pp. 521–6.

22 Neill Lochery, 'Israel and Turkey: Deepening Ties and Strategic Implications 1995–98', *Israel Affairs*, Volume 5, Number 1, Autumn 1998, p. 45.

23 William B. Quandt, *Peace Process and the Arab–Israeli Conflict Since 1967*, Berkeley: The Brookings Institution, University of California Press, 2001, p. 1.

24 David Frum, *The Right Man: An Inside Account of the Surprise Presidency of George W. Bush*, London: Weidenfeld and Nicolson, 2003, p. 246.

25 David Frum, ibid.

26 Bob Woodward, *Bush at War*, London: Pocket Books, 2003, p. 297.

Chapter 4

1 Michael Walzer, *Just and Unjust Wars: a Moral Argument with Historical Illustrations*, New York: Basic Books, 1992, p. 84.

2 Amnon Rubinstein, *The Zionist Dream Revisited: From Herzl to Gush Emunim and Back*, New York: Schocken Books, 1984, p. 76.

3 Nazih N. Ayubi, *Over-stating the Arab State: Politics and Society in the Middle East*, London and New York: I.B. Tauris, 1995, p. 143.

4 Even scholars sympathetic to the Arab cause such as Albert Hourani are forced to concede that such reports were 'probably' incorrect. Albert Hourani, *A History of the Arab Peoples*, London: Faber and Faber, 1991, p. 413.

5 Samir A. Mutawi, *Jordan in the 1967 War*, Cambridge: Cambridge University Press, 1987, p. 109.

6 For a detailed account of the fighting and the road to war, see: Michael B. Oren, *Six Days of War: June 1967 and the Making of the Modern Middle East*, London: Penguin Books, 2003.

7 Abdel Magid Farid, *Nasser: the Final Years*, Reading: Ithaca Press, 1996, pp. 143–4.

8 Walid Kazziha, 'The Impact of Palestine on Arab Politics', in Giacomo Luciani (edited), *The Arab State*, London: Routledge, 1990, p. 306.

9 Sami Al-Khazender, *Jordan and the Palestine Question: the Role*

of Islamic and Left Forces in Shaping Foreign Policy-making, Reading: Ithaca Press, 1997, p. 45.

10 Shimon Peres, *Battling for Peace: Memoirs*, London: Weidenfeld and Nicolson, 1995, p. 311.

11 Moshe Zak, 'Israel and Jordan: Strategically Bound', *Israel Affairs*, Volume 3, Number 1, Autumn 1996, p. 53.

12 Henry Kissinger, *Diplomacy*, p. 527.

13 On socio-economic gaps between the Ashkenazi Jews and the Orientals, see: Sammy Smooha, *Israel: Pluralism and Conflict*, London: Routledge and Kegan Paul, 1978, pp. 153–63.

14 Amos Oz, *In the Land of Israel*, London: Flamingo, 1984, p. 41.

15 On Begin's early days, see: Menachem Begin, *The Revolt*, London: W.H. Allen, 1983.

16 On the original various types of settlements, see: David Newman, 'Spatial Structures and Ideological Change in the West Bank', in David Newman (edited), *The Impact of Gush Emunim: Politics and Settlement in the West Bank*, London and Sydney: Croom Helm, 1985, pp. 172–81.

17 Mohammed Shadid, 'A Housing Strategy for the Palestinian Territories', in A.B. Zahlan (edited), *The Reconstruction of Palestine: Urban and Rural Development*, London and New York: Kegan Paul International, 1997, p. 49.

18 Chaim Herzog, *Living History: The Memoirs of a Great Israeli Freedom-Fighter, Soldier, Diplomat and Statesman*, London: Weidenfeld and Nicolson, 1997, p. 187.

19 Shabtai Teveth, *Moshe Dayan: the Soldier, the Man, the Legend*, London: Quartet Books, 1974, p. 379.

20 Teveth, *Moshe Dayan*, p. 380.

21 Peter Mansfield, *A History of the Middle East*, New York: Viking, 1991, p. 296.

22 Uri Bar-Joseph, 'Israel's 1973 Intelligence Failure', in P.R. Kumaraswamy (edited), *Revisiting the Yom Kippur War*, London and Portland: Frank Cass, 2000, p. 13.

23 On the failure of the Israeli intelligence services prior to the war, see: Uri Bar-Joseph, 'Israel's 1973 Intelligence Failure', pp. 11–35.

24 Chaim Herzog, *The War of Atonement: The Inside Story of the Yom Kippur War 1973*, London: Greenhill Books, 1998, p. 41.

25 Chaim Herzog, *Living History*, p. 187.

26 Patrick Seale, *Asad: the Struggle for the Middle East*, Berkeley: University of California Press, 1988, p. 206.

27 Moshe Ma'oz, *Syria and Israel: From War to Peacemaking*, Oxford and New York: Oxford University Press, 1995, p. 183.

28 See, for example: *Newsweek*, 25 February 1975.

29 On the US sponsored negotiations, see: Itamar Rabinovich, *The Brink of Peace: the Israeli–Syrian Negotiations*, Princeton: Princeton University Press, 1999.

30 Yitzhak Rabin, *The Rabin Memoirs*, Berkeley: University of California Press, 1996, pp. 274–5.

31 Neill Lochery, *The Israeli Labour Party: In the Shadow of the Likud*, Reading: Ithaca Press, 1997, pp. 44–59.

32 On the history of the Likud and its predecessor parties, see: Yonathan Shapiro: *The Road to Power: Herut Party in Israel*, Albany: State University of New York Press, 1991.

33 On Jabotinsky, see: Shmuel Katz, *Lone Wolf: a Biography of Vladimir Ze'ev Jabotinsky* (two volumes), New York: Barricade Books, 1996.

34 P.J. Vatikiotis, *The History of Modern Egypt: from Muhammad Ali to Mubarak*, London: Weidenfeld and Nicolson, 1991, p. 415.

35 Ezer Weizman, *The Battle for Peace*, London: Bantam Books, 1981, p. 86.

36 Boutros Boutros-Ghali, *Egypt's Road to Jerusalem: a Diplomat's Story of the Struggle for Peace in the Middle East*, New York: Random House, 1997, p. 136.

37 Kenneth W. Stein, *Heroic Diplomacy: Sadat, Kissinger, Carter, Begin and the Quest for Arab–Israeli Peace*, New York and London: Routledge, 1999, p. 252.

38 Richard Holbrooke, *To End a War*, New York: Random House, 1998, p. 205.

39 Ephraim Dowek, *Israeli–Egyptian Relations 1980–2000*, London and Portland: Frank Cass, 2001, p. 162.

40 Mohammed Heikal, *Autumn of Fury: the Assassination of Sadat*, London: Corgi, 1983, pp. 221–2.

41 For an account of the legal and political controversy surrounding Resolution 242, see: Musa Mazzawi, *Palestine and the Law: Guidelines for the Resolution of the Arab–Israeli Conflict*, Reading: Ithaca Press, 1997, pp. 199–238.

Chapter 5

1 For detailed analysis and background, see: Peter Medding, *The Founding of Israeli Democracy, 1948–1967*, Oxford: Oxford University Press, 1990, pp. 125–30.

2 Itamar Rabinovich, *The War for Lebanon 1970–85*, Ithaca and London: Cornell University Press, 1985, p. 59.

3 Ze'ev Schiff and Ehud Ya'ari, *Israel's Lebanon War*, London and Sydney: George Allen and Unwin, 1984, p. 304.

4 Ze'ev Schiff and Ehud Ya'ari, *Israel's Lebanon War*, ibid.

5 Dan Bavly and Eliahu Salpeter, *Fire in Beirut: Israel's War in Lebanon with the PLO*, New York: Stein and Day, 1984, p. 155.

6 Dan Bavly and Eliahu Salpeter, *Fire in Beirut*, p. 156.

7 Robert Fisk, *Pity the Nation: Lebanon at War*, Oxford: Oxford University Press, 1990.

8 Peter Medding, *The Founding of Israeli Democracy*, p. 128.
9 Harry Hurwitz, *Begin: a Portrait*, Washington DC: B'nai B'rith Books, 1994, pp. 230–1.
10 Conor Cruise O'Brien, *The Siege: The Story of Israel and Zionism*, London: Paladin–Grafton Books, 1988, p. 632.
11 Yezid Sayigh, *Armed Struggle and the Search for State: the Palestinian National Movement, 1949–1993*, Oxford: Oxford University Press, 1997, pp. 607–13.
12 Author's interview with Moshe Arens, 26 September 1994.
13 Giora Goldberg, 'Religious Zionism and the Framing of a Constitution for Israel', *Israel Studies*, Volume 3, Number 1, Spring 1998, p. 223.

Chapter 6

1 Jonathan Nitzan and Shimshon Bichler, 'The Impermanent War Economy: Peace Dividends and Capital Accumulation in Israel', in J.W. Wright (edited), *The Political Economy of Middle East Peace: The Impact of Competing Trade Agendas*, London and New York: Routledge, 1999, p. 73.
2 On Israel's political economy, see: Michael Shalev, *Labour and the Political Economy in Israel*, Oxford and New York: Oxford University Press, 1992.
3 Shimon Peres, *The New Middle East*, New York: Henry Holt, 1993.
4 Anita Shapira, *Land and Power: the Zionist Resort to Force 1881–1948*, Stanford: Stanford University Press, 1992, p. 366.
5 Asher Arian and Michal Shamir (edited), *The Elections in Israel 1996*, Albany: State University of New York Press, 1999, p. 13.
6 Asher Arian and Michal Shamir, *The Elections in Israel 1996*, p. 8.
7 Yoram Peri, 'Rabin: Between Commemoration and Denial', in Yoram Peri (edited), *The Assassination of Yitzhak Rabin*, Stanford: Stanford University Press, 2000, p. 357.
8 On the torture of so-called 'ticking bomb' terrorists, see: Alan M. Dershowitz, *Why Terrorism Works: Understanding the Threat, Responding to the Challenge*, New Haven and London: Yale University Press, 2002, pp. 131–64.
9 For an account of the history and examples of such torture, see: Tim Pat Coogan, *The Troubles: Ireland's Ordeal 1966–1995 and the Search for Peace*, London: Hutchinson, 1995, p. 149 and pp. 271–5.
10 Yossi Beilin, *Touching Peace*, p. 177.
11 Yossi Beilin, *Touching Peace*, p. 184.
12 Mahmoud Abbas (Abu Mazen), *Through Secret Channels: The Road to Oslo*, Reading: Garnet Publishing, 1995, pp. 44–5.
13 Yael Yishai, *Between the Flag and the Banner: Women in Israeli Politics*, Albany: State University of New York Press, 1997, p. 27.

Chapter 7

1 Elie Kedourie, *Politics in the Middle East*, Oxford and New York: Oxford University Press, 1992, p. 290.

2 George Stephanopoulos, *All Too Human: a Political Education*, London: Hutchinson, 1999, p. 191.

3 George Stephanopoulos, *All Too Human*, pp. 192–3.

4 Abba Eban, *The New Diplomacy: International Affairs in the Modern Age*, London: Weidenfeld and Nicolson, 1983, p. 353.

5 Edward Said, *Peace and Its Discontents: Gaza–Jericho, 1993–1995*, London: Vintage, 1995, p. 145.

6 Margaret Thatcher, *Statecraft: Strategies for a Changing World*, p. 246.

7 Khaled Hroub, *Hamas: Political Thought and Practice*, Beirut: Institute for Palestine Studies, 2000, p. 234.

8 Mohammed Shadid, 'A Housing Strategy for the Palestinian Territories', p. 32.

9 Rudolph W. Giuliani, *Leadership*, London: Little Brown, 2002, p. 338.

10 Rudolph W. Giuliani, *Leadership*, p. 337.

11 Bob Woodward, *Bush at War*, p. 324.

12 Benjamin Netanyahu, *Fighting Terrorism: How Democracies Can Defeat Domestic and International Terrorists*, London: Allison and Busby, 1995, p. 143.

13 Neill Lochery, *The Difficult Road to Peace: Netanyahu, Israel and the Middle East Peace Process*, Reading: Ithaca Press, 1999, p. 45.

14 David Grossman, *Sleeping on a Wire: Conversations with Palestinians in Israel*, London: Jonathan Cape, 1993, p. 250.

15 David Grossman, *Sleeping on a Wire*, p. 251.

16 On the latter, see: Bernard Lewis, *The Crisis of Islam: Holy War and Unholy Terror*, London: Weidenfeld and Nicolson, 2003, p. 71.

Glossary

Alignment: An election list that in 1965 comprised Mapai, Achdut Ha'avodah and Mapam, and in 1969 the Labour Party and Mapam.

Aliyah: A wave of Jewish immigration to Palestine/Israel. Each Aliyah is said to have a set of distinctive characteristics and period of time.

Ashkenazim: Jews whose background is usually from Eastern Europe.

Balfour Declaration: A frequently quoted statement made by the then British Secretary of State for Foreign Affairs in 1917 that gave support to the establishment of a Jewish homeland in Palestine.

Basic laws: In the absence of a formal written constitution, Israel has a series of these laws which are of a constitutional nature, for example on its elections.

Dominant party: A party that enjoys a long period of power; in ideological terms, this power includes a degree of spiritual dominance.

Eretz Yisrael: The Land of Israel that denotes the biblical Promised Land.

Greater Israel: Related to Eretz Yisrael: a Jewish State on both banks of the River Jordan.

Gush Emunim: The major settlers' movement in the territories that Israel conquered in the 1967 war. It is of a largely religious nature and is opposed to major territorial concessions.

Histadrut: The General Federation of Hebrew Labour, important in both the pre-state Yishuv and the state of Israel. Almost uniquely, it served as both a trade union and an employer, with large industrial and agricultural companies attached to it. In recent years, many of the companies that operated under the umbrella of the Histadrut have been sold off (privatised). The Labour Party (under various names) controlled the Histadrut until 1984, when a coalition of RAM–Meretz and Shas won control of it.

IDF: Israeli Defence Forces, founded in 1948.

Intifada: Palestinian uprising in the West Bank and Gaza Strip that began in 1987 and lasted until 1993.

Jewish Agency: An agency that concentrates on developing Israel using funds from world Jewry. Since 1971, it has worked in partnership with the World Zionist Organisation.

Kibbutz: A communal settlement with collective holding of property and earnings (pl. kibbutzim).

Knesset: The Israeli Parliament, which has 120 members.

Labour Alignment: An election list that included both the Labour Party and Mapam, 1969–84.

Moshav: A co-operative association of Israeli smallholders (pl. moshavim). The term is generally applied to agricultural settlements, many of which still exist today.

White Paper: British Government policy statement.

World Zionist Organisation: Founded by Theodor Herzl in 1897 to promote plans for Jewish nationalism.

Yishuv: Jewish settlement and organisations in Palestine in the pre-state period. In essence, this amounted to a state-within-a-state, and the institutions of the Yishuv transformed into the framework of the state of Israel in 1948.

Bibliography

Abbas, Mahmoud, *Through Secret Channels: the Road to Oslo*, Reading: Garnet Publishing, 1995.

Abu-Amr, Ziad, 'Hamas: a Historical and Political Background', *Journal of Palestine Studies*, Vol. 22, No. 4, Summer 1993, pp. 5–19.

Albright, Madeline, *Madam Secretary: a Memoir*, London: Macmillan, 2003.

Al-Haj, Majid, 'Strategies and Mobilisation Among the Arabs in Israel', in Kyle Keith and Joel Peters, *Whither Israel: the Domestic Challenges*, London: I.B. Tauris, 1993, pp. 140–60.

Al-Khazender, Sami, *Jordan and the Palestine Question: the Role of Islamic and Left Forces in Shaping Foreign Policy-making*, Reading: Ithaca Press, 1997.

Allen, Roger and Mallat, Chibli (eds), *Water in the Middle East*, London: British Academy Press, 1995.

Arens, Moshe, *Broken Covenant: American Foreign Policy and the Crisis between the US and Israel*, New York: Simon and Schuster, 1995.

Arian, Asher, *Security Threatened*, Cambridge: Cambridge University Press, 1995.

Arian, Asher, *The Second Republic: Politics in Israel*, Chatham: Chatham House, 1998.

Arian, Asher and Michal, Shamir (eds), *The Elections in Israel 1996*, Albany: State University of New York Press, 1999.

Aronoff, Myron, *Israeli Visions and Divisions*, New Brunswick: Transaction Books, 1991.

Aronson, Shlomo, *Israel's Nuclear Programme: the Six-Day War and its Ramifications*, London: King's College London Mediterranean Studies, 1999.

Ayubi, Nazih N., *Over-stating the Arab State: Politics and Society in the Middle East*, London and New York: I.B. Tauris, 1995.

Azmon, Yael and Dafna, Izraeli (eds), *Women in Israel*, New Brunswick: Transaction, 1993.

Bailer, Uri, *Between East and West: Israel's Foreign Policy Orientation, 1948–1956*, Cambridge: Cambridge University Press, 1990.

Bailey, Sydney, *Four Arab–Israeli Wars and the Peace Process*, London: Macmillan, 1990.

Bar-On, Mordechai, *The Gates of Gaza: Israel's Road to Suez and Back 1955–1957*, New York: St. Martin's Press, 1994.

Bavly, Dan and Salpeter, Eliahu, *Fire in Beirut: Israel's War in Lebanon with the PLO*, New York: Stein and Day, 1984.

Begin, Menachem, *The Revolt: the Story of the Irgun*, Tel Aviv: Steimatzky, 1952.

Beilin, Yossi, *Israel: a Concise Political History*, London: Weidenfeld and Nicolson, 1992.

Beilin, Yossi, *Touching Peace: from the Oslo Accord to a Final Agreement*, London: Weidenfeld and Nicolson, 1999.

Ben-Meir, Yehuda, 'Civil-Military Relations in Israel', in Kyle Keith and Joel Peters, *Whither Israel: the Domestic Challenges*, London: I.B. Tauris, 1993, pp. 223–43.

Ben-Meir, Yehuda, *Israeli Public Opinion, Final Status Issues: Israel–Palestinians, no. 6*, Tel Aviv: Jaffee Centre for Strategic Studies, 1995.

Ben-Zvi, Abraham, *The United States and Israel: the Limits of the Special Relationship*, New York: Columbia University Press, 1993.

Ben-Zvi, Abraham, *Decade of Transition: Eisenhower, Kennedy and the Origins of the American–Israeli Alliance*, Chichester, West Sussex: Columbia University Press, 1998.

Bernstein, Deborah (ed.), *Pioneers and Homemakers: Jewish Women in Pre-State Palestine*, Albany: State University of New York Press, 1992.

Biswas, Asit K. (ed.), *International Waters of the Middle East*, Oxford: Oxford University Press, 1994.

Bobbitt, Philip, *The Shield of Achilles: War, Peace and the Course of History*, London: Penguin, 2002.

Boutros-Ghali, Boutros, *Egypt's Road to Jerusalem*, New York: Random House, 1996.

Boutros-Ghali, Boutros, *Egypt's Road to Jerusalem: a Diplomat's Story of the Struggle for Peace in the Middle East*, New York: Random House, 1997.

Bulloch, John and Darwish, Adel, *Water Wars: Coming Conflicts in the Middle East*, London: Gollancz, 1993.

Carter, Jimmy, *The Blood of Abraham: Insights into the Middle East*, Boston: Houghton-Mifflin, 1985.

Churchill, Winston, *Never Give In: the Best of Winston Churchill's Speeches*, London: Pimlico, 2003.

Clinton, Hillary Rodham, *Living History: Memoirs*, London: Headline, 2003, pp. 517–18.

Cohen, Avner, *Israel and the Bomb*, New York: Columbia University Press, 1998.

Cohen, Mitchell, *Zion and State: Nation, Class and the Shaping of Modern Israel*, Oxford and New York: Blackwell, 1987.

Corbin, Jane, *Gaza First: the Secret Norway Channel to Peace between Israel and the PLO*, London: Bloomsbury, 1994.

Cordesman, Anthony, *The Arab–Israeli Military Balance and the Art of Operations: an Analysis of Military Trends and Implications for Future Conflicts*, Lanham: American Enterprise Institute, 1987.

Cordesman, Anthony, *Perilous Prospects: the Peace Process and the Arab–Israeli Military Balance*, Boulder: Westview Press, 1996.

Darboub, Leila, 'Palestinian Public Opinion and the Peace Process', *Palestine-Israel Journal*, Vol. 3, Nos 3–4, 1996, pp. 109–17.

Dayan, Moshe, *Diary of the Sinai Campaign*, New York: Da Capo Press, 1966.

Dayan, Moshe, *Breakthrough: a Personal Account of Egypt–Israel Negotiations*, London: Weidenfeld and Nicolson, 1981.

Dershowitz, Alan M., *Why Terrorism Works: Understanding the Threat, Responding to the Challenge*, New Haven and London: Yale University Press, 2002.

Diskin, Abraham, *Elections and Voters in Israel*, New York: Praeger, 1991.

Dowek, Ephraim, *Israeli–Egyptian Relations 1980–2000*, London and Portland: Frank Cass, 2001.

Eban, Abba, *The New Diplomacy: International Affairs in the Modern Age*, London: Weidenfeld and Nicolson, 1983.

Edelman, Martin, *Courts, Politics and Culture in Israel*, Charlottesville: University Press of Virginia, 1994.

Eisenstadt, Shmuel, *Israeli Society*, London: Weidenfeld and Nicolson, 1968.

Eisenstadt, Shmuel, *Israeli Society Transformed*, London: Weidenfeld and Nicolson, 1985.

Elazar, David, *Building a New Society*, Bloomington: Indiana University Press, 1986.

Farid, Abdel Magid, *Nasser: the Final Years*, Reading: Ithaca Press, 1994.

Feldman, Shai, *US Middle East Policy: the Domestic Setting*, Boulder: Westview Press, 1988.

Feldman, Shai and Levite, Ariel (eds), *Arms Control and the New*

Middle East Security Environment, JCSS Study No. 23, Boulder: Westview Press, 1994.

Feldman, Shai and Toukan, Abdullah, *Bridging the Gap: a Future Security Architecture for the Middle East*, Oxford: Rowman and Littlefield, 1997.

Fisk, Robert, *Pity the Nation: Lebanon at War*, Oxford: Oxford University Press, 1990.

Flamhaft, Ziva, *Israel on the Road to Peace: Accepting the Unacceptable*, Boulder: Westview Press, 1996.

Freedman, Lawrence and Karsh, Efraim, *The Gulf Conflict 1990–1991*, London and Boston: Faber and Faber, 1993.

Freedman, Robert, *The Middle East and the Peace Process: the Impact of the Oslo Accords*, Gainesville: University Press of Florida, 1998.

Friedland, Roger and Hecht, Richard, *To Rule Jerusalem*, New York and Cambridge: Cambridge University Press, 1996.

Friedman, Isaiah, *Palestine: a Twice Promised Land – The British, the Arabs and Zionism*, New Brunswick and London: Transaction Publishers, 2000.

Fromkin, David, *A Peace to End All Peace: the Fall of the Ottoman Empire and the Creation of the Modern Middle East*, London: Phoenix Press, 2000.

Frum, David, *The Right Man: an Inside Account of the Surprise Presidency of George W. Bush*, London: Weidenfeld and Nicolson, 2003.

Garfinkle, Adam, *Politics and Society in Modern Israel: Myths and Realities*, Armonk, New York: M.E. Sharpe, 1997.

Gilbert, Martin, *Jerusalem in the Twentieth Century*, London: Chatto and Windus, 1996.

Gilbert, Martin, *Israel: a History*, London: Doubleday, 1998.

Gilbert, Martin, *The Routledge Atlas of the Arab–Israeli Conflict*, London and New York: Routledge, 2003.

Gilmour, David, *Lebanon: the Fractured Country*, London: Sphere Books, 1987.

Giuliani, Rudolph W., *Leadership*, London: Little, Brown, 2002.

Golan, Galia, *Yom Kippur and After*, Cambridge: Cambridge University Press, 1977.

Golan, Galia, *Soviet Policy in the Middle East: from World War II to Gorbachev*, Cambridge: Cambridge University Press, 1990.

Gordon, Haim, *Looking Back at the June 1967 War*, Westport and London: Praeger, 1999.

Gorst, Anthony and Johnman, Lewis (eds), *The Suez Crisis*, London: Routledge, 1997 (collection of documents).

Govrin, Yosef, *Israeli–Soviet Relations from Confrontation to Disruption*, London and Portland: Frank Cass, 1998.

Gresh, Alain, 'Turkish–Israeli–Syrian Relations and their Impact on the Middle East', *Middle East Journal*, Vol. 52, No. 2, Spring 1998, pp. 188–203.

Grossman, David, *Sleeping on a Wire: Conversations with Palestinians in Israel*, London: Jonathan Cape, 1993.

Gruen, George, 'Dynamic Progress in Turkish–Israeli Relations', *Israel Affairs*, Vol. 1, No. 4, Summer 1995, pp. 40–70.

Hahn, Peter, *The United States, Great Britain and Egypt 1945–1956: Strategy and Diplomacy in the Early Cold War*, Chapel Hill and London: The University of North Carolina Press, 1991.

Halberstam, David, *War in a Time of Peace: Bush, Clinton and the Generals*, London: Bloomsbury, 2003.

Hammel, Eric, *Six Days in June: How Israel Won the 1967 Arab–Israeli War*, New York: Charles Scribner's Sons, 1992.

Harkabi, Yehoshafat, *Israel's Fateful Hour*, Philadelphia: Harper and Row, 1986.

Hashem, Talhami Ghada, *Palestinian Refugees: Pawns to Political Actors*, New York: Nova Science Publishers, 2003.

Hattis-Rolef, Susan (ed.), *Political Dictionary of the State of Israel*, Jerusalem: The Jerusalem Publishing House, 1993.

Heikal, Mohammed, *Autumn of Fury: the Assassination of Sadat*, London: Andre Deutsch, 1983.

Held, Colbert, *Middle East Patterns: Places, Peoples and Politics*, Boulder: Westview Press, 1994.

Heller, Joseph, *The Birth of Israel, 1945–1949*, Gainesville: University Press of Florida, 2000.

Heller, Mark, *A Palestinian State*, Cambridge: Cambridge University Press, 1983.

Herzog, Chaim, *The Arab–Israeli Wars*, New York: Vintage Books, 1984.

Herzog, Chaim, *Living History: The Memoirs of a Great Israeli Freedom-Fighter, Soldier, Diplomat and Statesman*, London: Weidenfeld and Nicolson, 1997.

Herzog, Chaim, *The War of Atonement: the Inside Story of the Yom Kippur War 1973*, London: Greenhill Books, 1998.

Hillel, Dan, *Rivers of Eden: the Struggle for Water and the Quest for Peace in the Middle East*, New York: Oxford University Press, 1994.

Hinnebusch, Raymond, 'Syria and the Transition to Peace', in Robert Freedman (ed.), *The Middle East and the Peace Process: the Impact of the Oslo Accords*, Gainesville: University Press of Florida, 1998, pp. 134–53.

Hiro, Dilip, *Dictionary of the Middle East*, London: Macmillan, 1996.

Holbrooke, Richard, *To End a War*, New York: Random House, 1998.

Hourani, Albert, *A History of the Arab Peoples*, London: Faber and Faber, 1991.

Hroub, Khaled, *Hamas: Political Thought and Practice*, Beirut: Institute for Palestine Studies, 2000.

Huntington, Samuel P., *The Clash of Civilizations and the Remaking of World Order*, New York: Simon and Schuster, 1996.

Hurwitz, Harry, *Begin: a Portrait*, Washington, DC: B'nai B'rith Books, 1994.

Inbar, Efraim and Sandler, Shmuel (eds), *Middle East Security: Prospects for an Arms Control Regime*, London and Portland: Frank Cass, 1995.

Israel Yearbook, Jerusalem: IBRT, published annually.

Jones, Clive, *Soviet Jewish Aliyah 1989–92: Impact and Implications for Israel and the Middle East*, London and Portland: Frank Cass, 1996.

Joyce, Miriam, *Kuwait 1945–1996: an Anglo-American Perspective*, London and Portland: Frank Cass, 1998.

Kaplan, Robert D., *The Arabists: the Romance of an American Elite*, New York: Free Press, 1993.

Karsh, Efraim (ed.), *From Rabin to Netanyahu: Israel's Troubled Agenda*, London and Portland: Frank Cass, 1997.

Karsh, Efraim, *Fabricating Israeli History*, London and Portland: Frank Cass, 1997.

Katz, Shmuel, *Lone Wolf: a Biography of Vladimir Ze'ev Jabotinsky* (two volumes), New York: Barricade Books, 1996.

Kedourie, Elie, *The Chatham House Version and Other Middle Eastern Studies*, London: Weidenfeld and Nicolson, 1970.

Kedourie, Elie, *The Crossman Confessions and Other Essays*, London and New York: Mansell, 1984.

Kedourie, Elie, *Politics in the Middle East*, Oxford: Oxford University Press, 1992.

Kelly, Saul and Gorst, Anthony (eds), *Whitehall and the Suez Crisis*, London and Portland: Frank Cass, 2000.

Khadduri, Majid and Ghareeb, Edmund, *War in the Gulf, 1990–1991: the Iraq–Kuwait Conflict and its Implications*, Oxford and New York: Oxford University Press, 1997.

Kimche, David and Bawly, Dan, *The Sandstorm, the Arab–Israeli War of June 1967: Prelude and Aftermath*, London: Secker and Warburg, 1968.

Kimmerling, Baruch and Migdal, Joel, *The Palestinians: the Making of a People*, Cambridge, MA: Harvard University Press, 1994.

Kinross, Lord, *The Ottoman Empire*, London: Folio Books, 2003.

Kissinger, Henry, *Diplomacy*, New York: Touchstone, 1994.

Kissinger, Henry, *Years of Renewal*, London: Weidenfeld and Nicolson, 1999.

Kretzmer, David, *The Legal Status of the Arabs in Israel*, Boulder: Westview Press, 1990.

Kumaraswamy, P. (ed.), *Revisiting the Yom Kippur War*, London and Portland: Frank Cass, 2000.

Kurzman, Dan, *Genesis 1948: the First Arab–Israeli War*, New York: Da Capo Press, 1992.

Kyle, Keith, *Suez*, New York: St. Martins Press, 1991.

Landau, Jacob, *The Arabs in Israel*, Oxford: Oxford University Press, 1969.

Laqueur, Walter and Rubin, Barry (eds), *The Arab-Israeli Reader: a Documentary History of the Middle East Conflict*, New York: Facts on File Publications, 1985.

Laqueur, Walter, *A History of Zionism*, New York: Schocken Books, 1989.

Levran, Aharon, *Israeli Strategy after Desert Storm: Lessons of the Second Gulf War*, London and Portland: Frank Cass, 1997.

Lewis, Bernard, *The Middle East: 2000 Years of History from the Rise of Christianity to the Present Day*, London: Phoenix, 1996.

Lewis, Bernard, *The Multiple Identities of the Middle East*, London: Weidenfeld and Nicolson, 1998.

Lewis, Bernard, *The Crisis of Islam: Holy War and Unholy Terror*, London: Weidenfeld and Nicolson, 2003, p. 71.

Liebman, Charles and Don-Yehiya, Eliezer, *Civil Religion in Israel*, Berkeley: University of California Press, 1983.

Lochery, Neill, *The Israeli Labour Party: in the Shadow of the Likud*, Reading: Ithaca Press, 1997.

Lochery, Neill, *The Difficult Road to Peace: Netanyahu, Israel and the Middle East Peace Process*, Reading: Ithaca Press, 1999.

Lucas, Noah, *The Modern History of Israel*, London: Weidenfeld and Nicolson, 1974.

Mahler, Gregory, *Israel: Government and Politics in a Maturing State*, San Diego and New York: Harcourt Brace Jovanovich, 1999.

Makovsky, David, *Making Peace with the PLO*, Boulder: Westview Press, 1996.

Malki, Riad, 'The Palestinian Opposition and Final-Status Negotiations', *Palestine-Israel Journal*, Vol. 3, Nos 3–4, 1996, pp. 95–9.

Mansfield, Peter, *A History of the Middle East*, London and New York: Viking, 1991.

Ma'oz, Moshe, *Syria and Israel: from War to Peacemaking*, Oxford and New York: Oxford University Press, 1995.

Masalha, Nur, 'A Critique of Benny Morris', in Illan Pappe (ed.), *The*

Israel–Palestine Question: Rewriting Histories, London: Routledge, 1999, pp. 211–20.

Massalha, Omar, *Towards the Long Promised Peace*, London: Saqi Books, 1992.

Mazzawi, Musa, *Palestine and the Law: Guidelines for the Resolution of the Arab–Israeli Conflict*, Reading: Ithaca Press, 1997.

McIntyre, Ian, *The Proud Doers: Israel After Twenty Years*, London: BBC, 1968.

Medding, Peter, *Mapai in Israel: Political Organisation and Government in a New Society*, Cambridge: Cambridge University Press, 1972.

Medding, Peter, *The Founding of Israeli Democracy 1948–1967*, Oxford: Oxford University Press, 1990.

Milton-Edwards, Beverley, *Islamic Politics in Palestine*, London: Tauris Academic Press, 1996.

Milton-Edwards, Beverley, *Contemporary Politics in the Middle East*, Cambridge: Polity Press, 2000.

Morris, Benny, *Righteous Victims: a History of the Zionist–Arab Conflict, 1981–1999*, London: John Murray, 1999.

Morris, Edmund, *Dutch: a Memoir of Ronald Reagan*, London: Harper Collins, 1999.

Mutawi, Samir A., *Jordan in the 1967 War*, Cambridge: Cambridge University Press, 1987.

Neff, Donald, *Warriors at Suez: Eisenhower Takes the US into the Middle East in 1956*, Brattleboro, Vermont: Amana Books, 1988.

Netanyahu, Benjamin, *Fighting Terrorism: How Democracies Can Defeat Domestic and International Terrorists*, London: Allison and Busby, 1995.

Newman, David (ed.), *The Impact of Gush Emunim*, London: Croom Helm, 1985.

O'Brien, Conor Cruise, *The Siege: the Saga of Israel and Zionism*, London: Paladin, 1988.

Oren, Michael, *The Origins of the Second Arab–Israeli Conflict*, London and Portland: Frank Cass, 1992.

Oren, Michael B., *Six Days of War: June 1967 and the Making of the Modern Middle East*, London: Penguin Books, 2003.

Ovendale, Ritchie, *The Origins of the Arab–Israeli Wars*, London: Longman, 1992.

Owen, Roger, *State Power and Politics in the Making of the Modern Middle East*, London: Routledge, 1992.

Oz, Amos, *In the Land of Israel*, London: Flamingo, 1984.

Pappe, Ilan (ed.), *The Israel/Palestine Question: Rewriting Histories*, London and New York: Routledge, 1999.

Peres, Shimon, *The New Middle East*, New York: Henry Holt, 1993.

Peres, Shimon, *Battling for Peace: Memoirs*, London: Weidenfeld and Nicolson, 1995.

Peretz, Don and Doron, Gideon, *The Government and Politics of Israel*, Boulder: Westview Press, 1997.

Pope, Juliet, 'The Place of Women in Israeli Society', in Kyle Keith and Joel Peters, *Whither Israel: the Domestic Challenges*, London: I.B. Tauris, 1993, pp. 202–22.

Quandt, William B., *Peace Process: American Diplomacy and the Arab–Israeli Conflict Since 1967*, Berkeley: The Brookings Institution, University of California Press, 2001.

Rabin, Yitzhak, *The Rabin Memoirs*, Berkeley: University of California Press, 1996.

Rabinovich, Itamar, *The War for Lebanon 1970–85*, Ithaca and London: Cornell University Press, 1985.

Rabinovich, Itamar, *The Brink of Peace: the Israeli–Syrian Negotiations*, Princeton: Princeton University Press, 1998.

Rahman, H., *The Making of the Gulf War: Origins of Kuwait's Longstanding Territorial Dispute with Iraq*, Reading: Ithaca Press, 1997.

Randall, Jonathan, *The Tragedy of Lebanon*, London: The Hogarth Press, 1990.

Ranstorp, Magnus, *Hezbollah in Lebanon*, London: Macmillan, 1997.

Reich, Bernard and Kieval, Gershon, *Israel: Land of Tradition and Conflict*, Boulder: Westview Press, 1993.

Reinharz, Jehuda and Shapira, Anita (eds), *Essential Papers on Zionism*, New York: Cassell (New York University Press), 1996.

Richards, Alan and Waterbury, John, *A Political Economy of the Middle East: State, Class and Economic Development*, Boulder and Oxford: Westview Press, 1990.

Rubin, Barry, *Revolution until Victory: the Politics and History of the PLO*, Cambridge, MA: Harvard University Press, 1994.

Rubin, Barry, Ginat, Joseph and Ma'oz, Moshe (eds), *From War to Peace: Arab–Israeli Relations 1973–1993*, New York: New York University Press, 1994.

Rubinstein, Amnon, *The Zionist Dream Revisited: from Herzl to Gush Emunim and Back*, New York: Schocken Books, 1984.

Sachar, Howard, *A History of Israel: from the Rise of Zionism to Our Time*, New York: Knopf, 1979.

Sachar, Howard, *Israel and Europe: an Appraisal in History*, New York: Knopf, 1999.

Said, Edward, *The Politics of Dispossession: the Struggle for Palestinian Self-Determination, 1969–1994*, London: Chatto and Windus, 1994.

Said, Edward, *Orientalism: Western Conceptions of the Orient*, London: Penguin, 1995.

Said, Edward, *Peace and its Discontents: Gaza–Jericho, 1993–1995*, London: Vintage, 1995.

Sandler, Shmuel, *The State of Israel, the Land of Israel: Statist and Ethnonational Dimensions of Foreign Policy*, Westport: Greenwood Press, 1993.

Sayigh, Yezid, *Armed Struggle and the Search for State: the Palestinian National Movement, 1949–1993*, Oxford: Oxford University Press, 1997.

Schiff, Ze'ev and Ya'ari, Ehud, *Israel's Lebanon War*, London and Sydney: George Allen and Unwin, 1984.

Schiff, Ze'ev and Ya'ari, Ehud, *Intifada: the Palestinian Uprising, Israel's Third Front*, New York: Simon and Schuster, 1990.

Seale, Patrick, *Asad: the Struggle for the Middle East*, Berkeley: University of California Press, 1988.

Shadid, Mohammed, 'A Housing Strategy for the Palestinian Territories', in A.B. Zahlan (ed.), *The Reconstruction of Palestine: Urban and Rural Development*, London and New York: Kegan Paul International, 1997.

Shalev, Michael, *Labour and the Political Economy in Israel*, Oxford: Oxford University Press, 1992.

Shapira, Anita, *Land and Power: the Zionist Resort to Force 1881–1948*, Stanford: Stanford University Press, 1992.

Shapiro, Yonathan, *The Road to Power: Herut Party in Israel*, Albany: State University of New York Press, 1991.

Sharkansky, Ira, *The Political Economy of Israel*, New Brunswick: Transaction Books, 1987.

Sheffer, Gabriel (ed.), *US–Israeli Relations at the Crossroads*, London and Portland: Frank Cass, 1997.

Shepherd, Naomi, 'Ex-Soviet Jews in Israel: Asset, Burden or Challenge', *Israel Affairs*, Vol. 2, No. 1, Winter 1994, pp. 245–66.

Shepherd, Naomi, *Ploughing Sand: British Rule in Palestine, 1917–1948*, London: John Murray, 1999.

Sherman, Martin, *The Politics of Water in the Middle East: An Israeli Perspective on the Hydro-Political Aspects of the Conflict*, London: Macmillan, 1999.

Shimoni, Gideon, *The Zionist Ideology*, Hanover and London: Brandeis University Press, 1995.

Shlaim, Avi, *The Iron Wall: Israel and the Arab World*, New York and London: W.W. Norton and Company, 2000.

Shulewitz, Malka Hillel (ed.), *The Forgotten Millions: the Modern Jewish Exodus from Arab Lands*, London and New York: Cassell, 1999.

Smooha, Sammy, *Israel: Pluralism and Conflict*, London: Routledge and Kegan Paul, 1978.

Smooha, Sammy, 'Jewish ethnicity in Israel', in Kyle Keith and Joel Peters, *Whither Israel: the Domestic Challenges*, London: I.B. Tauris, 1993, pp. 161–76.

Sofer, Sasson, *Zionism and the Foundations of Israeli Diplomacy*, Cambridge and New York: Cambridge University Press, 1998.

Statistical Abstract of Israel, Jerusalem: Central Bureau of Statistics, published annually.

Stein, Kenneth W., *Heroic Diplomacy: Sadat, Kissinger, Carter, Begin and the Quest for Arab–Israeli Peace*, New York and London: Routledge, 1999.

Stephanopoulos, George, *All Too Human: a Political Education*, London: Hutchinson, 1999.

Stothard, Peter, *Thirty Days at the Heart of Blair's War*, London: Harper Collins, 2003.

Swirski, Shlomo, *Israel: the Oriental Majority*, London: Zed Books, 1989.

Swirski, Barbara and Safir, Marilyn (eds), *Calling the Equality Bluff: Women in Israel*, New York: Pergamon, 1991.

Tessler, Mark, *A History of the Israeli–Palestinian Conflict*, Bloomington and Indianapolis: Indiana University Press, 1994.

Teveth, Shabtai, *Moshe Dayan: the Soldier, the Man, the Legend*, London: Quartet Books, 1974.

Thatcher, Margaret, *Statecraft: Strategies for a Changing World*, London: Harper Collins, 2002.

The Middle East and North Africa, London: Europa Publications, published annually.

Vatikiotis, P.J., *The History of Modern Egypt: from Muhammad Ali to Mubarak*, London: Weidenfeld and Nicolson, 1991.

Vital, David, *The Origins of Zionism*, Oxford: Clarendon Press, 1975.

Vital, David, *Zionism: the Formative Years*, Oxford: Clarendon Press, 1981.

Vital, David, *Zionism: the Crucial Phase*, Oxford: Clarendon Press, 1987.

Walzer, Michael, *Just and Unjust Wars: a Moral Argument with Historical Illustrations*, New York: Basic Books, 1992.

Watson, Bruce (ed.), *Military Lessons of the Gulf War*, London: Greenhill Books, 1993.

Weizman, Ezer, *The Battle for Peace*, London: Bantam Books, 1981.

Woodward, Bob, *The Commanders*, New York: Simon and Schuster, 1991.

Woodward, Bob, *Bush at War*, London: Pocket Books, 2003.

Wright, J., *The Political Economy of Middle East Peace: the Impact of Competing Trade Agendas*, London: Routledge, 1999.

Yapp, Malcolm, *The Near East Since the First World War: a History to 1995*, London and New York: Longman, 1996.

Yishai, Yael, *Between the Flag and the Banner: Women in Israeli Politics*, Albany: State University of New York Press, 1997.

Zak, Moshe, 'Israel and Jordan: Strategically Bound', *Israel Affairs*, Vol. 3, No. 1, Autumn 1996, pp. 39–60.

Ziberfarb, Ben-Zion, 'The Israeli Economy in the Era of Peace', *Israel Affairs*, Vol. 3, No. 1, Autumn 1996, pp. 1–12.

Websites

There are a number of websites of mixed quality that cover Israel and the Middle East. However, the ones listed below are excellent sources of information. Type the exact title given below into a search engine and use for both reference and analysis of current events. A few of the search engines that deal specifically with Israel and the Middle East have been included to help you search further afield.

Arab Internet Directory Media List
Begin–Sadat (BESA) Center for Strategic Studies (Middle East strategic and political issues)
Center for Palestine Research and Studies (polls, Israel studies, research papers)
The (almost) Complete Guide to WWW in Israel (news, politics, government, peace)
The Leonard Davis Institute for International Relations (Hebrew University)
Moshe Dayan Center for Middle Eastern and African Studies (very good free database of materials)
Globes Business Magazine (daily coverage of Israeli and regional economic issues with good archive)
Globes Arena Middle East Press Review (guide to media sources in region)
Ha'aretz (English edition)
Haifa University Middle East History Department (links to newspapers and Islamic studies sources)
Institute for Palestine Studies (Washington-based, publication lists)
Israel Defense Forces (only official site of Israel's military)
Israel Internet News Service (daily free e-mail publication with archives)

Israeli Central Bureau of Statistics (Israeli economic, census data, statistical abstract)

Israeli Knesset (English version) (Israel's parliament)

Israeli Ministry of Foreign Affairs (a good starting point)

Israeli Prime Minister homepage (official policy statements and more)

IsraeLine (government daily news summary, subscribe by e-mail)

Israel's Government Press Office (press clips, releases, e-mail list, links to government sites)

Jaffee Center for Strategic Studies (Israeli and Middle East strategic issues)

Jerusalem Post (main English language daily newspaper)

Jerusalem Report (fortnightly magazine)

Libraries with MidEast Collections (an overview of university libraries)

Palestinian National Authority Central Bureau of Statistics (official site, laws and statistics)

Palestinian National Authority (official site: statements, speeches, press summaries)

PALNET media links (Arabic) (includes al-Quds, al-Ayyam, al-Hayat al-Jadedah, al-Bilad)

UNSCO site (economic data and UN reports)

Washington Post, Middle East articles (Washington Post and AP articles, by country and finding engine)

Who's Who at the PNA (PNA Information Ministry) (lists/contact data, ministers/Assembly members)

Zionism: The First One Hundred Years

Index

Other political titles available from Icon Books

'Bold, original and immensely thought-provoking.'
Francis Wheen

'Anyone concerned with the state of the world cannot afford to miss this important book.'
Ziauddin Sardar, co-author of *Why Do People Hate America?*

Fundamentalist World
The New Dark Age of Dogma
Stuart Sim

The collapse of the Argentinian economy, the rise of the far right, 9/11, suicide bombings in the Middle East, campaigns against multiculturalism, anti-abortion terrorism, the militia movement in America, teaching creationism in schools, riots at Miss World: what ties these seemingly unrelated phenomena together?

All are products of a fundamentalist mentality, determined to crush all opposing ideas. Belief in these kinds of universal theories was, until recently, assumed to be in decline. Stuart Sim argues that this is far from true.

Fundamentalism is no fringe enthusiasm, but an increasingly mainstream and powerful influence. Whether it's religious, political, imperialist, nationalist or even market fundamentalism, believe it: we live in an increasingly fundamentalist world.

Stuart Sim
is Professor of Critical Theory in the English Department at the University of Sunderland. He is the author of *Derrida and the End of History*, *Lyotard and the Inhuman* and *Irony and Crisis: A Critical History of Postmodern Culture*, all published by Icon. His work has been translated into nine languages, and he is a Fellow of the English Association.

UK £12.99
ISBN 1 84046 532 8

Trust ... From Socrates to Spin
Kieron O'Hara

Who do we trust and why? Do we trust the government to act responsibly? Do we trust experts to be accountable? Do we trust corporations to work within the law? Do we trust newspapers (and books) to tell the truth? Should we be less trusting – or more?

A crisis in trust is currently gripping the West. Polls record an all-time low in levels of trust in politicians, businessmen and scientists. In this exhilarating ride through recent news events, literature, philosophy and history, Kieron O'Hara examines the vital questions of how trust is built up and how it collapses.

From Aristotle to Nick Leeson, from Machiavelli to Naomi Klein, from the Book of Job to Blairite newspeak and from Enron to nanotechnology, *Trust* explores the impact of this crisis on our daily lives, offering few easy answers but seeking out the questions we should all be asking.

Kieron O'Hara
is a Senior Research Fellow at the University of Southampton. He is involved in the Office of Science and Technology's Cybertrust and Crime Prevention Programme, is the author of *Plato and the Internet* (Icon, 2001) and has contributed to many journals and magazines including the *New Statesman*.

UK £12.99
ISBN 184046 531 X

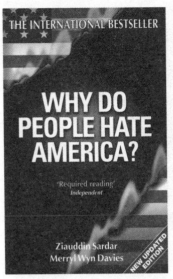

'THE INTERNATIONAL BESTSELLER'

WHY DO PEOPLE HATE AMERICA?

'Required reading'
Independent

Ziauddin Sardar
Merryl Wyn Davies

NEW UPDATED EDITION

Why Do People Hate America?
Ziauddin Sardar and Merryl Wyn Davies

The economic power of US corporations and the virus-like power of American popular culture affect the lives and infect the indigenous cultures of millions around the world. The foreign policy of the US government, backed by its military strength, has unprecedented global influence now that the USA is the world's only superpower – its first 'hyperpower'.

America also exports its value systems, defining what it means to be civilised, rational, developed and democratic – indeed, what it is to be human. Meanwhile, the US itself is impervious to outside influence, and if most Americans think of the rest of the world at all, it is in terms of deeply ingrained cultural stereotypes.

Many people *do* hate America, in the Middle East and the developing countries as well as in Europe. Ziauddin Sardar and Merryl Wyn Davies explore the global impact of America's foreign policy and its corporate and cultural power, placing this unprecedented dominance in the context of America's own perception of itself. Their analysis provides an important contribution to a debate which needs to be addressed by people of all nations, cultures, religions and political persuasions.

Ziauddin Sardar
is a writer, broadcaster and cultural critic. He has written a number of books for Icon's *Introducing* series and is a regular contributor to the *New Statesman* and national and international newspapers and magazines.

Merryl Wyn Davies
is a writer and anthropologist. Her most recent books are *Darwin and Fundamentalism* (2000) and *Introducing Anthropology* (2002).

UK £7.99
ISBN 184046 525 5

10% of the world is at war
One B2 Bomber costs more than the UN's annual budget
24.5 million people in Africa are HIV positive
Cars kill 2 people every minute in the developed world

facts that should change the world

Jessica Williams

50 Facts that Should Change the World
Jessica Williams

- In Kenya, monthly bribery payments add a third to the average household budget.
- The US spends $10 billion on pornography every year. In 2001, the US spent $10 billion on foreign aid.
- Landmines kill or maim at least one person every hour.

From the inequalities and absurdities of the so-called developed West to the vast scale of suffering wreaked by war, famine and Aids in developing countries, this book paints a picture of shocking contrasts. YOU need to know these facts.

Each fact from this eclectic range is followed by explanation and lively analysis. Some facts will make you rethink things you thought you knew. Some illustrate long-term, gradual changes in our society. Others concern local issues that people face in their everyday lives. All of the facts remind us that our world is deeply interconnected – and that civilisation is a fragile concept.

Jessica Williams
is a journalist and television producer for the BBC, where she has researched and produced interviews with such disparate figures as the political philosopher Noam Chomsky, President Paul Kagame of Rwanda, Sir David Attenborough, Northern Ireland First Minister David Trimble, and the American academic Edward Said.

UK £9.99
ISBN 184046 547 6
Published 6 May 2004